THE MULTICULTURAL PATH

h

THE MULTICULTURAL PATH

Issues of Diversity and Discrimination in Democracy

Gurpreet Mahajan

Sage Publications
New Delhi • Thousand Oaks • London

First published in 2002 by

Sage Publications India Pvt Ltd
M–32, Greater Kailash–I
New Delhi 110 048

Sage Publications Inc. Sage Publications Ltd
2455 Teller Road 6 Bonhill Street
Thousand Oaks, California 91320 London EC2A 4PU

Published by Tejeshwar Singh for Sage Publications India Pvt Ltd, typeset in 10.5/12.5 Garamond medium by S.R. Enterprises, New Delhi, and printed at Chaman Enterprises, Delhi.

Library of Congress Cataloging-in-Publication Data

Mahajan, Gurpreet.
    The multicultural path: issues of diversity and discrimination in democracy/ Gurpreet Mahajan.
        p. cm.
    Includes bibliographical references and index.
    1. Multiculturalism. I. Title
HM1271 M345 305.8—dc21   2002   2002017323

ISBN: 0-7619-9579-X (US-HB)   81-7829-098-7 (India-HB)
         0-7619-9630-3 (US-PB)   81-7829-099-5 (India-PB)

Sage Production Team: B.P. Sharma, N.K. Negi, Rajib Chatterjee and Santosh Rawat

To
Gunvir *and* **Amrita**

Contents

Acknowledgements

This book began more than five years ago when I initiated and taught a course on Multiculturalism and Democracy at the Centre for Political Studies, Jawaharlal Nehru University. It has grown through discussions in the classroom and has been put to test by the students who studied this course and whose research in this field I had the privilege of supervising. I am grateful to all of them, particularly to Papia Sen Gupta and Amir Ali, for always ensuring that I was sufficiently acquainted with new work in this area. I would also like to thank my colleagues in the department and the University.

The present form of the book owes, in no small measure, to animated discussions at seminars and in the relatively less formal environment of the lunch room. Were it not for the severity of these contestations, this book may have been in the making for a much longer time. I am indebted to Aswini K. Ray, Dhirubhai Sheth, Dipankar Gupta and Sarah Joseph for readily expressing their disagreements. The clarity of their thought has enriched my understanding of multiculturalism and helped enormously in giving my views a sharper focus and, I hope, some intelligibility. Discussions with Romila Thapar helped me understand the issues of plurality and difference in ancient India. She drew my attention to vital literature on the subject and, above all, shared her historical and archaeological knowledge which was far beyond what I could get from the published materials in this field. For all this, and much more, I am extremely grateful to her. I would also like to thank Professors Kuldeep Singh and Surjit Singh Narang of Guru Nanak Dev University for providing important empirical details on the Sikh minority community.

Over the years, this study has received the support of several institutions and individuals. I would specially like to thank The Fulbright Foundation, The Shastri-Indo Canadian Institute and Maison des Science d'le Homme, Paris. Their support enabled me to study the resistance and the support that multiculturalism has received in different parts of the world from governments as well as minority groups. They also gave me an opportunity to meet and learn from scholars whose writings have influenced the thinking on multiculturalism in our times. Among the many who were extremely generous with their time and who shared with me their ideas and work, I would like to thank Bhikhu Parekh, Joseph Carens, Melissa Williams, Patrick Macklem, Jenny Nedelsky, Rodney Bobbiwash, Jeff Spinner, Suzanne Rudolph and Lloyd Rudolph. My work has benefited greatly from interaction with them, and I remain extremely grateful to all. This book will, I hope, continue the unfinished dialogue with them and other theorists of multiculturalism.

Last, but by no means the least, I would like to thank my family and friends. Their constant support and encouragement made it possible for me to undertake this work. I am particularly indebted to Harpreet for her generous help in locating and providing books that were not available in India. I would also like to take this opportunity to thank Omita Goyal at Sage for her patience and professional efficiency. To Bhanu Pratap Sharma, who edited the manuscript, I owe an apology for making this task more difficult. I do appreciate the flexibility and consideration that I received from all at Sage in the process of publishing.

New Delhi
January 2002

Gurpreet Mahajan

1

Introduction: Beyond Pluralism, Towards Multiculturalism

Cultural pluralism is not a modern phenomenon. History provides many examples of different communities and cultures living side by side within the same society, co-existing peacefully, and sometimes, even amicably. The ancient empires of Persia, Egypt and Rome were culturally diverse. In India, similarly, people of diverse religions and languages have lived together for several centuries. In some pre-modern societies, differences of religion were even legally recognised and accommodated. The Ottoman Empire, while affirming Islam as its own religion, gave formal recognition to Orthodox Greeks, Jews and Orthodox Armenians. In fact, under the Millet system, each of these three communities had certain legal rights to govern their own communities (Walzer, 1997: 17).

The co-presence of different communities within the same polity is, therefore, not a new occurrence. Cultural plurality has been a hallmark of many societies for a very long time. However, the existence of plurality at the societal level does not imply that multiculturalism as a value prevailed in these societies. The simultaneous presence of many cultures and communities within the same social space points to a plural social fabric, but it does not betoken the presence of multiculturalism. The latter entails something more than the mere presence of different communities or the attitude of tolerance in society. Multiculturalism is concerned with the issue of equality: it asks whether the different communities, living peacefully together, co-exist as equals in the public arena.

It is this emphasis on equality that distinguishes multiculturalism from pluralism. Within the framework of plurality, the major concern is peaceful co-existence and amity. So long as communities have some degree of freedom to live by their own religious and cultural practices, their position *vis-à-vis* other groups and communities in the public arena is a non-issue. Pluralism, in other words, indicates the presence of differences and marks a departure from policies aimed at annihilating the other, but that is all. It remains silent about the public status of these communities. Indeed, in most pre-modern societies, pluralism prevailed against the backdrop of a widely accepted hierarchy of cultures and communities.

The Millet system, which is regarded by many scholars as a prime example of tolerance, provided a fairly elaborate system of legal pluralism. It conceived the three acknowledged religious minority groups as semi-autonomous entities with rights to manage and govern the life of their members. So long as they paid their taxes and lived peacefully, it did not interfere in the affairs of these communities. In fact, it communicated with them primarily through their leaders. Thus, it was the communal heads of the Millets who 'were summoned to receive news on behalf of their constituencies' while the rest of the population were 'communicated by public criers' (Lerner, 1958: 114). Yet, even within this system, the recognised religious communities enjoyed a relative degree of autonomy only *vis-à-vis* their own members. They were subject to the same restrictions with regard to such issues as dress, proselytising, intermarriage, etc., *vis-à-vis* the Muslims, who constituted the ruling community (Walzer, 1997: 17–18). In this respect, the Ottoman Empire was not an exception. Here, like in many other plural societies, multiple communities co-existed but within an acknowledged framework of hierarchy with the ruler's religion and culture occupying the highest position (see Gupta, 1996: 192–211).

Pluralism and tolerance are often most visible when the dominance of one community is unambiguously acceded. In medieval India, for instance, plural and syncretic existence was much in evidence when the subject population or its patron avowed their loyalty to the ruler. 'Thus we find Akbar allowing high-ranking Rajput officers in his service to build their own monumental temples in the provinces to which they are posted, as in the case of the Govind Deva temple in Brindavan, patronized by Raja Man Singh' (Eaton, 2001: 71). By the same logic, when the implicit structure of dominance is challenged openly or even indirectly, tolerance swiftly vanishes. What we witness at such moments are acts of repression or unequivocal assertion of supremacy through such actions as desecration of the places of religious worship (see Eaton, 2000 and 2001). A plural social fabric or stories of collective participation in festivals and processions are, therefore, no indication of the absence of hierarchy and inequality. In fact, it often exists when the authority of the dominant community and the symbols of its power are readily accepted by others.

Hierarchy and dominance can of course be expressed and acknowledged in a variety of ways. What characterises structures of pluralism is that power is displayed and conceded frequently in the domain of the symbolic. The dominant community asserts its supremacy by stamping its presence in public places, and *vice versa*, challenges to these symbols are taken as a sign of rebellion, to be strongly resisted. In India, from the sixth century AD onwards, rulers established their dominance by removing the idols of the local deity and replacing them with their own gods. At times, as in the case of Tirunelveli in the sixth century, Jain caves were completely taken over by the Shaiv community (Thapar, 1994: 17), but in many other cases the dominance was asserted by merely capturing the inner womb of the temple. To take another example, in much of the seventeenth century, officers of the Mughal court initiated the renewal of the Jagannath cult, but by establishing quite clearly the supremacy of the rulers. 'By sitting on a canopied chariot while accompanying the cult's annual festival, Shah Jahan's officials ritually demonstrated that it was the Mughal emperor, operating through his appointed officers (*mansabdar*), who was the temple's—and hence the god's —ultimate lord and protector' (Eaton, 2001: 71).

The presence of close interaction between communities and the existence of plural legal systems should not, in other words, be read as a sign of equality between communities. We need to go beyond the fact of co-presence and interaction and raise the issue of group equality by examining whether the different communities occupying the same social space—and at times even living amicably together—and participating in each other's cultures, have the same status in the public domain. This is essential because inequality in the public domain can, and often does, co-exist with degrees of legal and social pluralism. In Germany, for instance, we find that the Turks of Muslim faith enjoy a certain amount of religious freedom. They can assemble for collective prayers so long as they do so in structures that look more like 'warehouses' rather than 'mosques' (Ewing, 2000: 35). The state had no problem giving these rights provided their presence in the form of a mosque, was not publicly visible.[1] The British Empire, likewise, had no objection if the local rulers, over whom it had established dominion, displayed their status by wearing bejewelled turbans or some other form of decorative headgear as long as it was not a crown, since that was a symbol of the Raj.

Thus, in plural societies, dominance is frequently expressed in political and symbolic terms. It is by capturing and gaining exclusive control over public spaces that structures of inequality are put in place. It is, therefore, hardly surprising that in late nineteenth century India, the visibility of the *Shivalaya* from the area around the *mazaar*, where the Muslim community met for its Friday prayers, became a subject of considerable rancour between the communities in Mubarakpur. Even though Manohar Das had built this temple (*Shivalaya*) in the compound of his own house, the leaders of the Muslim community protested that it could not be allowed to dwarf the *mazaar* of Raja Mubarak Pur (Pandey, 1990: 134). Examples of this kind can be multiplied *ad infinitum*. It is sufficient here to reiterate that the co-presence of different religions, races, castes and other communities is not an indicator of their equal status in the public domain.

Contemporary discourses on multiculturalism have, more than all else, brought home the reality that inequalities of this kind may prevail even after some basic degree of political and civil

---

[1] The first free-standing mosque with minarets and a domed structure is currently being constructed by Diyanet Isleri Turk Islam Birligi, an organ of the Turkish government which propogates moderate Islam. However, before permission was granted for the construction of this mosque, objections were raised on such grounds as, the mosque would 'disrupt the Berlin skyline' and that it would be a 'constant reminder of the presence of foreigners in the heart of Germany' (Ewing, 2000: 35).

rights are granted to all. It is hardly a coincidence that multiculturalism surfaces within the framework of democracy because only when equality becomes a central norm is it possible to move beyond the concern for peaceful co-existence. Democracy, as I have argued elsewhere (1998b: Introduction), values the principle of non-discrimination. It aims to ensure that socially ascribed identities, such as those of caste, race, religion or gender, are not a source of discrimination and disadvantage in the public domain. Multiculturalism, as a political theory, extends this democratic concern. It probes areas of cultural discrimination that may exist even after legal equality has been established. Reflecting upon what constitutes fair and equal treatment for minority cultures and communities within the nation-state, multiculturalism explains why people committed to enhancing democratic citizenship should be concerned about the fate of other cultures in our society.

The focus of contemporary multiculturalism is, therefore, radically different from earlier notions of pluralism and cultural difference. Unlike pluralism, which points to the amicable co-existence of different cultures, multiculturalism makes a value statement. It asserts that the many cultural communities that are present in our society must live as equals in the public domain. As such, multiculturalism is not just an assertion of tolerance; nor is it, for that matter, a celebration of eclecticism of tastes. Multiculturalism speaks of equality of cultures and argues that in a democracy, all cultural communities must be entitled to equal status in the public domain. That is, fair treatment as an equal citizen is a matter of right; it is not—and must not be—dependent upon the largesse or benevolence of the majority community. Indeed, it is what all individuals, as citizens and members of different communities, might legitimately expect and receive in a democracy.

Multiculturalism thus speaks of issues that are central to democracy. On the one hand, it extends democratic sensibilities, and on the other, it is itself an expression of the democratic urge. The current engagement with multiculturalism and the attention that this theory has received in the recent past can best be appreciated against this wider backdrop of democracy. Since multicultural political theory has revealed patterns of cultural discrimination engendered by the nation-state, it has raised questions that no democratic polity can ignore. At the same time, by successfully articulating the sentiments of the subordinated and marginalised minority communities the world over, it has become a synonym for the assertion of their difference.

In India, however, multiculturalism as a theory of democracy and citizenship has received little attention. It appears quite paradoxical that in a country, which was among the first few democracies to endorse the principle of equality between groups,[2] there has been no serious attempt to theorise the idea of a multicultural democracy. The multicultural design of the Indian polity emerged as a consequence of the political negotiations between assertive and highly mobilised communities. This does not mean that the framework devised for incorporating diverse communities as equal partners in the polity lacked reflection or legitimacy. On the contrary, and notwithstanding the disclaimers of a few groups in the recent past, the constitutional schema was informed by a deep understanding of the different sites of group inequality within the Indian polity. The Constituent Assembly debated at length the issue of cultural majoritarianism and it also incorporated a framework of minority rights to safeguard religious and cultural minorities. Yet, the rights that were given at that time were essentially an outcome of the political consensus that emerged in that historical context. This was not backed by a theoretical defence, either of the idea of special rights for minorities or of the rights that were actually given to specific kinds of minorities in the Constitution of India.

Perhaps a philosophical justification was not considered necessary because there was a wide-based agreement on the issue of special consideration for the Scheduled Castes and the

---

[2] The concern for group equality was expressed quite explicitly in the Sub-Committee on Fundamental Rights. Here, representatives of minority communities argued that '[I]t is difficult to expect that in a country like India, where most persons are communally minded, those in authority will give equal treatment to those who do not belong to the community' (Rao, 1968: 98). Consequently, to allay such fears, special safeguards were provided to ensure equal treatment to all communities.

Scheduled Tribes, and a long-standing commitment that India would protect the rights of its religious minorities.[3] Hence, considerations of group equality received considerable weightage but remained more or less untheorised. In the prevailing circumstances, it was assumed that community identities are an integral part of our self-understanding. Their centrality to any conception of the self was a given fact that seemed to require no further affirmation. Thus, while a multicultural polity was designed, the principles of multiculturalism were not systematically enunciated.

It is not surprising that this task has eventually been undertaken in western democracies which are marked by a high degree of individualism. Here, arguing against the tide of liberal ethos, political theorists had to offer a systematic defence of the ideals of multiculturalism. In an environment where the autonomy of the self was greatly prized, they had the onerous task of convincing others that cultural community identities are constitutive of the self, and hence, need to be acknowledged and respected within a democratic polity.

Multiculturalism as a coherent political theory, with its distinct conception of democracy and citizenship, has emerged only in the recent past. Perhaps the most distinguishing mark of these recent enunciations is that they question the idea of universal citizenship and speak instead of 'differentiated citizenship' with group-differentiated rights. The view that people must be incorporated not merely as citizens but also as members of discrete communities possessing multiple loyalties, has challenged the most cherished norms of liberal democracy. It has, at the same time, provided a framework within which special rights for minorities may be discussed and debated. Collectively, these elements

---

[3] The extent and intensity of this resolve can perhaps be illustrated here through the voice of Sardar Patel, a person who worked to integrate India territorially and politically and was known to be attentive to the sentiments of the Hindu majority community. On receiving a letter from B.M. Birla suggesting that after the creation of a Muslim state in the form of Pakistan, it would now be possible to consider India as a Hindu state, Patel wrote: 'I do not think it is possible to consider Hindustan as a Hindu state.... We must not forget that there are other minorities whose protection is our primary responsibility. The state must *exist for all irrespective of caste and creed*' (Patel to B.M. Birla, 10 June 1947, quoted in S. Mahajan, 2001: 5; emphasis added).

have outlined a new vision of democracy: one in which cultural community identities are not only treasured but also sought to be protected and made secure.

Contemporary multiculturalism is, therefore, more than a theory of minority rights. It is a conception of democracy in which diverse cultures are represented as equals in the public domain. The idea that different individuals and communities should be treated as equals within the nation-state is steadily gaining wider acceptance. However, the actual task of abandoning a coherent, homogeneous national culture and replacing it with a heterogeneous public culture has raised a host of questions. Can heterogeneity of all kinds be expressed in the public domain? Indeed, should all forms of heterogeneity be endorsed and permitted in a democracy? What does a heterogeneous public domain entail? Does it imply endorsement of diverse community cultures? Does it affirm separate political space for each community? These, and many other issues, have come up along with the multicultural agenda and they need to be considered carefully. More so, as they raise deep anxieties about fragmenting the state and making communities, rather than individuals, the main unit of political analysis.

This book attempts to explore the conception of democracy that accompanies multiculturalism. It understands the salience of multiculturalism against the background of its analysis of cultural discrimination. By pointing to the existence of cultural discrimination in liberal democracies, even those of the western world, it suggests that multiculturalism has raised issues that democracies everywhere need to address. However, while appreciating the importance of these issues, the following pages argue that contemporary theories of multiculturalism counter culture-related discrimination by protecting and preserving minority cultures. In the pursuit of equal treatment, they privilege the ideal of diversity. While some votaries value diversity of cultures in itself, others claim that survival of marginalised minority cultures is a necessary condition for their being treated as equal. In either case, multiculturalism pleads for policies that promote diversity of cultures by enabling minority cultures to protect themselves. This response to the issue of cultural discrimination is quite problematic. While we need to take cognisance of the ways in which policies of the liberal nation-states continue to disadvantage some groups, it is equally important to take a critical look at the multicultural response to the question of minority discrimination.

The discussion on multiculturalism as well as an assessment of its core agenda is split into eight chapters in this book. The first three chapters elucidate the ideas that define multiculturalism and set it apart from other political theories. The opening chapter makes a distinction between the existence of multiple cultures in society and the theory of multiculturalism. It links multiculturalism to the project of democracy and argues that unlike assertions of plurality, multiculturalism seeks equality for diverse cultures. In particular, it asks whether the different cultures existing in society enjoy an equal status in the public arena. This concern for equality between groups distinguishes multiculturalism from previous theories of tolerance and composite culture.

The next chapter spells out two related dimensions of multiculturalism: its critique of the policies of homogenisation and its reading of cultural community membership. It argues that the value accorded to the latter privileges the goal of protecting minority cultures and promoting diversity of cultures within the polity. The third chapter focuses on the idea of diversity. It distinguishes between the notion of plurality and diversity and suggests that multiculturalism leans heavily on the latter. Beginning with the belief that the different cultures present in society are heterogeneous and incommensurable, it underlines the value of preserving cultural diversity. The commitment to promoting cultural diversity further reinforces the need to make minority cultures secure so that they survive and flourish. It is this attempt to protect marginalised cultures that differentiates multiculturalism from hermeneutic and anthropological studies of other cultures.

The fourth chapter explores the idea of differentiated citizenship. Since claims for special rights for marginalised minority cultures flow directly from the multicultural analysis of cultural discrimination and diversity, this chapter looks at the multicultural challenge to the notion of universal rights of citizenship. It further examines different kinds of special rights that are justified within the framework of multiculturalism with a view to separating rights that enhance options for individuals located within communities, and those enabling cultural communities to preserve their distinct way of life. The latter, it is argued, do not simply minimise discrimination faced by minority communities within the nation-state, but also pursue the agenda of protecting and preserving vulnerable cultures.

The next two chapters reflect upon the problems posed by the multicultural response to the issue of cultural discrimination. They draw upon the feminist and liberal critiques of multiculturalism and make a plea for re-thinking the goal of protecting and preserving minority cultures. The seventh chapter analyses the ways in which theorists of multiculturalism have attempted to address their critics. It analyses four different theories of multiculturalism that try to accommodate the concern for intra-group equality with inter-group equality. While some respond to liberal anxieties by limiting special rights to some minority cultures, others advocate a contextual approach. A few privilege differences unconditionally. However, what merits serious consideration is that all of them endorse the agenda of protecting minority cultures. More importantly, they fail to take a relational view of identities. Consequently, they assume that asserting an identity in the public domain implies protecting and preserving that identity.

The concluding chapter questions these dimensions of contemporary multicultural theory. It emphasises the need to replace the multicultural reading of community identity and membership with the idea of non-conformist membership. The latter, it is argued, is sensitive, both to the contextual dimension of identities as well as to the role that they play in the construction of the self. It also enables us to make a distinction between having an identity, asserting it against the homogenising policies of the nation-state, and preserving that identity. A distinction of this kind is particularly significant because many of the difficulties with contemporary multiculturalism arise from its agenda of protecting diversity and marginalised minority cultures. Under these circumstances, the concept of non-conformist membership allows us to separate policies that challenge the homogenising agenda of the nation-state from those that value diversity in itself.

The discussion here further points to the fact that the prevalent enunciations of multiculturalism are deeply marked by the experiences of Europe and North America. The multicultural analysis of minorities, its identification of the nation-state as the primary site of culture-related discrimination, its advocacy of special rights that give priority to the community over the state, are all shaped by the specific history of those states. Consequently, to re-conceptualise multiculturalism, this section draws upon the experiences of India to argue that the state is only one of the many sources of minority marginalisation. Quite often, it is the actions of other groups in society rather than the cultural orientation of the state that are the major source of discrimination in a polity. Multiculturalism needs to be cognisant of these diverse sites of culture-related discrimination for they call for disparate strategies. Policies that are required for curbing cultural majoritariansim or assimilation are different from those that are needed for battling discrimination that stems from the actions of other groups in society.

Besides, when we take stock of these diverse sources of minority discrimination it becomes evident that the postulated dichotomy between individual and group rights is quite unproductive. Instead of differentiating rights on the basis of different categories of claimants, it is preferable to think of rights that are necessary for minimising discrimination against rights that are essential for promoting other collective goals, such as promoting cultural diversity. If multiculturalism is to challenge minority discrimination, it must therefore reinvent itself. In particular, it must re-think both the idea of community membership as well as special rights and policies necessary for dismantling structures of cultural discrimination. However, this may not be possible in a framework that privileges and values cultural diversity by itself. Consequently, the following pages take a closer and more critical look at the core agenda of multiculturalism. Hopefully, they will affirm the need for re-conceptualising multiculturalism in a way that it acknowledges the presence of a cultural context of experience without attempting to protect it.

As we noted earlier on, the idea of differentiated citizenship and group-differentiated rights which defines contemporary multiculturalism has found the most systematic expression in the writings of political theorists in western democracies, particularly North America and England. In India, by comparison, where multicultural practices have been in operation for a much longer period of time, these issues have been debated more politically, than analytically or academically. Hence, the theory of multiculturalism in this book tilts towards western scholarship. Yet, their appreciation is mediated by the richness of the Indian experience. Hopefully, this work will show that it is the cross-fertilisation of analytical conceptions and political practices that enriches social and political theory.

2

Cultural Discrimination and Community Identity

Different but equal: this is the leitmotif of multiculturalism. While living with differences is a fact of our social existence, multiculturalism reflects upon the status of different cultural communities within a polity. Are diverse cultural communities accommodated as equals in the public arena? Do they receive equal respect and equal treatment in the state? Does the civic culture reflect the heterogeneity of these diverse ways of life? These are the questions through which multiculturalism examines the subject of democratic citizenship within a society. It raises the issue of group equality to underscore the point that cultural community memberships continue to be a source of discrimination in most liberal democracies. Even when legal equality and political rights are given to all persons, some cultural communities continue to be marginalised and disadvantaged in the public arena.

Discrimination on cultural grounds is perpetuated, directly or indirectly, by the policies of the nation-state. It is, in its view, further reinforced by the ideology of liberalism. The liberal principle of neutrality as well as the emphasis on universal rights of citizenship has, in some contexts, sustained the dominance of the majority community in society. Multiculturalism asserts that these principles, along with the policies of the nation-state, have nurtured structures of cultural discrimination. We need to take cognisance of these sources of discrimination, and in the interest of enhancing democracy, ensure that all cultural communities are treated as equals within the political and the public domain.

The question of cultural discrimination lies at the very centre of multiculturalism. Indeed, by identifying the sites of cultural discrimination, multiculturalism has contributed and enriched the discourses of democracy. Over the last four centuries, democratisation has occurred by steadily minimising and eliminating the existing sources of discrimination within social and political life. When religion, race, gender, caste and class were identified as the primary basis of discrimination, the attempt was to include people of all identities in the political domain by extending the same rights of citizenship to all persons. Subsequently, as formal equality became a reality, equality in the public arena became the major concern. Setting aside legal barriers that stood in the way of including people of all identities as citizens of the polity was an important step in actualising the principle of non-discrimination. However, to be an effective reality, non-discrimination entailed that all public spaces be opened to persons of all categories. In particular, it required that no one should be kept away from positions that are economically and socially prestigious. In more positive terms, this meant that as citizens all persons must have access to public spaces and facilities. They should be able to ride in buses and trains, take water from the village wells, eat at public restaurants, enter educational institutions and live in neighbourhoods of their choice.

This project of democratisation is even today far from complete. While identity-based discrimination has been minimised in some areas of life, there are still many pockets where some communities continue to be disadvantaged. Contemporary writings on multiculturalism reaffirm this conclusion by pointing to a site of oppression that has received relatively less attention in previous theories of democracy. They speak of culture-related discrimination that exists in almost all societies, including the most advanced democracies of the modern world, to show that the ideal of equal treatment has not been realised even within liberal democracy.

Through its analysis, multiculturalism makes us aware that promoting sameness may itself be a mode of unequal treatment. Classical theories of democracy were apprehensive about protecting differences. Since the assertion of differences, for example, between men and women, whites and blacks, coloniser and colonised, had been a means of excluding and segregating populations, democracies were expected to set aside these differences by extending the same status and the same rights to all persons. In other words, they weighed differences negatively. Multiculturalism alters this understanding of differences and equal treatment substantially by arguing that the eclipse of differences from the public arena is also a source of discrimination. While no one should be denied the basic rights of political participation on account of their difference, complete uniformity and sameness in public domain entails cultural assimilation, and this too is a mode of discrimination. In a democracy, both exclusion and assimilation are sources of discrimination and we need to guard against each of them. Since inclusion requires, most often, conferring the same status on all persons as citizens, we need to be cautious that identical status is not appropriated by the majority community, or on its behalf by the nation-state, to imply identity in every respect.

The idea that sameness may be oppressive, and that it may disadvantage minority populations, is a lesson that multiculturalism brings home to us. Through its analysis, multiculturalism also makes us aware that cultural nationalism discriminates by using the language of equality to justify its intolerance of cultural differences in public life. Multiculturalism mistrusts the pursuit of uniformity because it is usually a way of establishing the hegemony of the majority community within the polity. Historically, in the formation of the nation-states in Europe, officially recognised religion and language structured the norms that defined the public sphere. While they helped weld together a political community, they did so by eliminating minorities and differences. Multiculturalism builds upon these experiences to underline the need for heterogeneity and diversity in the public sphere.

As we will notice, contemporary discourses on multiculturalism make a plea for a heterogeneous public sphere. What are the notions of equality that prevail in a heterogeneous public sphere? At what level must differences exist in the public sphere? These are questions that can be examined carefully once we recognise the ways in which the notion of complete identity and sameness discriminate some communities in the nation-state. The multicultural reading of cultural differences, particularly its analysis of the sites of cultural discrimination, is important in this context. We need to begin with this dimension before exploring the multicultural agenda and the notion of democratic citizenship incorporated within it.

Liberal Nation-state as the Context of Discrimination

Multiculturalism begins with the understanding that liberal democracies have not been able to ensure equal citizenship for all their members. While they have, by and large, included all communities by granting them equal rights to participate in the public and political domain, they have not been able to incorporate them as equals. Discrimination, in other words, exists and takes many different forms within the nation-state. It is evident in the laws and the policies of the state as well as in the forms in which communities are represented in the public arena. Indeed, representations of other-ness, particularly in the form of negative stereotypes, are some of the most resilient and pervasive modes of discrimination that continue to exist even today.

In many cases, negative images of the other are figured into the cultural narrative of the nation-state itself. Advocates of multiculturalism point to the fact that modern European nation-states, in the process of creating a political community, constructed images of 'us' and 'them'. Through myths, shared past, memories and intermingling of fact and fantasy (Suarez-Orozoco, 2000: 7) they represented some communities as the 'other', the outsiders, who did not belong there. Historically, Islam or Muslim populations, people from the Orient, African races and native populations were represented as the quintessential 'other' (see Said, 1979). These groups were identified as 'inferior racial groups', 'half-castes' (Radhakrishna, 2001: 1), ethnics, barbarians or uncivilised people, and on that basis 'excluded, pathologised, dominated, marginalised and distanced' (Gandhara, 1993: 28). Images of this kind, which were invoked in the course of building the nation-state, have continued to exist despite the multi-ethnic and democratic nature of these polities. Indeed, they are a major source of marginalisation and alienation of individuals and communities in society.

For the multiculturalists, these representations of other-ness are important for they play a crucial role in the way institutions of state and society perceive minority populations. Take, for instance, the reactions of the educational institutions, state authorities and the vast majority in France to the issue of wearing *hijab*. In September 1989, when three Muslim girls wore the traditional headscarf (*hijab*) to their school in Creil, the principal barred them from attending class on the ground that religious symbols could not be worn or publicly displayed within the school premises (see Parekh, 1997: 135–54; Ewing, 2000: 40–44). Here, the minority practice of wearing *hijab* was identified as a religious symbol, and for this reason, disallowed. On the other hand, the practice of wearing a cross, clearly a religious symbol for the Catholic community, did not meet with the same censure. Minority religious practices received different treatment, and what is perhaps even more significant is that these aroused greater suspicion. It was seen as being 'outrageous, ostentatious or even meant to proselytize' (Ewing, 2000: 41). Similar perceptions across the border led the cultural minister of Baden Wurtemburg to deny a regular teaching position to Fereshta Ludin, an Afghan refugee in Germany, who wanted to wear the headscarf in the classroom (*Ibid.*: 42–43). In all these cases, the government and school authorities, as also the vast majority of the people, saw the headscarf as a symbol of an alien religion and oppressive patriarchal culture. Although subordination and oppression of women is not peculiar to Islam, and similar charges can be levelled against Christianity and Judaism, the representation of Islam as a non-liberal and oppressive way of life justified the action against the Muslim girls (see Carens and Williams, 1996: 157–62).

From the perspective of multiculturalism, the issue of *hijab* merely illustrates the way minority cultural practices often get represented within the nation-state. It also reveals the deep-seated bias against minority cultures that still exists in many liberal democracies of the West. Adverse and inhospitable construction of the 'other' is, however, only one of the ways in which minorities are marginalised and disadvantaged in society. In many cases, minority communities get discriminated against because the majority enjoys special privileges, either on account of the past policies of the state, or its current practices.

The disadvantages faced by some communities on account of the past commitments and policies of the state became the focus of multicultural discourse during the Rushdie affair. Votaries of multiculturalism pointed out that some laws that were formulated in the context of extreme religious orthodoxy and intolerance have continued to exist. In particular, laws that recognised, endorsed or even protected dominant religious practices, remain in effect. In England, for instance, this has happened in the case of laws of blasphemy. Even after these laws have been altered, they continue to provide protection to Christians (in particular, the Anglican Church), against desecration of their faith. However, the blasphemy laws provide legal options only for Christianity against obscene vilification. In the debate that followed the Rushdie affair, Muslims argued that their community was being treated unfairly as it alone had no protection against defamation of its religion. Neither the blasphemy laws nor the Race Relations Act of 1976, which declares incitement to racial hatred an offence, have been able to provide protection to Muslims against calumny and discrimination (see Madood, 1993; Bano, 1999). While the Christian majority is provided legal protection against vilification of its religion, the Muslim minority—which is a marginalised and disparaged community—is victimised. It is left open to ridicule and offensive utterances.

The historically advantaged position of the majority community is only one of the many sources of discrimination in contemporary liberal societies. On many occasions, it is the cultural policies and orientation of the nation-state that place minority communities at a disadvantage. Theorists of multiculturalism maintain that most states, including western liberal democracies, have a majoritarian cultural bias, i.e., their policies and practices express the culture of the majority. The choice of the official national language, declaration of public holidays, curriculum of educational institutions, norms pertaining to the preparation of food in public institutions, accepted dress codes in public life, rituals of the state, etc., all exhibit the culture of the majority. This cultural orientation of the nation-state places ethnic and cultural minorities at a disadvantage in the public arena. It even discriminates against them. For instance, the decision to have Sunday as a weekly holiday may appear to be a routine matter, neutral and completely without bias. Yet, in real terms, the decision to close businesses and offices on Sunday conforms to the practices of the Christian majority. It complies with the Christian belief that Sunday is a day of rest. This public endorsement of a religious belief places other minorities at a disadvantage. The Jews in the US argued that this policy of the state restricts them to a five-day week. Complying with their religious beliefs, the Jews observe Saturday as their Sabbath. Since the state compels them to shut their businesses and trades on Sunday, they are disadvantaged in the public arena. While devout Christians can observe Sunday as a day of rest in conformity with their religion, devout Jews, who wish to observe Saturday as a day of rest, are penalised. Similarly, in England, Muslims claimed that a public holiday on Sunday worked only to the advantage of the majority. While practicing Christians could, with Sunday off, go to church for their customary prayers, a religious Muslim could not act in a like manner. As the prescribed day of prayer for Muslims is Friday, which is a working day, the policies of the state only took care of the majority interests. Minorities were unequally treated as their preferences were not given the same consideration by the nation-state (see Parekh, 1997: 124).

The fact that public culture reflects the mores of the majority community is only a small part of the multicultural framework. It, however, gains significance because a public sphere that expresses only the traditions of the majority, places minorities at a disadvantage. When religious festivals of the majority, such as Christmas or Easter, are declared public holidays and the same consideration is not extended to the minorities, the latter are unequally treated. When a dress code is prescribed keeping in mind the preferences of one community or ignoring the practices of others, the latter are placed at a disadvantage. For instance, when the British Home Stores says that it is mandatory for women employees to wear a dress at the place of work, it *de facto* excludes Asian women, who feel that their culture does not allow them to reveal their legs. Similarly, when the Royal

Canadian Mounted Police prescribes a specific headgear for its men, it in effect keeps out the Sikhs who maintain that wearing a turban is an essential requirement of their religion (see Parekh, 1994b: 289–96). In these, and many other cases, minorities alone are seen as being disadvantaged because the preferences of the majority are accommodated in the public sphere. Moreover, the continued presence of majority culture in national and public life gives that culture certain legitimacy. Its customs and practices appear to be neutral, and are often treated as symbols of the nation-state rather than those of a community. Thus, for instance, wearing a crucifix causes no concern and it does not appear to violate the separation of religion from politics, but wearing a *chador* does. What could be a cultural symbol is transformed here into a religious one and conjures up images of the 'other' that become a matter of public outcry.

According to the multiculturalists, disadvantages of this kind that accrue from the prescription of norms in social and public sphere are reinforced by the nation-state through its policies on language and education. The choice of the official national language creates a distinction between the majority and the minority as it distributes resources and opportunities unequally in society. To take an example: the selection of English as the national language invariably places the French-speaking populations of Canada at a disadvantage. On the one hand, it popularises the English language. As English becomes the medium of instruction and government work, more and more people aspire to learn it. On the other hand, it links jobs and opportunities with competence in English and this places populations whose mother tongue is English at an advantage in the public arena. To occupy prestigious positions and jobs, people must learn and excel in the English language and absorb the culture associated with it. This necessarily disadvantages people whose mother tongue is not English. French speakers, for instance, suffer. They have to try harder to compete for open public positions. To be successful they need to have fluency in a language that is not their mother tongue and this requires special effort.

What is perhaps even more important, linking opportunities to facility in English speaking places pressure on the French speakers to learn that language. Young members of these communities try to assimilate into the mainstream by learning the official language and the way of life that comes with it. Parents also encourage this; they send their children to English medium schools so that they can compete for, and occupy, prestigious public positions. Pressures and incentives to integrate into the majority culture eventually result in the disintegration of the minority culture. In addition, it places heavy costs on the minority communities. As the children assimilate into the culture of the majority, they become more and more alienated from their own communities and families. They feel awkward publicly associating with their families as they feel their parents and elders do not fit in with the rest of society. This triggers off inter-generation conflicts and leaves the young with a sense of anxiety and insecurity that manifests itself in a variety of adolescent and teenage problems (Parekh, 1992: 65–67). The school curricula, particularly, representations of the nation's history in textbooks, the role ascribed to different groups within the polity, accentuate this sense of alienation. Together, these policies exclude, marginalise and disadvantage minority communities (see Gilroy, 1987).

Multiculturalism uses the case of language and education policies to show that the nation-state has a majoritarian cultural bias. It is not, in other words, neutral or indifferent to considerations of ethnicity and community identity. In some democracies, ethnicity is quite obviously linked to citizenship. In Germany, for example, 'most of the grandchildren of Turkish guestworkers are not citizens even though they, and often their parents, have lived all their lives in Germany' (Carens, 2000: 10). However, even in polities where citizenship is not defined entirely in ethnic terms, the state is not completely neutral. Institutions, through which the principles of liberal democracy are operationalised, themselves reinforce a particular value orientation. Take the case of representation, whether a state endorses first-past-the-post system or proportional representation, single-member geographically defined constituency, or represents communities of interest by creating rural ridings or black-majority ridings, each choice embodies a specific political and moral conception. What is perhaps equally significant is that they play an important role in including or marginalising communities.

Theorists of multiculturalism question the presumed neutrality of the liberal democratic state. In their view, no state can be entirely neutral. Almost everywhere, the state legislates on such matters as marriage, divorce, rights of illegitimate children, homosexual marriages, incest, compulsory education of children, • abortion, rules for adoption of children, capital punishment, public hangings, permissible initiation rights, rights of inheritance to parental property, etc. Legislation in each of these spheres reflects, and is anchored in, a specific conception of good life. It is not, in this sense, morally or culturally neutral. Indeed '[A] morally neutral state, making no moral demands on its citizens and equally hospitable to all human choices, is logically impossible' (Parekh, 1994c: 207).

A few theorists take the argument even further. They claim that the liberal state cannot be neutral because it has a moral universe in which individual freedom and autonomy are values that trump all else (Mendus, 1989: 107). Hence, it is not hospitable to all forms of life, or even all forms of diversity. Liberalism celebrates diversity but only at the level of the individual. It values differences of tastes, opinions and lifestyles but is less accommodative towards differences of culture. According to Bhikhu Parekh, nineteenth century onwards, the ideology of liberalism, and with it the practices of the liberal state, have been largely intolerant of cultural differences (Parekh, 1994a). They have been 'ethnocentric and narrow, dismissing non-liberal ways of life and thought as primitive and in need of the liberal civilizing mission' (Ibid.: 11). Parekh illustrates this through the writings of John Stuart Mill. He states that Mill characterised European states, rooted in the ethic of individualism and freedom of choice, as being 'civilized' societies, and represented the non-European states as 'backward' societies, 'continents without history' (quoted in Parekh, 1994a: 11). For him, non-European societies were in a state of 'infancy'. In the absence of the spirit of individualism, they lacked the ability to grow and develop themselves unaided. John Stuart Mill justified British colonialism on this ground, and he saw no injustice in subordinating these so-called 'backward' cultures and absorbing them within the culture of the colonisers (Ibid.).

Liberals such as Mill used judgements of this kind to defend colonialism and to argue that it was a 'right', if not the 'responsibility', of the colonisers to civilise the colonised by introducing them to the liberal way of life (*Ibid.*). According to Parekh, the missionary zeal of Millian liberalism has not ended with decolonisation. Even today, liberals justify the need to 'liberalise' the culture of the immigrant populations that live in the West (*Ibid.*: 11–13). In their view, most immigrants carry with them 'threatening values and alien ways of life' (Carens and Williams, 1996: 157) that breed fundamentalism and gender inequality. Hence, these cultures need to be transformed radically. The only difference between the old and the new incarnation of liberalism is that the former rationalised coercive and forced assimilation of diverse populations. The latter hopes to alter these ways of life through cultural engineering, i.e., by cultivating liberal values through educational system, funding liberal groups among these communities, and by adopting suitable immigrant policies (Parekh, 1994a: 13).

For the multiculturalists, liberal intolerance of cultural differences is a cause for concern because it disadvantages some forms of life. Typically, ways of life that are not rooted in the individualist conception of society, such as 'traditional and customary ways of life, as well as those centred around the community' are denounced as being inferior, inhuman and stifling (Parekh, 1994a: 12). To quote Joseph Raz, there are 'certain conceptions of good that are worthless and demeaning...political action may and should be taken to eradicate or at least curtail them' (Raz, 1986: 133). Eventually, only those religious and cultural communities are protected which value and accommodate individual choice and autonomy (Horton, 1993). While non-liberal communities can exist and, in principle, people are free to join them, the liberal framework does not provide a fertile ground for the survival of communities that endorse a strong commitment to a set of collective moral and religious values[1] (Chaplin, 1993).

---

[1] According to Jonathan Chaplin, isolated experiments that go against the thrust of the whole society are doomed to fail in a liberal polity. A socialist workers' cooperative would find it difficult to survive in a society governed by capitalist rules of competition, exchange and profit. It would not be able to convince

Not all votaries of multiculturalism share in this assessment of liberalism but they nevertheless accept that the policies of cultural homogenisation are a major source of minority discrimination. Homogeneity promotes, in their view, assimilation. It encourages uniformity in social and public life and this tends to disadvantage minorities. The emphasis on uniformity obliterates group differences and, at times, does not even allow differences of form to exist within the public arena. Since uniformity works to the disadvantage of minority communities and often camouflages the dominant position of the majority culture within the nation-state, multiculturalism is deeply sceptical of the ideal of uniformity. Indeed, it questions the very principle of formal equality or identical treatment, particularly because it eclipses differences.

Formal equality entails that all individuals as citizens must be treated alike in law and they must receive the same identical treatment under like conditions. It further assumes that ascriptive community identities must not be regarded as relevant differences that justify different or unlike treatment. As such, formal equality rests upon what Svensson calls, the 'generalizability principle'. It supposes that 'if Y is right for A and if A and B are relevantly similar persons in relevantly similar situations, Y is

---

investors or even workers in advance that it will succeed. 'The "whole thrust" of a libertarian society will have educated people to doubt the success of a socialist organization of industry. Even heroic voluntary sacrifices by workers would be unlikely to sustain a cooperative in such an inauspicious environment. Thus, while Nozick's libertarian utopia would appear not to be directly intolerant towards a workers' cooperative—they would be legally free to exist—it would very likely be indirectly intolerant towards them. Parallel problems would face any communities characterized by strong moral, social or religious obligations.... A libertarian framework would create a libertarian ethos in which the idea of open-ended or unquantifiable commitment to moral or religious values would be difficult to get off the ground—or seriously eroded—if it already existed' (Chaplin, 1993: 37).

Commitment to religious and collective communities is, in his view, equally jeopardised in Rawls' liberal society (*Ibid.*). Since Rawls does not recognise 'cultural identity as a primary good and a source of legitimate claims on the state', in his society 'citizens may follow the religious, communal and other ways of life, but the basic thrust of social structure is against them. Enjoying neither public recognition nor public support, they are on the defensive and at a disadvantage compared to the officially institutionalized liberal ways of life and thought' (Parekh, 1994a: 13).

right for B' (Svensson, 1979: 428). While stipulating a fundamental similarity between individuals as citizens, this principle sets aside differences of race, religion, gender and ethnicity. Multiculturalism is critical of this neglect of group differences. It maintains that in certain circumstances, group memberships and cultural identities are significant and must be seen as relevant differences. Further, negating these differences can yield unequal and unjust treatment of some.

Taking the example of a tribal woman who tattoos the cheek of her eight-year old child and that of a white woman who causes bodily harm to her child, multiculturalists argue that within the framework of formal equality, both these women would be treated alike. Their actions, leading to bodily harm to the child, would appear to be just the same; and hence, both would receive the same punishment. However, judgements of this kind that are based on the notion of sameness, are blatantly unfair to the tribal woman. They eliminate the relevant differences between the two women and their respective actions. They ignore that the white woman acts with the intention of harming the child, while the tribal woman tattoos the cheek under ceremonial conditions and in accordance with her community practices. In other words, she does not act with the intention of harming the child (Parekh, 1994c: 210). Differences of this kind, according to advocates of multiculturalism, become evident only when the law pays attention to the cultural identity and community practices of the agents. When differences in the cultural context of experience are set aside, identical treatment can be a source of discrimination against the marginalised groups whose practices are not reflected in the laws of the state.

In part, these objections to the principle of formal equality arise from the recognition that law also uses the framework of the hegemonic culture to understand an action and infer its meaning. Since it does not take note of the difference that minority cultures represent, it remains insensitive to the meaning that a seemingly similar action may have in another culture. However, by suggesting that cultural differences may be relevant in determining what is fair and just, multiculturalism implies that the mere presence of plurality or multiplicity of form is not enough.

It is essential but not sufficient. If diverse communities have to be treated as equals, then we need to think of a heterogeneous public sphere that is constituted by, or accommodative of, different ways of life.

Constructing a public domain where many different cultures are present as equals is the primary agenda of multiculturalism. The need to protect minorities and their culture through a system of special rights is, within this framework, seen as a necessary step in the realisation of that goal. This step becomes necessary because of the prevailing structures of culture-based discrimination; and it is believed that a heterogeneous public sphere would help check and dismantle these sites of discrimination. Most supporters of this viewpoint, however, accept that there are limits to what may be accommodated in the public sphere; and they also accept that the entire range of existing diversity cannot always be represented in a like manner. But these are issues that we will take up a little later. It is essential at this stage to recall that multiculturalism holds the nation-state, including the liberal democratic state, responsible for engendering the marginalisation and discrimination of minority communities within the nation-state.

Further, in its analysis of this pattern of discrimination, multiculturalism does not differentiate between the majority and the minority on the basis of numerical strength. Numbers matter but what is of utmost importance is the cultural orientation of the nation-state. The community whose culture is endorsed by the state and expressed in national public culture constitutes the majority, irrespective of its numerical size. Public endorsement does, however, ensure that the culturally dominant community will, over time, become the numerically larger community. When the nation-state, for instance, grants official recognition to the language of a community, other languages and cultures existing within the state are inevitably devalued. People living in the nation-state try to learn the official language in their quest for jobs and opportunities. They also try to ensure education for their children, not in their own mother tongue, but in the language endorsed by the state. The recognition given to a particular language by the nation-state thus gives it a certain advantage in the public arena. With state support it is transmitted more effectively to others, and even members of other communities find it necessary and profitable to learn that language. As a consequence, the national language gradually becomes the language of a numerical majority while other linguistic cultures, which may have been previously dominant in certain places, get marginalised. They are reduced to the status of a minority language and culture (Mahajan and Sheth, 1999: 10).

Hence, the crucial factor is endorsement by the state rather than numerical size. The majority community is one whose culture is recognised by the state while minorities are those whose cultures are not represented in the public domain. This notion of the majority and the minorities follows from the multicultural reading of cultural discrimination and marginalisation. Minorities are said to be marginalised because these cultures are excluded from the public arena and policies of the state which eventually makes them a less attractive option. The multicultural agenda of preserving marginalised minorities through a system of group-differentiated rights is supposed to protect minority cultures from this fate: namely, gradual disintegration and extinction.

Community Identities and the Public Domain

Within multiculturalism, the issue of cultural discrimination is coupled with the idea that community identities are constitutive of the self. Multiculturalism underlines the importance of collective identities in everyday life. Indeed, it finds fault with liberalism for neglecting the cultural context of experience and action. Cultural discrimination, according to supporters of multiculturalism, remains unattended within liberalism because this framework imagines individuals as separate, atomised selves, delinked from their cultural context. It sees individuals as autonomous persons whose moral agency lies in their ability to make choices. The notion of a freely choosing atomised self invariably ignores the constitutive dimension of personal identity. It forgets that individuals are, in addition to being citizens, members of diverse communities and located in different cultures.

To emphasise the importance of cultural community as a context of experience, multiculturalism argues that community membership gives individuals a specific history. It influences their predicaments and structures the way other people relate to them. As such, cultural community identities are important. They define, at least in part, who we are. The idea that cultural communities constitute, in this minimalist sense, an 'anchor for self-identification' (Margalit and Raz, 1990: 447) and the 'context of experience' (Kymlicka, 1995: 89) is, in their view, eclipsed within liberalism (also see Chandhoke, 1999; Bhargava et al., 1999: 9). Even when John Rawls acknowledges the presence of community identities in his later writings, he sees these memberships as being relevant only in the private sphere of life. They constitute the 'non-public identity' (Rawls, 1985: 241) of the person. In limiting these identities to the private realm he does not sufficiently recognise that our projects and engagements in the polity may arise out of social and cultural identities. When the policies and the practices of the 'procedural republic' advantage some communities, individuals cannot be expected to participate in the public arena as 'unencumbered selves'. Indeed, people may participate to promote certain shared community goals. Some may even complain of 'unequal and discriminatory treatment, and question their obligation to obey the state' (Parekh, 1994a: 13). As such, community memberships cannot be completely effaced from the public domain, nor can they be restricted to the private sphere alone.

Cultural community membership, according to theorists of multiculturalism, structures individual experience. It influences choices and provides a framework within which things come to acquire value. To assume as many liberals do that all associations and engagements are freely chosen, or that individuals enter into the cultural supermarket, shop around and select what they like, is to grossly misunderstand the nature of self. The idea that all associations are voluntary in nature and people can join or leave them as they please is a compelling liberal utopia, but it misapprehends the nature of community membership.

Community memberships are neither permanently fixed nor freely chosen. They are malleable and open to construction and individuals may choose to exit from them, yet memberships cannot be relinquished so easily. Just as communities are not formed deliberately for the sake of pursuing shared interests, similarly they cannot simply be forsaken by a single act of volition. People may disavow the beliefs of their community but others may continue to represent them as members of that community. For instance, a person born in a Muslim family may chose not to live by the religious precepts of Islam. But by designating him as 'anti-nationalist' who must prove his loyalty to the Indian nation-state, others may force that community membership upon him, and he cannot escape his identity even if he wishes to. These representations by others cannot be simply set aside. They influence our self-perceptions. Consequently, to assume that community memberships can be taken on or abandoned at free will misrepresents the formation and functioning of identities in society.

In locating the individual within the community, multiculturalism acknowledges the existence of collective communities and identities. Contra liberalism, it maintains that people inhabit two worlds: they are members of a political community as well as members of specific cultural communities. Hence, what matters to them in this dual capacity must receive consideration within the democratic state. What is perhaps even more important from the perspective of multiculturalism is that individuals value collective memberships. While arguing that cultural communities constitute the context in which individuals live, experience and form judgements, multiculturalism does more than assert the existence of cultural community identities. It claims that a secure cultural context is essential for the wellbeing of the self. When cultural community is either not recognised or subject to disintegration by the policies of the nation-state, some individuals and groups are disadvantaged within the polity. Hence, in the interest of ensuring fair treatment to all, it suggests that marginalised minority cultures be protected by creating conditions in which these cultures flourish. The multicultural agenda flows from this understanding of the value of cultural community membership and it is this assessment of community membership that shapes its commitment to ensure that minority cultures survive and flourish within the nation-state.

The Agenda of Preserving Minority Cultures

Recognition of the importance of community identities and the accompanying awareness that some minorities are disadvantaged in the nation-state has structured the agenda of multicultural-ism. The concern for preserving minority cultures works with the belief that the nation-state is not one, homogeneous entity. It encompasses within it people of different communities. What is even more important, it has two kinds of communities within its boundary: the majority community and the minority communities. The former is placed at an advantageous position because it enjoys a hegemonic position in the public arena. The minorities, by implication, are disadvantaged in public life. They have to work harder to compete for jobs and positions, their cultures are undervalued, and they are faced with pressures to assimilate into the majority. The visible gains of endorsing the majority culture embodied by the nation-state, make it attractive for them to assimilate into the dominant culture. But assimilation comes at a cost. It undermines minority cultures and results in their disintegration. Such processes of marginalisation place minority communities at a disadvantage. It denies members of these communities access to their culture. In the absence of a secure culture, they are deprived of an environment that gives meaning to their lives. Within multiculturalism, special treatment for minorities, by way of protecting their culture, is strongly advised to minimise these structures of minority discrimination.

Most multiculturalists accept that assimilation into the majority culture is not always induced through coercion. Indeed, given the gains of endorsing that culture, members of the minority communities themselves seek the 'instrumental' aspects of that culture (Suarez-Orozoco, 2000: 20). They want their children to receive education in the national language and to go to schools where they can absorb the culture and manners of the dominant community. Such choices are generally guided by the unequal positions that the majority and the minority cultures have in the marketplace. According to theorists of multiculturalism, minorities do not have an equal opportunity to continue with their own way of life for they have to pay a heavy price for that choice.

Besides, given the inequality of circumstance, minorities have to use all their resources just to ensure the survival of their cultural structures (Kymlicka, 1991: 189). It is these forms of disadvantage and inequality of cultural circumstance that multiculturalism targets and hopes to remedy through a system of group-differentiated rights.

The agenda of protecting minority cultures by giving special rights to identified minorities has brought communities into the discourse of democracy. Although on previous occasions, both the advocates of welfare state as well as the supporters of affirmative action differentiated between citizens and identified vulnerable groups that required special treatment, they involved the community in very different ways. Within the framework of affirmative action, community identities were not valued in themselves. They were merely a means of targeting sections of the population who, on account of their discrimination in the past, were marginalised.

Further, the intention of these policies was to bring the identified groups and communities into the mainstream. The background assumption being that groups that had been victims of historical injustices could not compete with others on equal terms. They required special assistance to help minimise the effects of past discrimination. Affirmative action was to ensure this; it was expected to create conditions necessary for ensuring that the race was fair and no one had a head start, particularly on account of what Rawls calls 'natural lottery'. Thus, measures of affirmative action were to promote assimilation. Through specially designed programmes, it was believed that hitherto segregated and excluded communities would be able to overcome barriers that were imposed on account of their identity. Hence, all such policies were supposed to be temporary in nature, and intended to last till such time these communities merged into the larger totality.

Multiculturalism deviates significantly from this framework. Unlike the schema of affirmative action, it values community identities and finds fault in the present system for not acknowledging the importance of these identities. Since it prizes cultural identity, there is no question of transcending the identity or assimilating into the mainstream. Moreover, as cultural community identity is perceived as being a mark of who we are, multicultural policies are supposed to be permanent measures that enable these groups to be included as equals. They ensure equality of cultural circumstance rather than equality of opportunity. Besides, these measures are not restricted to communities that have, in the past, suffered on account of the policies of the state and society. Although western theories of multiculturalism have focused on 'indigenous people', who have suffered injustices for centuries together, in principle multiculturalism is supportive of the claims of all marginalised minority communities. Since multiculturalism identifies present policies of the state and its cultural orientation as the source of cultural discrimination, it is assumed that minority communities, irrespective of their past position, may require special rights. New immigrants may legitimately seek rights to construct their mosques and wear turbans. All such claims for recognition and equal treatment are entertained within multiculturalism.

Consequently, multiculturalism needs to be distinguished from affirmative action. Even though references are made to the community in each of these frameworks, it occupies very different position in each. Indeed, the agenda of multiculturalism and affirmative action are significantly different, and must be separated. The difference in the logic of these two schema comes sharply into focus when we turn to the Indian Constitution. Here, when the concern was to include hitherto segregated and excluded communities who were disadvantaged on account of past prejudices, the framers identified the Scheduled Castes and the Scheduled Tribes as groups that deserved positive discrimination. However, when the question was one of incorporating all communities as equals with the same rights, it identified Muslims, Sikhs, Christians and Parsees as minorities who deserved special rights to protect and preserve their culture. The difference between these two sets of groups was based on the understanding that the former needed temporary measures to make up for the loss they had suffered by being excluded. The latter, on the other hand, were communities that had a distinct culture and wanted an assurance that the state would not take on the culture of the majority. As such, they sought, and were given, minority rights that were permanent in nature. These rights represented conditions for ensuring equal space for all communities, and hence, did not require periodic confirmation, as was the case with measures of positive discrimination and affirmative action.

Multiculturalism, as we noticed earlier, places special rights for minority communities against the backdrop of existing structures of cultural discrimination. However, these claims are further reinforced by the value that it places upon culture and community. Multiculturalism regards community membership as a valued collective good. It argues that personal identity is shaped by community membership. Consequently, we cannot respect individuals without respecting the values they uphold and deeply cherish. A democratic polity must, therefore, accommodate individuals not only in their capacity as citizens, but also as members of specific communities. The multicultural agenda rests upon this proposed link between the self and the community. Hence, it is necessary to dwell upon this aspect in a little more detail.

Locating the Individual in Community

Multiculturalism sees individuals not simply as citizens or rational, autonomous and self-directing persons, but also as members of communities. Indeed, it emphasises the importance of collective community identities in individual life. In asserting the value of community identities, multiculturalism invariably distances itself from mainstream liⁱ ʳalism. It maintains that liberalism gives little consideration tᴜ this dimension of individual life and personal identity. Political philosophers from Hobbes to Mill speak only of the individual or the state. Free, consenting individuals form the basic unit of the state; they are the possessors of rights; and it is they who come together voluntarily to sign the contract and constitute the commonwealth (Van Dyke, 1977). As such, within the theoretical schema of liberalism, community memberships are rarely acknowledged, let alone valued. In fact, the individual is defined in 'austere and minimalist terms' (Parekh, 1993). Liberalism abstracts the person from all contingent relations with other people, and draws a sharp boundary between the self and others. Each individual is seen as a distinct person, separate and distinguishable from others. Furthermore, the individual is conceived primarily as an autonomous person who makes his or her own choices about values and goals to pursue in life. Since liberals prize free will, they only recognise voluntary groups and associations that emerge from chosen affiliations. Communities that are not chosen, communities in which individuals are born or find themselves in, win no favour with them. In fact, from the liberal perspective, all such ascribed identities and community memberships which are inherited rather than chosen, constrain individual action and freedom. As such, they are not regarded as valued goods in society.

Multiculturalism challenges this account of the community and, with it, the liberal conception of the individual self. For it, bonds of cultural community identity define personal identity. They provide an anchor for self-identification (Kymlicka, 1995: 89). Individuals see themselves as members of a specific community and their expectations and experiences are formed, to a considerable extent, by their community membership. Moreover, cultural community moulds the 'context of experience' (*Ibid.*). It shapes their attachments and influences their conceptions of good life. In addition, it constitutes a framework through which they judge and evaluate life-plans. Cultural practices, it is argued, structure the life of individuals and yield norms by which they distinguish between right and wrong, sacred and profane, meaningful and inane. As such, individuals enter the public domain and often participate as members of specific communities (*Ibid.*).

Beginning with the view that cultural community memberships define personal identity, theorists of multiculturalism argue that these memberships must be regarded as a valued collective good. Consequently, no one should be expected to give up their cultural identity. While some may voluntarily relinquish this bond, no one must be expected to do without this resource. 'We should treat access to one's culture as something that people can be expected to want, whatever their more particular conception of good. Leaving one's culture, while possible, is best seen as renouncing something to which one is reasonably entitled' (Kymlicka, 1995: 86).

In addition to valuing cultural community membership, advocates of multiculturalism maintain that 'a concern for equality and freedom requires us to respect claims about culture and identity' (Carens, 2000: 1). Since individuals are defined, at least in part, by community membership, respect for the individual requires respect for their community membership, respect for their values and for what they consider to be good and desirable. 'One's sense of personal identity is closely bound up with one's language, characteristic modes of thought, customs, collective memories, and so on, in a word, with one's culture. To ignore the latter is to denude individuals of, and reject, what constitutes them as particular kinds of persons and matters most to them, and that is hardly a way of showing them respect' (Parekh, 1994c: 206). Consequently, respect for an abstract humanity must be replaced by respect for 'historically articulated humanity' (*Ibid.*), and this requires respect for individuals in their particularity and uniqueness.

Respect for cultural community identity is valued within multiculturalism for yet another reason. Cultural membership is, to use Kymlicka's phrase, 'crucial for personal agency and development' (Kymlicka, 1991: 176). While individual identity is shaped by the community in which the individuals are situated, their self-perception is affected by the way they are perceived by others. Individual members suffer if their community membership is not valued by others and if it has low prestige in the public arena (Taylor, 1994). They become diffident, nervous and unable to perform successfully in the public domain (Parekh, 1994c: 66–67). Alternately, they respond to their low cultural self-esteem by distancing themselves from their own families. Instead of locating themselves in their respective cultural norms, they aspire to conform to values that are, in their view, endorsed by the majority. The alienation of the self from family, relatives and friends places a heavy toll on the community and its members, particularly the young ones. On the one hand, it creates inter-generation conflicts, and on the other, it deprives the individual of a secure social environment that is necessary for proper growth and development of the self. As a result, there is a much higher incidence of poverty, unemployment, drug addiction, health risks, juvenile delinquency among individuals from these marginalised communities (see Kymlicka, 1991; Macklem, 1996).

Misrecognition or absence of recognition of one's identity can, in this way, cause real damage. Besides being a social stigma, it is a 'potent instrument of one's oppression' (Taylor, 1994: 25–28) and can be an instrument of self-depreciation. Since adverse representations of one's cultural identity can cause grievous harm to the self, we 'owe' it to others to give them due recognition. This conclusion is affirmed by most multiculturalists, albeit by invoking different arguments. Kymlicka, for instance, does not emphasise a person's moral responsibility to other human beings, but states that a rich and secure cultural context is essential for exercising options and making meaningful choices. People can make rational choices and rethink their inheritances only when their culture is secure and valued in society. When cultures are threatened or devalued, they tend to become more closed. Consequently, even for the sake of creating space for individual expressions of difference, it is necessary to make all cultures, particularly, marginalised minority cultures, secure. However, this is possible only when we recognise the existence of cultural community memberships and appreciate the value they have in the lives of individuals.

Multiculturalism and Communitarianism

The multicultural conception of individual self and community that has just been outlined, bears a strong resemblance to communitarianism. Both locate the individual in community; both cherish community memberships and argue that the community forms the backdrop against which individuals give meaning to their lives. Like multiculturalism, communitarianism begins with a critique of liberalism. It questions the view that the world consists of discrete individuals, and that these separate, atomised selves enter into relationships voluntarily, for the sake of realising some specific goals. In its place it, too, argues that individuals see themselves as members of specific communities. They are situated in a social matrix and a web of relationships that define their personal identity. 'I am someone's son or daughter, someone else's cousin or uncle; I am a citizen of this or that city, a member of this or that guild or profession; I belong to this tribe, that clan, this nation' (MacIntyre, 1981: 204–05). Individuals recognise and acknowledge the embedded nature of their identity. They see themselves as members of specific communities. Instead of representing themselves as attributeless persons or as 'abstract instances of human species' (Gray, 1988: 39), they see themselves as 'articulators of definite ways of life that reflect their circumstances and, at once, express and confer on them a distinctive identity' (*Ibid.*).

This idea that individuals are situated in specific communities, and that they approach their 'circumstances as bearers of particular social identity' (MacIntyre, 1981: 204–05) is endorsed by both multiculturalism and communitarianism. However, even as both 'isms' situate the individual in the community, there is a slender line that differentiates the two. One needs to take cognisance of this fine distinction to understand the specific agenda of multiculturalism and to avoid communitarian appropriations of the multicultural agenda.

Communitarianism sees individuals as being constituted by their communities. The notion of a constituted self entails two things: (*i*) collective community identity 'give my life its moral particularity' (*Ibid.*), i.e., in 'the absence of constitutive communal frameworks, the very idea of morality as a rational or intelligible enterprise drops out' (Mulhall and Swift, 1992: 92) and (*ii*) as members of specific communities, individuals are defined by shared collective goals. Effectively, this means that they cannot stand back or distance themselves from these goals to assess them. Conceptions of good life are not perceived here as being objects of choice. Individuals endorse moral ideals that are shaped by the community and presented in the language of the community. They are expected to affirm received goals, and value them above all else, even the right to revise or rethink those commitments.

Several theorists of multiculturalism consciously dissociate themselves from this idea of a constituted self. They place the individual within her cultural community but in principle at least they accept the possibility of shared practices and collective goals being revised. According to Kymlicka, it 'is not easy or enjoyable to revise one's deepest ends, but it is possible, and sometimes a regrettable necessity. New experiences and circumstances may reveal that our earlier beliefs about the good are mistaken.... No matter how confident we are about our ends at a particular moment, new circumstances and experiences may arise...that cause us to re-evaluate them. There is no way to predict in advance when the need for such a reconsideration will arise' (Kymlicka, 1995: 91). Since our ends and goals may change, for the multiculturalists, community membership does not foreclose options of questioning or revising the existing way of life. Thus, unlike many communitarians, advocates of multiculturalism abandon the notion of a deeply or 'radically situated self'. Even though they do not reject the belief that a community is marked by shared values, they do create some space for revision of these common norms, practices and institutional structures. However, what must be underlined here is that multiculturalism does not see the individual as the subject of change. It, too, locates agency in the community rather than the individual. It maintains that a given way of life may change and the group may decide to reject existing practices and community structures, but all such changes are to be initiated by the community itself. Indeed, many multiculturalists claim that when communities enjoy a degree of political and cultural autonomy, they are likely to re-think existing practices. Will Kymlicka, in fact, maintains that a secure cultural context is a pre-condition for revising received inheritances. According to him, not all circumstances allow individuals to reconsider their received traditions and beliefs. When cultures are insecure, people are more inclined to affirm collective community goals; but when a culture is secure, individuals can distance themselves from, and re-think, received norms.

There is another distinction that needs to be made between multiculturalism and communitarianism. Communitarianism perceives communities to be collectivities with a shared conception of good life. Indeed, it values community membership because a common language of morality is only conceivable within a community. To put it the other way around, communitarians maintain that it is difficult to envisage any kind of public good in a polity where individuals come together only to pursue their voluntaristic goals or personal advantages. Commitment to shared values and conceptions of good are the essential conditions for the existence of a political community. Without these shared conceptions of good, they claim, it is impossible to envisage any kind of public good. It is equally difficult to legitimise and justify goals that the state wishes to pursue. Collective enterprise and pursuit of common goals, including those of welfare and distributive justice, require commitment to shared goals. They demand 'a national political community of shared purposes' (Sandel, 1987: 206).

However, since shared purposes can only exist within a community whose members are bound to each other antecedently, communitarianism moves between two extreme positions. It seeks to empower and strengthen small collectivities such as the family, neighbourhood, church, caste groups, etc., i.e., communities that can express a shared conception of good life. Alternately, it envisages the nation-state as a community of persons who share a conception of what is good for the self and the community. In both cases, it sees shared commitment to substantive goals and conception of good life as the defining elements of community life.

Multiculturalism, by comparison, is particularly wary of imagining the nation-state as a political community committed to shared conceptions of what is good and desirable. Against the communitarian vision of a nation-state that is anchored in the politics of common good, multiculturalism aims to construct a nation-state that can represent and accommodate diverse conceptions of good life. Besides, multiculturalists fear that a prior commitment to substantive notions of good is likely to re-entrench the hegemony of the majority culture in the public domain. Consequently, they question the very pursuit of common good at the level of the nation-state, though not always at the level of the community.

Moreover, while critiquing liberalism and pursuing the politics of common good, communitarians give primacy to participation over rights. Accordingly, they want to strengthen political institutions such as legislatures and political parties rather than judiciary or bureaucracy. To quote Michael Sandel: 'The political institutions that come to the fore in the neutral state are institutions like the judiciary and the bureaucracy. These institutions are designed, in principle at least, to be insulated from democratic pressures, and so better able to define and defend individual rights. Despite their great importance in such areas as civil rights, these are not democratic institutions' (Sandel, 1987: 208). They have alienated citizens and made them powerless.

To counter these trends, the communitarians underline the need to build a less fragmented, if not a more cohesive, collective identity that is rooted in shared conception of what is good and desirable. Multiculturalism, by comparison, is concerned with the fate of minority cultures and communities within the nation-state. Hence, it is reluctant to leave everything open to popular pressures for that is likely to allow the majority community to determine decisions. To protect minorities from the tyranny of the majority, multiculturalism, in fact, favours a regimen of special rights. In any case it refuses to privilege conceptions of shared good within the polity.

Thus, there are significant differences between multiculturalism and communitarianism. However, multiculturalism affirms the premise that individual identity is shaped, in part, by cultural community membership, and that individuals value these memberships. It is because these community memberships are deeply cherished that it makes sense to protect and preserve them. What bears repetition here is that the presence of cultural majoritarianism and assimilationist policies point to the need for heterogeneity. Further, the conclusion that promoting heterogeneity entails preserving marginalised minority cultures gains salience when the issue of cultural discrimination is linked to the view that collective cultural identities are deeply cherished by individuals; and that their non-recognition, or even misrecognition, can cause considerable harm to the self.

It is this emphasis on the value of community membership that shapes the multicultural agenda for making minority cultures secure. And, it is this that differentiates multiculturalism from liberalism. Although liberalism and multiculturalism approach the individual and the community from vastly divergent perspectives, several multiculturalists claim that the concerns of these two frameworks are fairly similar. Multiculturalism, in their view, points to the existing patterns of cultural discrimination with the aim of making liberalism more self-critical and true to its own conceptions of fairness. Liberalism, they feel, is not 'liberal' enough; it is unjust to some cultures and communities, and it is this that they seek to remedy. They hope that multicultural analysis will enable liberal democracies to realise the values that they cherish deeply, in particular, the principle of value pluralism. Liberalism, they argue, does not favour a society which establishes some 'universally binding higher-order purposes' (Galston, 1996: 9). It cherishes a procedural republic on the assumption that different people may cherish different goods and that no one group can encompass the entire range of goods that we regard as desirable. Multiculturalists build on this idea and maintain that no one culture can encompass the entire range of values that we, as human beings, prize deeply.

A more systematic statement of the link between liberalism and multiculturalism is articulated in the writings of Will Kymlicka. He explains that liberalism does not simply value individual autonomy and the freedom to choose one's preferred way of life. It strongly favours the freedom to *revise* and rethink our preferences. From the liberal perspective, individuals must not only have the freedom to choose but also the freedom to make informed choices and the accompanying freedom to interrogate those choices. If individuals so desire, they must have the liberty to reject a conception of life that they once opted for and choose another vision of good life. The ability to revise and rethink our choices is thus central to any conception of liberalism. The difficulty however is that received traditions and conceptions can be revised only under certain circumstances. Revisability requires, among other things, a secure cultural context and the availability of options and information about alternatives. By protecting minority cultures and sustaining cultural diversity, he feels, we can fulfil these conditions and create an environment in which the liberal ethos can flourish (Kymlicka, 1991: 9–19).

For Kymlicka then, both multiculturalism and liberalism are committed to the ideal of 'revisability'. However, while affirming the ideal of revisability, multiculturalism locates the individual within the community and stresses the need to provide a secure context. Liberalism, on the other hand, gives centrality to the idea of individual autonomy, and in this it visualises an autonomous and unencumbered self. As a consequence, the two isms follow different routes: liberalism protects the rights of individuals as citizens while multiculturalism speaks of the rights of minority cultures within the nation-state.

In this chapter we noted that multiculturalism critiques the practices of the liberal nation-state on the ground that its policies disadvantage and discriminate against minorities. However, analysis of the structures of cultural discrimination only constitutes one dimension of multiculturalism. The multicultural agenda of protecting and preserving minority cultures comes to the fore because it is assumed that people value cultural memberships. Both the majority and the minorities, it is argued, require a secure cultural context if they are to lead a meaningful life and inculcate liberal values. However, in an environment where minority cultures are threatened and misrepresented, members of these marginalised communities are harmed significantly. They develop negative perceptions of themselves and, even more importantly, they feel compelled to either assimilate into the majority culture or affirm their community identities more stridently. It is to prevent the disadvantages that stem from each of these predicaments that multiculturalism presents the agenda of preserving minority cultures through a framework of differentiated citizenship.

3

Valuing Diversity,
Preserving Minority Cultures

Multiculturalism responds to the issue of cultural discrimination by privileging the goal of protecting minority cultures. Based on the understanding that policies of cultural assimilation and homogenisation render minority cultures unviable, it aims to make these marginalised communities and cultures secure so that they can flourish within the nation-state. Creating a framework in which different societal cultures survive and grow is desired, both for the sake of minimising cultural discrimination, and for promoting cultural diversity. The latter is equally important; in fact, it is deeply cherished within multiculturalism. It is seen as a valuable resource for enriching our lives. More significantly, it is seen as the essential pre-condition for equality of cultures. Multiculturalism assumes that diverse cultures can only flourish in a context where different cultures are acknowledged and accorded respect in the public domain.

The notion of diversity receives a positive value within multiculturalism. It does not simply indicate the absence of cultural homogeneity. Rather, it points to the presence of several distinct and heterogeneous cultures. It suggests that each culture has an individualised particularity, and it must be appreciated in terms of that uniqueness. The concept of diversity further asserts that each culture has attributes that deserve our respect. It has something valuable to offer to us for which it must be cherished, protected and preserved. This perception of differences affirms the goal of preserving minority cultures and, in a way, supplements the importance given to cultural community membership within the multicultural framework. The belief that different cultures within the nation-state cannot be compared or collapsed into each other gives a distinct flavour to the multicultural notion

of difference and multiplicity. To comprehend the specificity of
the multicultural agenda we need, therefore, to look closely at
the concept of diversity.

Plurality and Diversity: Two Notions of Difference

In everyday conversation, the terms plural and diverse are used
interchangeably to describe societies that comprise different religions, races, languages and cultures. In common usage, it is
assumed that each of these expressions represents the same thing
—namely, the presence of many, different communities. However, a closer scrutiny will reveal that the ideas of multiplicity
and difference that they incorporate are dissimilar in significant
ways. Far from being synonyms, they are discrete concepts with
distinct meanings, contextual parameters and symbolic space.
We need to apprehend this dissonance because multiculturalism
endorses a conception of heterogeneity that is best expressed
by the concept of diversity rather than plurality.

Let us begin with the concept of plural. Plurality suggests the
presence of 'many' but it does not stipulate anything about the
nature of many. How the multiple forms are structured, and how
they relate to one another, are aspects on which the idea of
plurality is silent. Consequently, the many that it denotes could
be manifold representations of 'one', they could even be reduc-
ible to a single unified whole. Alternately, the 'many' may be
separate and unequal entities. As such, they may occupy different positions along a continuum; at times the 'many' may be
hierarchically arranged. All these possibilities can be envisaged
within the concept of plurality. Thus, for instance, the existence
and worship of many, different gods makes Hinduism a plural
religion even though the many are, in the ultimate analysis, re-
ducible to one supreme God.

Similarly, we may speak of a multi-racial society as a plural
society even when the different races are related to each other in
a relationship of domination and subordination. Then again,
we may see different caste communities in India as a sign of its
plurality, even though these castes are hierarchically arranged.
In another context, we could refer to plural associations and

plural centres of power within society, each of which seek to influence the centre—the 'one' that constitutes the core. We may associate the presence of many interest groups in a society with pluralism even when some groups are relatively powerless. Even when the lobbying groups are all members of one and the same class, the presence of several groups is seen as an indicator of its plural character. This is the idea of pluralism that political theorists employed in their study of industrialised western societies, and it is on the basis of this understanding that they distinguished between totalitarian and democratic polities. Here again, plurality symbolised the presence of more than one, but that is all.

The existence of many became a sign of democracy in the twentieth century because the presence of one ideology, one political party, one electoral candidate was regarded a sign of state coercion. Hence, the presence of many—such as, associations, interest groups, political parties—was seen as a minimum condition of freedom. The fact that these many entities might express different facets of the same ideology was an aspect that did not diminish the democratic content of a system. While this reading of democracy was insensitive to structures of inequality that continued to exist in these societies despite the presence of a multitude of groups, it was correct in one small respect: the presence of many is a pre-condition for the recognition of difference. We need to acknowledge the presence of many before we can speak of difference and diversity.

To say this is not to suggest a necessary connection between the concept of plurality and diversity. Plurality merely suggests the presence of many; diversity points to the existence of many that are different, heterogeneous and often incommensurable. To put it in another way, when we speak of diversity we refer to multiplicity that is not collapsible into one. The many, in this conception, are discrete and separate entities that are different from one another. The difference, in fact, limits comparison.

It was this notion of difference and diversity that German historians developed in the mid-eighteenth century. Theorists of Enlightenment in England and France noted the existence of plural cultures and civilisations. However, in keeping with their understanding of plurality, they arranged these cultures hierarchically.

The history of humankind, in their view, represented progress from the dark ages to the civilised, enlightened present. In making this assessment, the *Philosophes* used their contemporary sensibilities to judge all other cultures, and it was from the perspective of their own historical world that other civilisations in the past, as well as existing non-industrial, absolutist regimes, seemed to be lagging behind. The German historians, from Herder to Ranke, used the idea of cultural diversity to question this judgement of the enlightenment. They argued that human history was constituted by discrete and heterogeneous cultures, each with its own values, moral and aesthetic norms, and political and economic structures. Thus, each culture was 'in itself a whole' (Herder, 1969: 188), complete, with its own centre of happiness.

To emphasise the authentic and unique nature of each culture, Herder represented them as 'children' of God, destined to carve their own distinct identity and future. Subsequent historians and philosophers drew upon this idea of diversity to point to the heterogeneity and incommensurability of different epochs and civilisations. However, the peculiarity of this framework was that it accommodated diversity only historically. That is, it maintained that history is defined by a succession of diverse cultures or values, but each culture manifests a single idea. Thus, while each era was characterised by a defined 'spirit' or *Volkgeist*, historical succession provided evidence of difference and diversity.

The German historicists tradition elucidated the distinction between plurality and diversity. Since then, the idea of irreducible difference or diversity has been used in a variety of theoretical contexts. The occidentalists invoke this concept of diversity when they stress the difference between civilisations of Asia and western Europe, and argue that the former personify a set of values which are admirable in themselves. Advocates of ethno-social science also anchor their arguments in this conception of diversity or non-collapsible difference. They maintain that each society is unique in terms of its internal structure, institutions and values. Consequently, it must be studied in its own terms.

Contemporary multiculturalism also endorses the idea of difference and heterogeneity that is exemplified in the concept of diversity. It does not simply point to the presence of many cultures within the nation-state, rather it admits that these multiple cultures are discrete and often incommensurable. In a manner analogous to the German historicists, it too argues that each culture incorporates a distinct conception of good life and is organised around a set of values and norms that are its very own. Sensitivity to the fact that each of the many cultures present in a society are unique and heterogeneous entities eventually justifies the multicultural project, particularly the agenda of preserving marginalised and vulnerable cultures. It further suggests that the distinctive particularity of each culture needs to be recognised and represented separately. It is this reading of diversity that supports rights of separate representation for communities that have a distinct cultural identity and are keen to preserve that identity. By comparison, in a framework where difference is represented as plurality instead of diversity, claims for separate representations get somewhat mitigated. In India, for instance, the leadership of the national movement acknowledged the presence of different religions in the country. But, for them, different religions were just so many paths to reach the one, absolute unconditional truth. Since all religions were said to pursue the same truth and seek the same basic human values, they placed them alongside each other as equals. More importantly, they assumed that the multiplicity of religious groups could constitute a single fabric, or, one composite culture. As such, from their perspective—and this was best exemplified in the writings of Mahatma Gandhi—the presence of religious plurality was not a mark of complete distinction or separateness. Hence, the presence of differences did not point in the direction of separate representation for these religious communities. If anything, it suggested that these communities could be seen as a part of a wider oneness.

In sharp contrast to this perspective that prevailed in India, multiculturalism and the idea of differentiated citizenship that comes with it, begins with the belief that different cultures represent divergent conceptions of what is good. As each culture embodies different values or conceptions of good, and each is worthy of our respect, it follows that we should be concerned about the fate of diverse cultures in our society. Indeed, we should attempt to give each culture space to protect itself and represent its distinctive perspective in the public arena. The concept of cultural diversity thus constitutes the basic idea on which the edifice of multiculturalism is constructed. However, in the course of its enunciations, multiculturalism introduces three important elements which nuance the idea of diversity that was articulated in the historicist tradition.

First, multiculturalism places diversity within the boundaries of the nation-state. The German historians and philosophers spoke of a succession of diverse cultures in history and diverse patterns of national growth. As such, they acknowledged the presence of diverse cultures, albeit over time and space. The multiculturalists recognise diversity that is found across societies and civilisations, but they are concerned primarily with diversity of cultures within the liberal nation-state. Second, while locating diversity within a society, multiculturalism draws attention to the presence of heterogeneous communities within the state. While other theorists speak of, and even promote, homogeneity within the politically defined boundaries of a state, the adherents of multiculturalism point to the heterogeneity within, and support the preservation of this diversity of cultures.

Third, in the course of supporting cultural diversity, the multiculturalists distinguish between the majority community and the minorities. The diverse cultural communities are categorised as majority or minorities. In modern democratic polities, the state is generally identified with the majority culture, while other communities that are different are designated as minorities. Multiculturalism emphasises the irreconcilable differences between the majority and the minority cultures. To the extent that the state expresses the culture of the majority, it discriminates against the minorities. Theorists of multiculturalism are concerned about this. They use the concept of cultural diversity to analyse the fate of minority cultures in the state. Like the nineteenth century German historicists, they want different cultures to be treated equally. However, as they speak of diverse cultures within the state, they focus on the fate of different cultures within the polity. Do the diverse ethnic and national minorities receive equal and fair treatment in the public and political arenas? Do the policies of the state, national culture, or the adopted liberal principles, discriminate against these communities? What needs to be done in order to provide an equal status to these minorities? These are questions that multiculturalism brings into the discourse of diversity. Even as it incorporates the notion of heterogeneity that is embodied in the concept of diversity, it gives a new focus to this concept.

Valuing Cultural Diversity

The idea of diversity has two dimensions within multiculturalism. On the one hand, it connotes a specific notion of difference and, on the other, it represents a determinate value orientation. So far, while making the distinction between plurality and diversity, we have concentrated primarily on the first aspect. We now need to turn to the second dimension that suggests the presence of heterogeneous cultures is desirable, and we should be concerned about the fate of different cultures in our society. In particular, we should try to ensure that the many different cultures that exist in the polity, survive and grow within the polity. This assessment of the value of diversity is backed by the belief that each culture possesses some value and is worthy of our respect.

It is worthy of our respect because 'no culture can ever exhaust the full range of human possibilities' (Parekh, 1994c: 207). Each articulates an aspect of human potentialities. As such, the presence of different cultures contributes to the 'overall richness of society' (Parekh, 1994a: 13). Besides, '[H]uman beings lack a master Archimedian standpoint from which to look at themselves and their cultures...' Under the circumstances, the presence of different cultures, however, makes available to us 'several mini-Archimedian standpoints' (*Ibid.*). Through them we can encounter other ways of living and, in the process, come to understand the limits and possibilities of our own world-view.

Diversity of cultures is, for this reason, considered a valuable resource. It is both a condition of 'critical self-understanding' (Parekh, 1994c: 208) as well as a way of enhancing our options and choices. It makes freedom of choice real. Individuals can, as Kymlicka argues, exercise freedom of choice only if there are alternatives from which they can choose what they regard to be worthy of pursuit. Diverse cultures provide them with meaningful options (Kymlicka, 1991: 164–66). 'In deciding how to lead our lives, we do not start *de novo*, but rather we examine definite ideals and forms of life that have been developed and tested by innumerable individuals, sometimes for generations' (*Ibid.*: 164). As each culture incorporates a specific model of social life and organisation, diverse cultures present options and concrete alternatives from which individuals can choose. If cultural diversity was to disappear then there would be no concrete alternatives left for human beings to explore (Kymlicka, 1991: 165). Worse still, '[O]nce the long-established ways of life are destroyed in the dogmatic belief that the autonomous way of life alone is valuable, they are lost forever. If the liberal way of life were to run into unexpected difficulties, as it is beginning to do today, we would have no resources left from which to draw new inspiration and strength' (Parekh, 1994a: 13).

Within multiculturalism, cultural diversity is cherished not only as a derivative good. It is, at times, perceived as an 'intrinsic good' (Moore, 1977: passim; also see Haksar, 1998). That is, it is or 'would be a good, even if it existed quite alone, without any accompaniments or effects whatever' (Moore, 1977: 29). It is good by itself and valued for what it is rather than what it can contribute. By this reckoning, cultural diversity is to be cherished always, and under all circumstances. Two reasons are offered for this. First, it is argued that the vast diversity of cultures that exists is an expression of divine providence (Taylor, 1994: 72). It is not 'mere accident'; it was 'meant to bring about a greater harmony' (*Ibid.*). It is, therefore, our moral responsibility to acknowledge and treasure this diversity. Since we are still 'too far away from the ultimate horizon from which the relative worth of different cultures might be evident' (*Ibid.*: 73), we must not discount the fact that all cultures exist for a purpose. Indeed, it would be 'supreme arrogance to discount this possibility a priori...' (*Ibid.*: 73).

Second, it is argued that each culture has provided 'the horizon of meaning for large numbers of human beings of diverse characters and temperaments, over a long period of time' (Taylor, 1994: 72). It must, therefore, have something that is worthy of our respect and admiration. In any case, each culture must be valued as it has meaning for its practitioners. Even when there are elements within a culture that we may abhor or reject, their intrinsic value to humankind cannot, and must not, be dismissed. Keeping in mind the finitude of human beings, the limits of our present horizon and the value that a culture has for its members, all cultures are equally sacred (*Ibid.*). They must be valued in the same way as we value the individual, as entities that are irreplaceable and non-substitutable.

Preserving Minority Cultures

The belief that different cultures articulate diverse conceptions of good life, and that there is something worthwhile in each culture, underscores the value accorded to cultural diversity within the framework of multiculturalism. It also reaffirms the goal of protecting and preserving marginalised minority cultures. As was noted in the previous chapter, advocates of multiculturalism claim that to stem the discrimination of minorities within the nation-state, it is essential to protect their cultures. This conclusion is reinforced by the perception that diversity of cultures enriches our life and is a valuable good.

Although the agenda of preserving minority cultures is based on the multicultural reading of discrimination and diversity, these arguments are often supplemented by pragmatic considerations. Today, almost every society is internally plural. There are a large number of cultural communities living within the same polity. If our democratic fabric is to survive, we need to learn to live together. The empirical reality, therefore, necessitates that we inculcate an attitude that is sensitive to differences of culture. If we fail to do this, we are likely to face an endless prospect of ethnic violence and confrontations. Besides, marginalisation of minorities and unequal treatment to them is among the major reasons for ethnic conflict. We need to bridge the hiatus that has built between communities, particularly between the majority and the minorities in each polity. Multiculturalism believes and hopes that minimising cultural discrimination and enhancing the equality of cultures may well provide an answer to some of the most pressing concerns of our times.

· Joseph Carens points to another possible benefit of protecting minority cultures. Taking the example of indigenous people, he says that communities that have a secure culture are better able to survive dramatic changes in their material and political environment.

[W]hen North Americans think of indigenous peoples, they tend to think of people conquered by violence or ensnared by the deceit of European settlers and their descendants, people decimated by disease and driven from their lands, now impoverished and powerless minorities in countries overwhelmingly populated by the descendants of immigrants from other places. That has been the fate of indigenous peoples in North America and elsewhere.... By comparison with these other indigenous peoples, native Fijians appear to enjoy an enviable situation.... If they have not achieved as much success in economic endeavours as other segments of the population, they have enjoyed a relatively secure material and social life.... It seems reasonable to attribute much of the present situation of native Fijians, and hence, their relative well-being, to the fact that native Fijians have been able to maintain a relatively stable and coherent collective way of life over the last century or so. That fact, in turn, seems due in significant measure to the policies of cultural preservation pursued in Fiji. Moreover, it seems plausible to suppose that policies more in keeping with liberal individualism...might have had disastrous consequences for native Fijians as such policies did elsewhere.   (Carens, 1992: 575–76)

Pragmatic considerations of this kind are often asserted in the writings on multiculturalism. However, they are invoked primarily to underline the advantages of policies that aim to protect minorities. The agenda of preserving marginalised cultures gets its justification mainly from the multicultural analysis of cultural discrimination within the state and the assertion of the value of diversity in society. What is perhaps quite striking is that within multiculturalism, the principle of equality and diversity are placed alongside each other. While critiquing liberalism and the practices of liberal nation-states, multiculturalists tend to give centrality to the idea of equality. They point to the ways in which liberal policies and principles disadvantage minorities and treat them unfairly. However, while enunciating their own conception of a multicultural polity, it is the concept of diversity that tends to gain salience. A multicultural polity values diversity of cultures and aims to devise a system of special rights by which this diversity can grow and flourish. Although the presence of secure minority cultures is said to be an indicator of equality and non-discrimination, nevertheless, cultural diversity is desired, both for enhancing self-understanding and for increasing the available range of options.

When we place both these dimensions of multiculturalism together—namely, its critique of liberal state practices and the agenda of preserving cultural diversity—it becomes apparent that multiculturalism is more than a statement of fact. It does not simply point to the co-presence of many cultures, it asserts a value. It cherishes cultural diversity and envisions a society in which different communities forge a collective identity while retaining their cultural provenance. Consequently, when modern democratic societies are called upon to embrace multiculturalism, they need to demonstrate a deeper and more profound egalitarian impulse within them than the mere presence of plural cultures.

Multiculturalism acknowledges the existence of diverse communities but what is more important is that it grants positive value to the collective identities of all ethnic communities. It pictures a society that is characterised, not by multiple cultural solitudes or endemic cultural strife, but by communities living together and participating as *equal partners* in national political life. As such, multiculturalism represents a new kind of universalism—one where integration of individuals in the state is not predicated on a total disengagement from particularistic community ties. Rather, people are included in the nation-state as members of diverse but equal ethnic groups. And the state recognises that the dignity of individuals is linked to the collective dignity of the community to which they belong.

This radical redefinition of a democratic polity makes multiculturalism a normative value that is applicable as much to the modern liberal democracies of the West as it is to modernising polities like India. Contrary to the general expectation, community identities have not dissolved in market economies or liberal democracies. No society is so completely modern or homogenised that collective group identities have seized to be of relevance to its members. The democratic citizen remains simultaneously embedded in a variety of particularistic ties. To believe that he or she is a deracinated individual, unconstrained by previous loyalties and identities, is to grossly misread the human condition. Given this reality, multiculturalism endeavours to initiate policies that allow citizens to maintain their cultural distinctiveness. It sustains cultural diversity and helps in the forward movement of societies by engendéring a broad-based acquiescence which is not thwarted or prejudiced by religious or cultural intolerance.

If multiculturalism and democracy appear together in history, then this co-existence is neither fortuitous nor accidental. Only democracy can reach out and explore formats of interaction that presume equality and respect. It is this concern for equality that also precludes the possibility of democracy ever being associated with majoritarianism—either of the political or of the cultural kind. The dangers of political majoritarianism are by now widely accepted. They have become an assimilated ingredient in the metabolism of modern democracies. Multiculturalism adds to this awareness by sensitising us to the dangers of cultural majoritarianism. In particular, it points to the way in which cultural majoritarianism disadvantages minorities, alienates them, enhances conflicts between communities and limits self-understanding. It is to counter these forms of minority discrimination and to protect the diversity of cultures that multiculturalism eventually privileges the goal of preserving minority cultures.

Understanding Difference: Three Modes of Appropriating and Preserving Cultural Diversity

Awareness about the dangers of cultural majoritarianism, coupled with the emphasis on cultural diversity, has made preservation of minority cultures a primary concern of multiculturalism. As we noticed in the previous section, recognising cultural differences and valuing cultural diversity is a necessary condition for endorsing the goal of preserving minority cultures. Only when diverse cultures, and the differences that they express, are acknowledged and accorded a positive weightage, can we envisage the possibility of preserving cultures. This implicit association between the idea of preserving cultural diversity or minority cultures and valuing cultural differences fosters the impression that multiculturalism bears a strong affinity to theories of cultural anthropology and hermeneutics that emphasise cultural differences. Consequently, to understand the particularity of multiculturalism in this respect, it is important to examine these other perspectives on difference, diversity and preserving the other.

Over the last century-and-a-half, cultural differences have been noted and respected in two quite distinct contexts. In the first half of the twentieth century, anthropologists such as, Alfred L. Kroeber, attempted to record and reconstruct the cultures of diverse populations. Following upon the work of Franz Boas— the man who introduced him to anthropology—Kroeber collected and interpreted the culture of the Indian American tribes and other small marginalised communities that lived on the fringes of the 'great modern civilisation'. His emphasis on the historical study of custom and cultural diversity gave a new orientation to the study of culture. It enabled anthropology to move away from the earlier more positivist attempt to look for uniformities that pervade civilisations and to formulate laws of cultural development (see Tylor [1871], 1959: 3–20; Wolf, 1964: 1–33).

The historical perspective that Boas and Kroeber brought to bear upon the study of culture began with the belief that anthropology cannot begin with a unified image of man as it manifests itself in a given culture. Instead, our understanding of the nature of man must take cognisance of the many different but equally valid pictures that emerge in different cultures (Wolf, 1964: 10). This conception of heterogeneity of material, and the need to analyse the many forms in which the universal manifests itself, created space for the study of different cultures individually, in all their specific and localised detail. Careful and meticulous observation of aspects of daily life and culture thus gained importance within this framework. In fact, it accorded a positive value to the search for particularities.

Kroeber himself recorded the particular elements that constituted the cultural complex of the Indians of California. He collected their artefacts—from baskets to flint knives, canoes to arrows—and recorded their customs, religious practices, kinship structures, food habits, dress, myths, songs, spoken language and dialects. Through this carefully assembled information, Kroeber constructed in the museum a replica of the life-world of these people. The museum collection provided a picture of these diverse ways of life, and from the point of view of the anthropologist, it was here that these cultures were being preserved.

Kroeber recognised that many of the cultures—for instance, those of the Indian Americans—were changing significantly or becoming extinct. Consequently, he made every possible attempt to construct a picture of these people and keep a record of their history and culture in a museum. The point that needs to be emphasised here is that Kroeber and his associates were not attempting to keep these cultures alive in their original or pristine form. Nor were they trying to ensure that these cultures survive and continue to perpetuate themselves. Kroeber's concern stemmed from a certain humanism and respect for diversity. He recognised that many of the cultures that he was recording were significantly different from his own modern civilisation, and many of them were likely to become extinct. Hence, he and other like-minded anthropologists were keen to record these cultures. Just as a zoologist would like to make a register of different species of animals on the earth, these scientists wanted to catalogue the variety of existing cultures before they became extinct.

Theodora Kroeber describes the vision of her husband, Alfred Kroeber, and his associates, in the following way:

Everywhere over the land were virgin languages, brought to their polished and idiosyncratic perfection of grammar and syntax without benefit of a single recording scratch of stylus on papyrus or stone; living languages orally learnt and transmitted and about to die with their last speakers. Everywhere there were to be discovered Ways of life, many, many ways. There were gods and created worlds unlike other gods and worlds, with extended relationships and values and ideals

and dreams unlike anything known or imagined elsewhere,
all soon to be forever lost—part of the human condition, part
of the beautiful heartbreaking history of man. The time was
late; the dark forces of invasion had almost done their igno-
rant work of annihilation. To the field then! With notebook
and pencil, record, record, record. Rescue from historylessness
all languages still living, all cultures. Each is precious, unique,
irreplaceable, a people's ultimate expression and identity,
which, being lost, the world is made poorer as surely as it
was when a Praxitelean marble was broken and turned to
dust.   (T. Kroeber, 1970: 51)

This understanding of difference and the fate of other tribal
cultures permeated all aspects of Kroeber's work—his field work
among the various Indian tribes as well as his dealings with
Ishi. In August 1911, when the city papers announced the capture of a wild Indian, Kroeber intervened to have this man
released to his custody. He named him Ishi, which meant 'man
or one of the people in Yana' (*Ibid.*: 1970: 81). Kroeber soon
surmised that Ishi was the last of the Yana Indians who lived in
the Deer Creek region in the Yahi territory. Over the next five
years, Ishi spent much of his time with Kroeber at the museum
in San Francisco. Here he made Yana objects that were then
displayed at the museum. Through Ishi, Kroeber could represent authentically the life and culture of the Yana Indians. More
importantly, he could now provide the most genuine exhibit of
another culture or difference.[1] Every Sunday, people would come
to the museum to see Ishi. They would touch him, hear him sing
Yana songs, string a bow, use a fire drill or flake an arrowhead
with a metal-tipped pressure flaker that Ishi had used through his
life (T. Kroeber, 1961: 180–89). On occasions, Ishi would be dressed
in his native clothes and displayed with reconstructed artefacts
of his own world—most notably, a Yana style hut on which a
sign would read: Door 33 inches high (picture reproduced at

---

[1] 'For this event, the museum made simultaneous announcements in the city
newspapers to the effect that Professor Kroeber and the wild Indian Ishi would
be at the museum on Sunday afternoon, between two and four thirty for the next
several weeks to receive visitors who wished to meet them' (T. Kroeber, 1961: 135).

www.wnme.net/-amerabo/ishipage.htm). When it became evident that exposure to people from a different world made Ishi vulnerable to new diseases to which he had no immunity, Kroeber placed him in a glass enclosure, 'an exhibition case' and the display continued (*Ibid*.: 134). To Kroeber, Ishi was a symbol of the 'other', the difference. The fact that Ishi's world had changed considerably as he now lived among white Americans in California did not receive much consideration from Kroeber. For him, Ishi was a member of the Yahi tribe and he would always remain so.

Kroeber was aware that the Yahi dialect, of which Ishi was now the sole speaker, would soon die. Consequently, he made considerable effort to record the dialect and save it from extinction. Kroeber persuaded his friend and colleague, Waterman, and the linguist, Edward Sapir, to record Ishi's Yahi dialect of the Yana language. Ishi continued to work with Sapir, even during his illness, till such time he succumbed to tuberculosis. All through his friendship with Ishi, Kroeber encouraged him to draw pictures of his original homeland, and then he spent considerable labour in discovering the described land. He returned from the land of Yahi armed with objects that were once used by the Yahi, and an understanding of the violence that had been inflicted on the tribe by the white men (*Ibid*.: 214–16). Kroeber witnessed Ishi's bond with the original homeland as he identified and addressed with Yana names, the caves, hills, streams, plants and animals around him. Kroeber respected the cultural beliefs that structured Ishi's world. So much so that when he learnt in Europe of Ishi's deteriorating health, he wrote to say that the body must not be used for medical examination. It must be kept intact in accordance with the beliefs of the Yahi. Although these instructions were not carried out fully as a simple autopsy was performed and his brain preserved, yet, they reveal Kroeber's respect for Ishi's beliefs (*Ibid*.: 234–35). Even though some of the Yana beliefs might have appeared absurd to some, they nevertheless deserved our respect. For Kroeber, this respect for the other meant that Ishi must not be denied the right to live or, as in this case, to die in accordance with his own beliefs.

Kroeber's work with Ishi is perhaps the most important indicator of his conception of difference. Ishi was the symbol of the lost world that had been brutalised and destroyed by white settlers. Kroeber attempted to retrieve and preserve what was available of that world. In attempting this task, he challenged the racist and colonialist perspectives that were responsible for wrecking the native American ways of life. For Kroeber the latter were, in many ways, primitive worlds, yet this was no justification for their being annihilated. The existing variety of human cultures needed to be noted and preserved, even as relics in a museum.

Cultural anthropologists like Kroeber acknowledged the presence of diverse cultures and made considerable effort to record that diversity. However, their study was motivated by the desire to note the variety that existed. While documenting the multiplicity of cultural complexes, these anthropologists did not suggest that the study of diverse cultures could enhance our self-understanding. Nor did they endorse the view that there was something admirable in these cultures from which we might learn or adopt something. Theorists like Kroeber dissociated themselves from the romantic conception of pre-modern and tribal cultures and maintained that diversity could entail encounter with an otherness that appears as 'primitive' and 'lower-grade' when compared with our present sensibilities (Kroeber, 1946 and 1939, respectively). Kroeber realised that several tribal customs, for example, girl's puberty rites practiced by the Chibcha or passive homosexuality accepted by most Siberian and north American tribes, may appear to us to be a mark of their backwardness. But for him, the presence of these customs indicated that 'manifestations that are pathological, *or at any rate are so regarded by us*, are accepted and socially challenged in many *primitive* societies' (Kroeber, 1940: 317; emphasis added).

Kroeber recognised and recorded with care the difference between 'us' and 'them'. For him, heterogeneity was the given natural order and had to be treated as such. Hence, irrespective of whether we can learn anything from these cultures, they had a right to exist, and it was important to register the different ways in which human beings have organised their life and society. The pictures of difference that Kroeber created were museum pieces, and many of them were presented and preserved at the Museum of San Francisco, where he spent several years as a curator.

At the turn of the twentieth century, cultural anthropologists such as Kroeber acknowledged difference. However, the 'other' that they were analysing and preserving was placed at a certain distance from the self. As such, it was an object of scientific curiosity rather than moral value. Further, these anthropologists were interested in preserving these cultures as relics in a museum that indicated the diversity of forms, and from which we could reconstruct the history of humankind. As they tried to capture and represent the difference, they restricted judgements about the worth of other cultures and the validity of their own. A certain degree of distance and neutrality was maintained in this regard.

The idea of difference as well as the accompanying notion of preserving diversity that surfaced in Kroeber's writings was significantly different from that which is articulated in contemporary multiculturalism. Unlike Kroeber, theorists of multiculturalism seek to preserve minority cultures in society and argue that preserving diversity is both desirable and beneficial for humankind. The presence of diverse cultures enhances self-understanding and offers alternative ways of life from which we may choose what we favour most. As it enhances options for us, it contributes to our quality of life and allows liberals to pursue the ideals that they value most—namely, the right to choose and revise our inheritances. Preserving diverse minority cultures is also, in their view, a pragmatic way of dealing with ethnic conflicts and promoting liberal values. As such, preserving other minority cultures is in our collective self-interest, and is desirable for liberal democratic polities.

Furthermore, most multiculturalists offer a value judgement about other cultures that they seek to protect and secure. They believe that there is something admirable in all cultures. Each incorporates qualities that are valuable and worthy of our respect. At least, in part, it is this representation of the other that justifies their campaign to preserve diverse cultures. Advocates of multiculturalism attribute a positive value, both to the task of preserving differences, and to the qualities embodied by the other. This evaluation of the worth of the other differentiates them sharply from the perspective of cultural anthropologists like Kroeber. At the same time, it reveals the affinity of the multicultural position to conceptions of difference and diversity that emerged in Germany between the mid-eighteenth and mid-nineteenth centuries.

The historical–hermeneutic school of thought emphasised the historicality of human existence. Distancing himself from the Enlightenment conception of history, Herder, in the mid-eighteenth century, argued that history of humankind was marked by the succession of heterogeneous cultures, each with its own distinctive pattern of values, beliefs and practices. Each culture and form of life was, in his view, unique and complete in itself. As such, it could not be treated as a stepping stone for another culture (Herder, 1969: 188). '...[L]et us rest secure in the certainty that whatever is God's purpose with regard to human species upon earth remains evident even in the most perplexing parts of its history. All the works of God have this property that although they belong to a whole, which no eye can scan, each is in itself a whole, and bears the divine characters of its destination. It is so with the brute, and with the plant: can it be otherwise with man? Can it be that thousands are made for one? All the generations that have passed away, merely for the last? ...The Allwise sports not in this manner; he invents no finespun shadowy dreams: he lives and feels in each of his children with paternal affection, as though it were the only creature in the world' (Herder, 1966: 229).

This view about the nature and equal worth of diverse cultures was endorsed in Germany by historicists and hermeneuticians alike. Collectively, they emphasised two points: first, each culture must be judged in its own terms, i.e., in terms of the values which are internal to it rather than by norms that are esteemed in other cultures. Second, they argued that there was no unilateral progressive movement from one culture to another, or from one century to another. In the words of Ranke:

[If] one were to assume that the progress consisted in the fact that the life of humankind reaches a higher potential in every epoch—that is, that every generation surpasses the previous one completely and that therefore the last epoch is always the preferred, the epochs preceding it being only stepping-stones to one that follow—this would be an injustice on the part of the deity. Such a generation that, as it were, had become a means would not have any significance for, and in, itself. It would only have meaning as a stepping-stone for the following generation and would not have an immediate relation to the divine. But I assert: every epoch is immediate to God, and its worth is not at all based on what derives from it but rests in its own existence, in its own self. In this way the contemplation of history, that is to say of individual life in history, acquires its own particular attraction, since every epoch must be seen as something valid in itself and appears worthy of consideration. (Ranke (1906) in Sältzer, 1991: 84)

The belief that all cultures possess equal worth was anchored in the assumption that diverse cultures and civilisations, like various species on earth, were expressions of the divine order. For these German historians no one culture or way of life could be regarded as being better than the other because in each some values are realised while others get marginalised and submerged. In this way, different skills and values develop in different epochs.

...[H]istory shows us that in modern times art flourishes most in the fifteenth and in the first half of the sixteenth century, but in the seventeenth and in the first three-quarters of the eighteenth century it declined the most. The same is true of poetry: there are only brief periods when this art is really outstanding, but there is no evidence that it rises to a higher level in the course of the centuries.... The great spiritual tendencies that govern mankind go separate ways and, at other times, are closely related. In these tendencies there is, however, always a certain particular direction that predominates and causes the others to recede. So, for example, in the second half of the sixteenth century, the religious element predominated so much that the literary receded in the face of it. In the eighteenth century, on the other hand, the striving for utility gained so much ground that art and related activities had to yield before it. (*Ibid.*: 83)

Thus, different values emerge at different times, and in different epochs and cultures. Consequently, no one period of history and no single culture could be placed over others. Each contained something of value that was worthy of admiration. From this, Ranke and many of his contemporaries concluded that history did not manifest unilinear progression. While the Enlightenment *Philosophes* argued that history represented progress, from the dark ages to the enlightened present, these theorists found some value in each culture. They maintained that change may bring forth new values that had been eclipsed in the previous era, or it may involve the loss of desired norms and distinctive qualities for which the era is best known. Ranke noted this in his assessment of Asia. He wrote: 'The oldest epoch of Asian culture was the most flourishing; the second and the third epochs in which the Greek and the Roman elements dominated, were no longer as significant...' (*Ibid.*: 83).

Dilthey used the historicist understanding about heterogeneity of cultures to argue that each culture must be judged in terms of the values internal to it. Since no one value is valid for all nations or for all times (see Dilthey, 1961: 166–68), each world-view (*Weltanschauung*) must be hermeneutically reconstructed so that we can understand the other without imposing our present sensibilities on it. For Dilthey, each expression of the human mind (be it a word, an action, an event or practice) is a part of a particular life-world. It is a moment in the ongoing process of a life and must be placed in the context of that specific whole, if we are to understand it at all.

The German hermeneutic school developed this notion of understanding to challenge the Enlightenment's idea of progress and its representation of Germany as a backward society. Questioning the view that the world inhabited by French and British Enlightenment was the most advanced and civilised epoch in human history, they argued that history of humankind reveals the presence of heterogeneous cultures and civilisations. Each civilisation brings to fruition a set of historical values that are unique and worthy of respect. The idea that all epochs deserve to be treated as equals and that all civilisations are equally worthy of our respect shaped the perceptions of the hermeneutic school. On the one hand, it highlighted the need to understand the other in its own terms, and on the other, it attributed a positive value to difference and diversity.

The writings of Wilhelm Dilthey expressed both these aspects of hermeneutic thinking. He maintained that each historical–cultural entity is defined by a specific set of norms, practices and inter-subjective meanings. This shared complex of meanings and norms is reflected in an objective form in the customs, laws, institutions of the state, religion, art, science and philosophy. Collectively, these aspects of historical life constitute the 'objective mind' of a society, and it is the objective mind that makes available to us the world of the other (Dilthey, 1949: 118). To put it in another way, the 'other' is available to us, it can be known and understood, only to the extent that it survives in these objectifications. Conversely, to understand the other we need to reconstruct its world-view (*Weltanschauung*) from these objectifications, and then relate the given expression (or text) to that world-view.

For Dilthey the past or the historical–cultural other is permanently present for us in the objective mind. The latter reveals to us the world-view and shared practices that people belonging to a given society invoke when they communicate with others. Since the objective mind forms the backdrop against which people act or express themselves, we can understand the other only by acquainting ourselves with the objective mind of a given society and reading a text as an expression of that collective mind. Through the objective mind we can bridge the distance between the 'self' and the 'other', and understand the latter in its own terms. That is, understand it in terms of its own values rather than our present sensibilities and world-view. However, the objective mind is not always available directly. For the historian, or a person outside that world, it is not ready-at-hand. It has to be systematically constructed through historical and linguistic exegesis (see Mahajan, 1992: 50–60).

Hermeneuticians, like Dilthey, were not interested in preserving the other as a museum piece; nor were they attempting to ensure the survival of a given culture. Their focal point of enquiry was quite different. Dilthey, like many of his contemporaries, acknowledged difference. Indeed, living in Germany these theorists saw themselves as the 'other' of the British and French Enlightenment. Consequently, they wanted to create space for the existence and recognition of the worth of the other. Above all, they wanted to reveal the errors associated with judging Germany—the other—in terms of the values of the dominant tradition of Enlightenment.

Two things need to be emphasised with regard to the hermeneutic framework used by Dilthey. First, it recognised differences of world-views and maintained that each epoch or civilisation had some admirable qualities that needed to be acknowledged and respected. Second, it suggested that differences of *Weltanschauung* could only be recognised when we understand the other in its own terms, i.e., in terms of the norms and values internal to that historical world. According to Dilthey, when we judge the other, or make sense of its expressions in terms of our historical sensibilities, we misunderstand the other. To understand the other and to appreciate its value, we must relate its specific practices to the totality of that historical world. Learning about the world of the other, however, entails exegesis or systematic reconstruction. Through reconstruction of systems of culture and external organisation of society, a specific worldview comes to life. It is recreated from the objective mind in which it is permanently preserved. Unlike contemporary multiculturalists, Dilthey was not stipulating policies that must be adopted to ensure the survival of diverse cultures. He was merely emphasising the problems associated with imposing our present system of values to judge ways of life that are different from our own.

Towards the end of the eighteenth century, Herder had attempted to record the language, customs, myths, music and folklore of the people of German Highlands. He took note of their distinctive character and, as a historian, was interested in capturing this cultural whole before it was gradually transformed or wiped out. Herder cherished differences and recognised the need to analyse the domain of culture. Individuals, he maintained, are fashioned not only by their genetic dispositions and climatic conditions, but also by their culture. The traditions that they inherit play a crucial role in defining them. It was this conception of the role and significance of culture that prompted Herder's study. Presenting a wholistic picture of a culture was, for him, a mode of understanding a given people.

Dilthey retained a part of this orientation. However, he asserted that the study of culture—language, art, philosophy and religion—must be supplemented by an analysis of associations, such as state, church, city and other corporate bodies which express and structure human interaction. The latter, termed as external organisation of society, differ from systems of culture insofar as they embody relationships of power and dominance, property and community. However, like systems of culture, they reflect permanent and objective structures of human purposes, interaction and will. For Dilthey, the historical world was constituted by these twin dimensions of internal and external organisations (Dilthey, 1988: 105–28). Consequently, understanding the other required reconstruction of both these aspects of human life.

Hermeneutic understanding represented both a conception of difference as well as a method of apprehending the other. However, the point that needs to be emphasised is that for Dilthey, opening oneself to the other performed a latent critical function. By exposing ourselves to diverse world-views, we could experience states of mind which are otherwise not possible for us. For instance, on reading the letters of Luther, the writings of his contemporaries and the records of religious disputes, we can experience religious states that are beyond the experience of people of our time (Rickman, 1976: 227–28). In this way, encounter with difference widens our horizons and enriches our perception. In addition to it—and this was perhaps most significant for Dilthey—we come to recognise the finitude of the self through our encounters with diversity. Heterogeneous world-views reveal the immanence of historical consciousness. The disclosed plurality of human projects, aspirations and purposes make us aware of the limitations of our own perspective (also see Ricoeur 1981: 63–100). As such, it offers a moment of critique as well as the conditions necessary for realising our freedom. 'The historical consciousness of the finitude of every historical phenomenon, of every human or social condition, and of the relativity of every kind of faith, is the last step towards the liberation of man. With it man achieves the sovereignty to enjoy every experience to the full and surrender himself to the unencumbered, as if there were no system of philosophy or faith to tie him down' (Dilthey, 1961: 167).

Acknowledging difference and exposing oneself to diverse ways of life was thus a mode of enhancing liberty and self-knowledge. The hermeneuticians believed that learning about other people, no matter how different or distant they may be from the self, serves a practical and critical function. As we analyse the different ways in which human beings have organised themselves and the different projects they have pursued, we become aware of the historicity of our existence. We realise the distinctiveness of our world-view and see that our society may be structured differently. This awareness about alternative world-views reveals to us the strengths and limitations of our present world and, at the same time, opens new possibilities for us. As such, awareness of difference, or other ways of life, is valuable for the self.

Cultural anthropologists such as Kroeber, acknowledged the presence of diversity but they did not associate self-knowledge with the study of the other. For them, diversity was an ontological given and respected for just that reason. It had little epistemo-logical value. The hermeneutic tradition, by comparison, valued cultural and historical diversity for what it could suggest to us. It was a valuable source of knowledge and self-consciousness. In addition, it was a necessary condition for understanding the other.

Contemporary theories of multiculturalism endorse, to a con-siderable extent, these perceptions of the hermeneutic school. While acknowledging diversity of cultures, they caution against judging the other in terms of our present sensibilities. At the same time, they value cultural diversity because it can enrich our lives and widen our horizons. In their view, it is in our collective interest to ensure that diverse cultures survive. As such, their understanding of diversity as well as the value they at-tribute to cultural diversity is anchored in a conception of the self and the other that formed the basis of the hermeneutic school. This image is further reinforced by the fact that multiculturalism often points to the ways in which minority cultures are misunderstood in the nation-state. As these cultures express values that are different from those endorsed by the majoritarian culture, these populations are misrepresented and discriminated against. At least in part, treating these cultures as equals requires that we acknowledge difference and create space to accommodate it in the public arena.

In its conception of difference, its understanding of the value of cultural diversity and the necessity of understanding the other in its own terms, multiculturalism expresses a deep affinity to the historical–hermeneutic school. However, despite these fundamental similarities, multiculturalism differs from the hermeneutic tradition in at least three respects: (*a*) Multiculturalism is concerned about the survival of diverse cultures in a given society. Consequently, it explores ways by which different cultures can be preserved within the nation-state. The historical–hermeneutic school, by comparison, paid little attention to internal diversity. They spoke primarily of differences across nations and epochs, and alluded to this kind of diversity for the sake of understanding the other. As such, *understanding* rather than *preserving* the other was the focus of their study. (*b*) Within multiculturalism, preservation of cultures is linked to recognition of identity. The hermeneutic school recognised historical situatedness and it emphasised the need to understand the other in relation to the specifics of its own historical world. Theorists of multiculturalism speak more narrowly of being located within a community. They value cultural community membership and argue that the latter defines, to a considerable extent, the identity of a person. Who we are and what we aspire to be, they maintain, is influenced by our community membership. This shift in the conception of the self, from being historically situated to being embedded in the life of a community, is significant because it bestows a positive value upon cultural community membership. It also allows them to differentiate between the majority community and the minorities, and make a case for minority rights. Since community membership is valued by individuals, advocates of multiculturalism maintain that all cultures, particularly minority cultures within society, must be protected and made secure. (*c*) Within multiculturalism, preserving cultures is a way of recognising minority cultures and representing them as equals in the public arena. While the hermeneutic school focused on reconstructing the life of the other through the objective mind—or the texts in which the other is preserved for us—the multiculturalists are concerned about the fate of marginalised cultures within the nation-state. In their view, minority cultures require protection and special consideration to ensure equal treatment within the nation-state. Hence, their interest in preserving cultures is prompted by their assessment of the value of diversity as well as their commitment to democratic equality. Thus, even though the multicultural conception of difference and diversity has a strong affinity to the hermeneutic tradition, its notion of preserving cultures and its concern for the equal status of minority cultures within the nation-state, sets it apart from that tradition.

Minority Cultures and the Nation-state

Multiculturalism seeks to enhance cultural diversity by preserving minority cultures. The fate of minority cultures in a society is therefore its main concern. The singular emphasis on minority cultures is linked here to the understanding that the assimilationist policies of the liberal nation-state make minority cultures weak and susceptible to disintegration. It is to correct the cultural biases of the nation-state and to promote cultural diversity that multiculturalism aims to protect minority cultures. The focus on minority cultures is a distinctive attribute of multiculturalism and it is on this basis that we can distinguish it from the position of other cultural pluralists, such as Michael Walzer.

Michael Walzer, like most advocates of multiculturalism, begins by acknowledging the existence of diverse world-views. He maintains that our choice of socially valued goods is shaped by the historical and cultural context in which we live. Since social goods are the product of historical and cultural particularism, the distribution of particular goods must be understood in terms of a specific culture. To override the latter and impose a different criterion of rationality is tantamount to acting unfairly (Walzer, 1983: 314). However, while associating fairness or justice with the existence of diverse conceptions of social goods and values, Walzer maintains that in contemporary society all cultures, the majority culture and the minority cultures, are under siege. 'Confronted with modernity, all the human tribes are endangered species; their thick cultures are subject to erosion' (Walzer, 1994: 72). Consequently, the minority cultures cannot claim 'any absolute protection against the pressures and attractions of common life—as if they were endangered species' (*Ibid.*).

Multiculturalism does not endorse the latter proposition. From its perspective, the cultural policies of the nation-state are defined by the culture of the majority. As such, it is minority cultures, and not the majority culture, which are disadvantaged and discriminated against in the public arena. Special arrangements are, therefore, advocated to preserve culturally distinct ways of life that are currently being assimilated and eroded within the nation-state. It is to emphasise this point that theories of multiculturalism focus on the ways in which indigenous populations, immigrants and ethnic minorities are treated by the universalistic framework of the modern state.

While emphasising the preservation of minority cultures and diversity, multiculturalism accepts that cultures are not static entities. They change and evolve over time. Consequently, what it is concerned about is the injustice that stems from state policies of homogenisation. In other words, multiculturalism seeks to protect cultures from forced assimilation by the nation-state and the majority culture. To the extent that the majority does not face the same pressure to assimilate into a way of life that is hostile, alien and imposed, the fate of majority culture and the changes and challenges that it faces, are not the subject of multicultural discourse.

Within multiculturalism, the issue of cultural discrimination and diversity are discussed in the context of the nation-state. Even the majority and the minority communities are identified in that context. The nation-state forms the backdrop against which the relationship that is stipulated here between minorities and nation-state, marginalisation and homogenisation, preserving minority cultures and cultural diversity, needs to be placed and understood.

What Do We Preserve and How?

Discourses on multiculturalism underline the need to preserve a particular way of life. However, what is characteristic of a way of life is open to various interpretations. Does it entail preserving traditional occupations, patterns of economic life, social institutions, political and legal structures, or religious practices and moral norms? Most analyses of multiculturalism do not address these questions directly. In fact, a way of life is associated in different contexts with different things. At times, existing cultural and religious practices are associated with a way of life; at other moments, a way of life refers to community institutions and structures of authority. For instance, in the case of indigenous populations, their way of life is commonly related to their special relationship to land; in particular, with collective ownership of land. Other social, political, legal and religious practices such as adherence to a specific faith, expulsion of women who marry outside the band and nomination of tribal council members, are seen as incidental practices that do not define who they are. Likewise, adherence to traditional occupations and use of older technologies in the pursuit of traditional occupation is not seen as defining their way of life. It is believed that these practices may also change once the original relationship to land is restored. As such, it is the latter that emerges as the essential element of the indigenous way of life. And it is this that multiculturalists like Kymlicka and others would hope to protect in order to preserve these cultures.

However, with reference to other ethnic groups, preservation of a particular way of life is often associated with cultural and religious practices. Thus, preserving the 'way of life' of Muslim immigrants in western European societies is associated with recognition of their right to pray on Friday afternoon, wearing *hijab*, accepting polygamy and female circumcision. In the case of internal minorities like Jews, the focus is on the recognition of religious holidays, availability of Kosher foods and other cultural practices. In most of these cases, what is designated as worthy of preservation are practices, that a nation-state disallows or opposes. In more positive terms, existing cultural and religious practices, or even linguistic practices that are regarded to be collectively valued by a community are sought to be protected against liberal opposition. Thus, preservation aims to allow minority communities the rights to continue with practices that they see as being essential to their cultural self-definition.

The agenda of preserving minority cultures privileges a community's self-perception. It treats existing social and cultural practices as markers of a community's distinct way of life. Furthermore, it assumes that some practices are collectively valued in a community and perceived as being crucial to their identity. Hence, through its agenda of preserving minority cultures, multiculturalism seeks to protect cultural practices which are perceived by the community to be signs of their identity. This, as we will observe later on, privileges the voice of the present leadership and tends to silence the dissenting notes within the community. However, before taking up these issues, it is important also to note that the multicultural discourse often works with stereotypical images of communities and cultures. For example, the Quebecois way of life is associated with the preservation of a linguistic tradition; but the way of life of ethnic communities from West Asia and Africa is most often linked to their religious identity. Thus, in their case it is religious practices usually associated with Islam that become the object of multicultural debate. Even when the religious practices of these communities are defended, these people emerge as 'others', different and incommensurable with the modern West. Although, in part, these images surface because multiculturalists defend religious and cultural practices of these ethnic minorities against the liberal onslaught, these pictures get reinforced as these theorists select a few existing social, cultural and religious practices of these communities and associate them with their way of life.

Although preserving minority cultures involves protection for all those practices that are currently endorsed by the community, at least some theorists of multiculturalism maintain that they aim to shelter marginalised cultures only from external pressures of disintegration. Existing practices are, it is said, defended against the assimilationist policies of the nation-state and the pressures to conform that come from the larger society. To underscore this point, Kymlicka makes a distinction between internal and external pressures for change. According to him, a community faces two distinct sources of destabilisation: pressures that come from groups within the community, and external political or economic pressures that come from the larger society. It is the latter that must be resisted, and it is against this category of pressures that an attempt is made to preserve cultures. Although this distinction is fairly tenuous, it emphasises that multiculturalism does not, at least in principle, seek to arrest changes that members of the community may themselves desire in their culture (see Kymlicka, 1991).

In fact, multiculturalists maintain that change in operating practices must come from within the culture. Instead of stipulating minimum conditions that the culture must fulfil, any transformation in existing practices must be negotiated by members within the culture. It must not be imposed upon them from the outside. As the state is seen as the embodiment of majority culture, it is the community that is vested with the authority to determine whether change in the existing practices is necessary and desirable. A few multiculturalists do suggest the necessity of creating or activating institutions that allow all sections of the community to participate in their internal affairs. However, within the multicultural analysis, this too may be an imposition. Since it is assumed that communities value different notions of good life, it follows that they may opt for institutional structures that do not conform to liberal–democratic expectations. Yet, despite this, multiculturalism does not, in principle, preclude the possibility of changes occurring in the existing way of life.

The agenda of protecting and preserving minority cultures grants community the autonomy to determine what is to be protected. One might also add that many multiculturalists support preservation on the ground that the agents themselves desire to continue and protect these practices. Consequently, if they were to relinquish some of these elements themselves, then the question of preservation would not arise. To take an example: if native Fijians were to want the same things that other members of society do, the case for separate institutions needed for preserving the traditional way of life would decline (Carens, 1992: 595).

Hence, preservation is predicated on the view that members of a particular culture wish to continue with a specific practice or tradition; and multiculturalists seek to create conditions in which communities can resist pressures to assimilate; specifically, pressures that come from the market and the cultural majority within the state. Special rights for minorities are advocated to protect them against such external pressures. However, it remains to be seen whether the multicultural conception of culture and community can accommodate expressions of multivocality within the community. Indeed, in a framework where the community is included as a homogeneous entity, space for internal dissent is likely to shrink. Besides, as we will see in the next chapter, through the idea of differentiated citizenship it is the issue of inter-group equality that is foregrounded within multiculturalism. As a result, the equally important concern for intra-group equality often takes a backseat.

4

Citizenship and Group-differentiated Rights

Within multiculturalism, minority communities are singled out as a special category of citizens. They are differentiated from others on the ground that they are marginalised and discriminated against. Based on the understanding that the policies of liberal nation-states create conditions in which these cultural communities are susceptible to disintegration, multiculturalism argues that we should make an effort to promote cultural diversity. This would require, not just special consideration for marginalised minorities, but also special rights for them: rights that would enable them to sustain themselves and resist pressures of assimilation that come from the state and society. It is assumed here that by resisting homogenisation and preserving their cultures, minority communities would not only be able to fight existing patterns of cultural discrimination, they would also be able to participate as equal members of the polity.

Special rights of this kind for marginalised minority communities are located and defended within the framework of differentiated citizenship. Setting aside the ideal of universal citizenship with identical rights for all persons, multiculturalism claims that a system of group-differentiated rights is needed for ensuring equal citizenship. At the most general level, differentiated citizenship implies that people should be included not merely as citizens but also as members of communities, and that diverse categories of citizens be brought into the state by extending special or different rights to them. These claims challenge our most deeply ingrained ideas of justice and fairness as well as the dominant thinking within democratic theory. One needs, therefore, to take a closer look at the notion of citizenship and rights that is articulated within the framework of differentiated citizenship.

Going Beyond Universal Citizenship

Equality is commonly associated with uniform and identical treatment. Since at least the time of Aristotle, it has been linked with the idea that 'likes should be treated alike'. Living in fourth century BC, Aristotle, however believed that men were, by nature, different. Some had the rational capacity to deliberate, while others could only follow directives of others. Hence, for him, all persons within the *polis* were not alike. They needed to be treated differently. Accordingly, he distinguished between slaves and masters, women and men, children and parents, and prescribed different duties and obligations for each. When we come to the modern era, the assumption of natural inequality on which the Aristotelian system was built, is questioned systematically. In fact, through the struggles for democracy it is gradually argued that social identities with which we are born, such as race, religion, caste and gender, must not be the basis of differentiating between individuals. Just because people worship differently or the colour of their skin is different, we must not see them as being unlike each other. As human beings, they are members of a common humanity and must be considered alike, at least in the eyes of the law.

In particular, identities that are inherited rather than chosen must be regarded as irrelevant in the distribution of rights, and all persons, as citizens, must be considered to be the same. At least, in part, this understanding of equality gained acceptance because speaking of differences was a way of excluding some categories of people and denying them rights of citizenship. Consequently, to include them in the political process, it was believed that we must represent them as citizens, and in that capacity they must all receive the same, identical rights.

The fact that the ideal of universal citizenship has helped include people who were previously excluded from the public–political domain is today widely acknowledged. Multiculturalism does not deny this contribution. It, however, asserts that this ideal has not effectively realised the goal of equality. While it has enabled people of different identities to achieve *membership* of the state, it has not provided equality of democratic citizenship.

The principle of universal and uniform citizenship has, in fact, left many structures of discrimination untouched within the polity. Multiculturalism identifies three reasons for this: (*a*) universal citizenship acknowledges commonalities only at the level of the state; (*b*) it assumes the existence of a *homogeneous* public, and (*c*) it mandates identical treatment for all. Collectively these three elements have resulted in the marginalisation of some communities within the nation-state.

From the point of view of multiculturalism, a major problem with the idea of universal citizenship is that it speaks only of individuals as citizens. It recognises only one membership: namely, of the state, and dismisses all other affiliations and loyalties. As a consequence, it makes no attempt to accommodate the latter. Only individuals as citizens of the state receive consideration within it; they alone have rights and can make claims against the state and other individuals. Communities have no recognised standing within it. According to the multiculturalists, this 'unitary' model of citizenship is endorsed in the liberal tradition as well as the republican tradition (Carens, 2000: 162). The former sets aside all community memberships for it acknowledges only the moral worth of the individual. It sees the political realm as being constituted by unencumbered citizens. The latter, on the other hand, speaks of a community but it visualises the state as a political community. Thus, even though the civic republican tradition conceives citizenship as a bond entailing reciprocity and a sense of commonality, it assumes a sense of community and belonging arises through participation in common institutions and laws. Hence, it too speaks of only political and civil ties. It gives no significance to cultural ties, shared experiences and meanings, other than those that are represented in the state. Consequently, in this conception of citizenship too the importance and wellbeing of particularistic cultural communities remains largely unattended (see Carens, 2000).

Besides ignoring the existence of multiple loyalties, the ideal of universal citizenship assumes the presence of a homogeneous public. For advocates of differentiated citizenship, it judges everyone, even those belonging to different cultural contexts— and endorsing different values and ways of life—by the same

rules and standards. What is even more significant for multiculturalism is that the chosen standards generally express the culture of the majority community within the state, i.e., what is
permitted and prescribed as desirable is shaped by the preferences of the majority. As a result, the principle of universal rights
discriminates against the minority communities. The assumption
of sameness and identity disadvantages 'groups whose experience, culture and socialized capacities differ from those of the
privileged groups' (Young, 1990: 164). In a 'society where some
groups are privileged while others are oppressed, insisting that
as citizens persons should leave behind their particular affiliations and experiences to adopt a general point of view only
serves to reinforce that privilege' (Young, 1989: 260). It allows
'privileged groups to ignore their own group specificity' (Young,
1990: 165) and define, at least implicitly, 'the standards according to which all will be measured' (*Ibid.*: 164). Besides, by allowing norms expressing the point of view and experiences
of the privileged groups to appear neutral and universal,
(*Ibid.*: 165), it tends to perpetuate a kind of cultural imperialism'
(*Ibid.*: 164). As a result, some communities remain marginalised.
Their points of view and perspectives get gradually silenced and
excluded from the 'common culture of the state' (Kymlicka and
Norman, 1994: 370; also see Young, 1989: 257).

It is to include people of all cultures and communities as equals
within the nation-state that multiculturalism advocates a heterogeneous public culture. It pursues this ideal through the framework
of differentiated citizenship. The latter begins with the understanding that people have multiple identities and overlapping
loyalties. The identity of a person as a citizen is only one of the
many identities. More importantly, the presence of these other
community identities does not weaken or threaten his or her
identity as a citizen. Besides, individuals often carry their cultural
identities into the public domain. Consequently, one needs to
give due consideration to individuals as members of the state
as well as members of cultural communities. Their claims and
rights in this dual capacity must be taken into account. If, for
some reason, we neglect their claims as members of cultural
communities, they are likely to be alienated from the political

community and this would certainly weaken their commitment to the state.

Informed by this view of the value of cultural community identity, the concept of differentiated citizenship sees individuals, both as members of the political community, or the state, as well as members of a cultural community. Further, it envisages rights of persons in both these capacities. Since multiculturalism believes that the state is not neutral between different ways of life, it pays particular attention to the rights of marginalised minority communities within the state. Indeed, the framework of differentiated citizenship is invoked to argue that different categories of people may receive different rights for the sake of ensuring fair and just treatment. While some rights are to be given to all persons as citizens, a few may be extended to only a few individuals belonging to specific communities. Special rights may be given to individuals belonging to minority communities as well as to minority communities themselves. Thus, while all rights are supported for the value they have for the individual, not all rights are given to individuals. Some rights, accruing in the framework of differentiated citizenship, are collective rights that are given to communities. They may be given to communities so that they may protect their culture and resist assimilation into the majority culture. In most cases, special rights allow individuals to continue with their cultural community practices while also giving them a say in defining the public domain and the norms that govern it. Multiculturalism entertains collective rights of these diverse kinds within the system of differentiated citizenship.

The notion of differentiated citizenship approaches the issue of rights with the belief that equal citizenship is not always achieved by giving uniform rights to all persons. At times, special consideration is needed for a few so that they are neither excluded from the public culture nor compelled to endorse the culture of another. The latter is considered equally important by multiculturalism because the loss of their culture can create havoc in the lives of the individuals and leave them extremely vulnerable and marginalised. Cultural community membership enters into the picture because of its significance to the individual. In other words, the concern for the individual itself necessitates that the cultural community be accommodated and its rights be considered along with those of political community membership (see Haksar, 1998). Even when multiculturalism expresses concern about the wellbeing of marginalised cultural communities, it often does so with the belief that individuals can live a life of dignity and meaningfully exercise options only when the fate of their cultural community is secure. Thus, the individual remains directly—and at times indirectly—the focus of attention, albeit the individual is almost always located in some community. Thus, while special rights are mooted for promoting the wellbeing of the individual (see Chandhoke, 1999: 302) it is also believed that this task cannot be performed without taking care of the community to which he or she belongs.

The idea of differentiated citizenship that is often justified on grounds of enhancing democratic citizenship and fair treatment for all, assumes that people may be included with different rights within the polity. While no one may be denied the basic rights of participation, some may receive special rights in addition to those. Special rights of some cannot, however, be a means of excluding anyone from the political and public domain. These rights may exist only to enhance inclusion in a way that does not compel assimilation. Within multiculturalism, special rights that are required for resisting assimilation are often associated with—and at times even conflated with—rights that allow minority cultures to protect their community identity. It is assumed that protecting the cultural community identity and making it secure is itself a way of countering discrimination that minorities face in the polity. The postulated link between eliminating discrimination and protecting minority cultures is central to multiculturalism and it is this that needs to be seriously interrogated.

The notion of differentiated citizenship provides a framework within which multiculturalism discusses and upholds special rights of minority communities that are disadvantaged and discriminated against within the nation-state. Although rectifying sources of cultural discrimination is the postulated goal here, enhancing cultural diversity is perceived to be a way of addressing that issue. Indeed, it is to further this latter end that the idea of differentiated citizenship rather than substantive equality is advocated. While the latter too endorses the necessity of deviating, at least temporarily, from the norm of formal equality, differentiated citizenship abandons the goal for promoting 'a minimum set of resemblances' (see Gupta, 1998: 516–18).

In other words, differentiated citizenship values cultural diversity and is often operationalised to further that ideal. The centrality accorded to cultural diversity needs to be emphasised because it prioritises the controversial agenda of preserving minority cultures, and this is a dimension that has received relatively less attention. The debate on differentiated citizenship has revolved largely around the issue of communities being the subject of rights. In fact, theorists of multiculturalism have also accepted these terms of debate and attempted to justify the shift from the individual to the community by arguing that group differentiation is not peculiar to multiculturalism. 'The orthodox liberal view about the rights of states to determine who has citizenship rests on the same principles which justify group-differentiated citizenship within states' (Kymlicka, 1995: 124). Citizenship is 'an inherently group-differentiated notion' (*Ibid.*) for even the most liberal countries in the world do not open their borders to all. They turn down applications for immigration and refuse people the right to enter their state and participate in its affairs as they are not born in that country. As such, all of them treat people differently depending upon their group membership. Liberal democracies restrict citizenship to people born in a particular territory, and on most occasions, shape their immigration policies to bring in people who can endorse or conform to the cultural ethos of the nation-state. Since considerations of cultural identity have been historically quite important in the construction of the nation-state, it is said that liberals should not object to linking cultural community membership to the distribution of rights within the polity.

Arguments of this kind tend to ignore one major difference: namely, in contemporary democracies, the nation-state is the reference point of all discussions of fairness and justice. While cultural identities are rarely, if ever erased, and they do influence, directly or indirectly, decisions about membership of a state, yet, once the issue of membership is settled it is assumed that all citizens will be entitled to the same rights and treatment by law. The notion of differentiated citizenship however challenges this.

It argues for different treatment for different categories of citizens within the nation-state. Further, it maintains that different treatment on account of cultural community membership would not pose a threat to the territorial integrity of the nation-state. On the contrary, incorporating the legitimate claims of marginalised minorities is likely to build a stronger and more integrated nation-state.

While discussing the issue of special rights for minorities, multiculturalism concentrates on discrimination that occurs through the policies and cultural orientation of the nation-state. The focus, therefore, is on cultural rather than economic marginalisation. Although the latter is an important source of subordination, multiculturalism addresses culture-related discrimination. Some communities, in its view, remain vulnerable irrespective of the economic clout they possess. Lower economic status may significantly accentuate the feeling of marginalisation, but an improved economic position is not enough to overcome the disadvantages the community faces within the nation-state. Hence, it is the cultural identity rather than economic status that is seen as the crucial condition here. Furthermore, special rights are given to minority communities so that they can protect their culture and enjoy a life of equal dignity and respect. It is because special rights fulfil these conditions that they are perceived as a way of enhancing 'civic integration' (Carens, 2000). Against the critics who feel that special rights will fragment the national community, multiculturalists maintain that differential citizenship will promote a deeper sense of belonging to the state.

Elucidating this further, Joseph Carens argues that citizenship is not simply a legal status. It has a psychological dimension (Carens, 1996–97). Citizenship denotes a sense of belonging to a collectivity; and to belong, people must have an 'emotional attachment, identification and loyalty' (*Ibid.*: 113). However, forging a connection of this kind requires, in his view, a context in which minorities have a sense of collective participation and adequate representation. Special rights are intended to provide just this. They aim to include diverse communities, not by expecting conformity to a set of cultural norms, but by acknowledging cultural differences and creating space for the representation and participation of these differences. Consequently, it is argued that the majority should accept the necessity and value of special rights for minorities. 'Members of a political community should be able and willing to work together, to understand one another, to seek agreement on issues, to compromise where necessary to reach agreement, to respect each other's legitimate claims, to trust one another, and even to make sacrifices for one another. This is what belonging to a common community means or ought to mean' (Carens, 1995: 28). It is in this spirit of enhancing a sense of belonging that special rights for marginalised communities should be accepted within the polity.

Special Rights for Marginalised Minorities

Within the framework of differentiated citizenship, multiculturalism focuses on three categories of special rights that minorities may claim within the nation-state. These are: (i) *cultural rights* in the form of *exemptions, assistance* and *recognition*; (ii) *self-government rights*, and (iii) *special representation rights*. Both the rights to self-government as well as separate representation make community membership the basis of participation in the political process, and for this reason these rights, more than cultural rights, have been seen as a threat to the unity of the nation-state. So strong was this belief at the time of independence in India that the Constituent Assembly distinguished between the political and the cultural claims of the religious communities. The latter were accommodated quite readily in the belief that these were markers of a distinct community identity, and making space for them was essential for checking assimilation and promoting diversity. On the other hand, political claims for separate representation and a separate electorate for representation were regarded as measures that would divide the nation along communal lines and threaten its territorial integrity. The representatives of minority communities in the Constituent Assembly eventually endorsed this assessment of political claims, and consequently, in the final stages of the deliberations they withdrew their claims for separate representation in legislative bodies.

India is not the only country where demands for separate representation or self-government by a community have been perceived as a source of sedition and disunity. Similar sentiments have been expressed by several analysts with regard to the claims of the people of Quebec as well as the indigenous people of North America. The multicultural defence of these rights, particularly the argument that granting territorial and political autonomy to specific minority communities, gains significance against this backdrop. The claims for cultural rights have raised anxieties of a somewhat different kind. The issue that has been debated most closely here is the conflict between claims for equal and uniform treatment *vis-à-vis* accommodation of heterogeneity. Both the feminists and the liberals have been concerned overwhelmingly with this issue. However, even as we discuss these questions over the next few chapters, it is necessary to draw attention to the fact that cultural community rights serve two fairly different purposes. While some enhance options for community members, others enable communities to protect and preserve themselves. The former entail some deviation from the principle of uniform treatment but are not inimical to the concerns of democracy. The latter, by comparison, raise serious concern about intra-group equality and the agenda of promoting cultural diversity. It is these that need to be examined carefully for they do not fit well with the project of democracy. The following pages approach the issue of special rights from this perspective. They discuss the different kinds of cultural and political rights defended within multicultural discourses while simultaneously drawing attention to the fact that the collective rights defended by them support, not just rights that enhance options for community members, but also rights that enhance diversity by protecting cultures and communities.

CULTURAL RIGHTS

Exemptions

Cultural rights, or what are sometimes also called, 'polyethnic rights' (Kymlicka, 1995: 30–33), are by far the most frequently demanded special rights in liberal democracies. Almost everywhere minorities ask for an equal liberty to continue with their specific religious and cultural practices. However, this demand is couched in different languages at different moments in time. In western democracies with strong homogenised nation-states, minorities most often seek *exemptions*. Exemptions are desired to correct the majoritarian bias of the existing laws and to provide minorities with the right to live by their culturally distinct way of life. For instance, in America, Jews asked for exemptions *vis-à-vis* the Sabbath laws on the grounds that the religious practices of the majority placed them at a disadvantage in the public arena. The Sikhs in Canada and Britain sought exemptions from laws prescribing wearing of helmets by motorcycle riders, miners and police personnel on the plea that they restricted minority practices. These laws, they argued, imposed norms that violated the prescribed religious and cultural practices of the community. The Jews pointed to the disadvantages that emanate from the hegemony of the majority culture in the public domain, and the Sikhs revealed that insensitivity to group differences could deny some communities the right to their religion and culture. Both sought exemptions to rectify the existing modes of culture-based discrimination. In positive terms, they demanded exemptions to ensure that minorities enjoy the same right to religion that is granted to the majority.

Within multiculturalism, equal access to one's religion and culture is valued for it signifies equal treatment of minorities within the state. Ensuring that minorities have access to their culture requires rectifying the cultural biases of the state. More importantly, it requires that differences in group practices be respected and reflected in the public domain. Exemptions are, in this sense, a double-edged weapon. On the one hand, they correct the biases that emanate from the cultural orientation of the nation-state, and on the other, they provide equal opportunity to minorities to live in accordance with their own religious and cultural practices.

Exemptions from wearing helmets or the prescribed headdress for mounted police do not simply mitigate the disadvantages stemming from insensitivity to group differences; they enable Sikhs to wear the turban as prescribed by their religion. Likewise, exemptions from compulsory school laws allow the Amish to withdraw their children from schools at the age of fourteen, so that they do not build resistance to their own way of life. Special rights to hunt and fish on reservations allow American Indians to continue with their own way of life. Freedom to wear the *hijab* allows the Muslim girls to observe the customary practices of the community. Exemptions from the law on narcotics and hallucinogens take cognisance of the specific practices of the American Indians and enable them to continue with the use of Peyote for religious purposes. Thus, exemptions have been demanded, and often granted, for the sake of minimising majoritarian cultural biases, incorporating group differences into the public domain and giving minorities an opportunity to continue with their customary religious practices.

Although, in a large number of cases, exemptions have been sought to protect the religious practices of minority communities, it is only one of the many grounds for seeking exemptions. American Indians, for instance, seek exemptions from various fishing and hunting laws to preserve their own distinct way of life. At various times, the Irish citizens of South Africa, Canada and the United Kingdom have desired exemptions from compulsory conscription so that they were not forced to fight on behalf of England (see Levy, 1997: 26). Thus, while religious beliefs are often invoked in minority claims, a cultural way of life and freely chosen commitments[1] have also been the basis of minority demands for exemptions.

In the recent times, western liberal democracies have been more receptive to claims for exemptions that have come from minorities. Also, in comparison with other claims for minority rights, the demand for exemptions has met with a more positive response from state institutions. However, the relative success in this field has not come about without a struggle. Minorities have had to mobilise themselves and fight for each of these exemptions. However, today there are a number of exemptions that have been granted to specific minorities in each state. Exemptions have been granted to minorities so that their religious

---

[1] For instance, Jehovah's Witnesses in some states of America asked for, and have been given, exemptions from healthcare regulations.

and cultural norms related to worship, initiation ceremonies, dress codes, food habits, etc., can be accommodated in the public arena. For example, special provisions have been made to allow Sikhs to wear their turban, Muslim girls to wear a *chador* to school and for Asian women to wear their traditional dress to their workplace. Likewise, many states have provided special exemptions for *halal* and *kosher* foods to accommodate the special needs of Muslims and Jews, respectively. In another instance, ceremonial use of wine by Catholics and Jews has been exempted from laws dealing with prohibition of alcohol. The Amish community has been granted exemptions so that it can withdraw children at the age of fourteen from school. In addition, in some states the Amish have also been granted exemptions from participating in unemployment insurance and worker's compensation plans (see Ferrarra, 1993). Jehovah's Witnesses and Christian Scientists have been exempted from healthcare regulations in some states in America. The Indian American community has been exempted from laws protecting certain species of birds and fish, and allowed special hunting and fishing rights in this regard on reservation land.

The list of exemptions is steadily increasing in western liberal democracies. Indeed, exemptions have been given to various kinds of communities, such as indigenous people, immigrants, internal religious minorities (e.g., Jews in America) and ethnic groups (e.g., Francophones in Canada). Also, exemptions have been given on a wide variety of issues. Yet, in most cases these have been a product of political negotiations. There is no one rule that has been consistently applied while considering these diverse demands. Indeed, even retrospectively it is exceedingly difficult to identify a single principle which can explain why some claims have been yielded more readily than others. At times, accommodation of cultural symbols has been strongly contested, but at other moments there has been a greater willingness to negotiate and grant exemptions. In Germany, for instance, Muslim girls can wear the headscarf to the school but there are cases where women have lost school jobs for wearing the headscarf in the classroom. In Canada, to take another example, military veterans of the Sikh community faced a great deal of resistance when they sought permission to wear turbans to the annual fil-lip. Since the turban, unlike the hat, would not be removed at dinner, officials claimed that wearing the turban would be a sign of disrespect to the crown. By comparison, the exemption to wear turbans in the Royal Canadian Mounted Police was conceded more readily (Levin, 1999). In the recent past, however, a great deal of controversy has been generated around the issue of a Sikh boxer fighting his match while continuing to keep his beard. While the Sikh community has maintained that having a beard was a religious requirement, the Canadian Amateur Boxing Association (CABA) stated that keeping a beard violated the norm of the International Boxing Association. Even when lawyers got an injunction from the court allowing the Sikh boxer to participate in the competition, the CABA cancelled all the matches in his flyweight category (*Ibid.*). Thus, the response of the democratic state to demands for exemptions has varied. Even within the same country, what exemptions are granted, and to whom, depends upon a number of issues. Eventually, the outcome depends on a number of contingent conditions.

It is perhaps necessary to note that claims for exemptions have arisen overwhelmingly in western liberal democracies. By comparison, in countries like India, there are in relatively fewer demands for exemptions. This is not because India is not sufficiently democratic, or that western democracies are more strongly committed to the principles of liberalism. Rather, this difference has arisen on account of the success of the homogenising project of the nation-state in western democracies. Since the latter have had a long history of religious and cultural homogenisation, many existing laws reflect the culture of the majority. They accommodate majority cultural practices and place minorities at a disadvantage. Over the last three decades, minorities have pointed to this discrepancy and put pressure upon the nation-state to make suitable adjustments in the form of exemptions. In India, greater attention was given to the cultural and religious claims of minorities at the time of framing the Constitution. In fact, the Constitution ensured protection to religious practices of all communities in the chapter on fundamental rights. It also granted minorities special rights to preserve their language and culture. Hence, exemptions were not needed for protecting religious freedom. While there were—and still are—challenges to the exercise of religious freedom, they needed to be countered through other kinds of measures, and not just exemptions. However, in western democracies where there has been an officially recognised religion for a long period of time, many laws and policies implicitly—and sometimes even explicitly—reflect the culture of the ruling majority. In most cases, exemptions have been demanded, and granted, to correct this kind of bias, and through it, to realise the ideal of equal treatment for all religious and cultural minorities.

When exemptions have been demanded for the sake of giving minorities an equal freedom to practice their religion and culture, minority claims have often been defended within the broader framework of the right to religious liberty. In fact, some theorists represent claims for exemptions as the voice of the conscientious objector seeking freedom for the individual against coercion by the state and society (see Levy, 1997; Raz, 1986: 252). Others associate exemptions with the right of the individual to carry out his or her religious duties. Both sets of arguments, however, agree that exemptions given to protect a religious and cultural way of life strengthen communities.

Multiculturalism adds to these arguments by suggesting that exemptions are needed to accommodate markers of minority religious and cultural identity in the public domain. Since it maintains that majority identity is already visible and incorporated in the practices of the state, exemptions are sought only for minority communities. Further, exemptions allow minority communities to continue with their customary cultural practices while simultaneously making the public sphere more heterogeneous. Although exemptions are supported for the sake of including marginalised communities into the nation-state, they do allow communities to protect and continue with their distinct way of life. While some of these collective rights introduce heterogeneity by giving members the option of endorsing a way of life, others empower communities and give the right to ensure that a given way of life is made secure.

To put it in another way, exemption claims entail two different kinds of rights: (*i*) those that enhance options for internal members and (*ii*) those that enable communities to protect their way of life, often by minimising options for community members. Although contemporary discourses of multiculturalism make no distinction between these two fairly different kinds of collective rights, it is essential to disaggregate them for they have different implications for a democracy. To take an example: exemptions from helmet wearing allow members of a community to be treated differently. This takes note of their distinct headgear prescribed by community religious and cultural practices, and accordingly, makes exceptions for them. Exemption is here granted on the basis of community membership: that is, only individuals belonging to a specific community are granted exemptions. However, it is individual members of the community—and not the community—who exercise the special right. It is they who decide whether to wear their traditional turban or to opt for the helmet. Hence, exemptions of this kind have the potential of enhancing options for community members so long as the community does not institute any punitive measures against those who choose to wear the helmet rather than the turban. In contrast to this, an exemption given to the community to withdraw its children from school before they reach a specific age allows the community to safeguard its identity, but only by minimising options for its members. While exemptions of this sort seek to accommodate the distinctiveness of a cultural community they do so by restricting the options for the children and their parents.

To enable the community to preserve itself, an exemption here allows the community to make the choice on behalf of its members. Further, the choices are made in a way that give the young members no real possibility of moving out of the community even at some future date. Consequently, special rights of this kind empower communities; they preserve the existing institutional and power structures. While they increase diversity and enable a community to survive, they do restrict options for their members. Since multiculturalism advocates special rights for enhancing cultural diversity and for ensuring a secure cultural context for all persons, it remains largely inhospitable to these distinctions. The value that it accords to the ideal of cultural diversity in fact enables it to justify claims that enhance options for community members as well as claims that enable communities to protect their way of life. Needless to say, communitarian appropriations of multiculturalism arise primarily from the conflation of these two fairly different claims. It is essential therefore to separate rights that protect cultures from those that challenge the assimilationist policies of the nation-state. Indeed, a distinction of this kind may be necessary for accommodating claims of collective cultural rights within a democracy.

State Assistance for Minority Cultures

Seeking exemptions is perhaps the most common form in which minorities in western democracies have represented their claims for equal religious and cultural rights. However, it is not the only form in which cultural rights are claimed by minorities. To overcome the disadvantage that minorities face in observing their own distinct way of life, communities frequently supplement exemption claims with those of special assistance from the state. The nation-state, according to the multiculturalists, protects the culture of the majority community. The heritage of the majority—its art, language, architecture, music and other such artefacts—receive state patronage. Or else, on account of its dominant position in society it is protected in the public arena. As a consequence, the majority enjoys access to its culture. It knows that its culture is secure within the nation-state. The minorities, by comparison, feel vulnerable. The pervasiveness of the majority culture as well as the rewards that go with acquiring that culture, disadvantage minority cultures. They threaten the very existence of these marginalised cultures.

To offset marginalisation of this kind, minorities frequently seek *assistance* from the state to promote their culture and to give it some space within the public arena. At the very least, they may request financial support or other related state resources for sustaining their cultural institutions, such as minority educational institutions, museums for ethnic arts and crafts, theatres, community newspapers, cultural clubs and institutions for the learning of ethnic languages. However, in certain spheres they can, and often do, expect the state to play a more proactive role. On the issue of language, for instance, minorities ask the state to facilitate the use of minority languages and enable the meaningful exercise of language rights by minorities. Special assistance for both these activities receives strong support within multiculturalism. As language is regarded to be a primary pole of individual identity, giving due recognition to a person's language and the rights to use that language is considered important. Following upon the Heideggerian maxim that to have a language is to have a world, it is argued that recognition to a language is a necessary condition for recognising a culture and giving it an equal status.

However, since the status of language is closely related to the position of a culture and community, a variety of different strategies are endorsed within multiculturalism in this regard. At the very least, access to one's language entails the opportunity to receive education in the language of the community, use of minority languages in state institutions and the right to address public authorities in those languages. Since 'the freedom to use one's own language in addressing (state) authorities is ineffective if those authorities have no corresponding duty to understand and act upon that language' (de Witte in Levy, 1997: 30), what is also advocated is the right of minorities to expect the state to undertake routine administrative and judicial work in the languages of the minority communities. In effect, this means that the state must either promote bi/multi-lingualism among its personnel, or provide interpreters for members of minority communities.

However, this is not the only way in which access to a language may be protected for community members. As the experience of several democracies shows, the presence of minority educational institutions and the availability of education in the language of a minority is not always enough for keeping a language alive or attractive for its members. In India, for instance, the presence of minority educational institutions established for Urdu-speaking population in areas where Urdu is a spoken language, has not helped to check the decreasing interest in Urdu (Shahabuddin, 2000: 2). Indeed, the decline of Urdu language users has been a matter of some concern among members of the Muslim community. Many of them feel that the loss of language users will adversely affect the survival of the culture and literature associated with that language. Consequently, to keep a language alive and to make it a viable option which community members may themselves choose, multiculturalists often recommend public recognition for minority languages. To put it in another way, what is advocated is not merely the right of community members to use a language if they so desire, but the re-organisation of territorial boundaries in a way that a minority language can become the language of the majority in a designated region. It is assumed here that public endorsement of a minority language, particularly its designation as the official language of the region, would protect the language and promote linguistic and cultural diversity within the polity.

Both sets of policies begin with the belief that language constitutes self-identity, however, they address the issue of linguistic identity quite differently. While policies that seek bi/multilingual education give individuals the option to read in their language, policies that sustain a language by making it the official language of a region often minimise options for community members. Even though some internal minorities may, at times, have the option of receiving education in their own language, these options are rarely made available to the rest of the population. The paradox, therefore, is that formal recognition to a minority language helps a language flourish and boosts the number of language users, but promoting diversity in this way places heavy costs upon community members. Even though the culture survives and enjoys a higher prestige, choices for members get restricted.

Symbolic Claims

Besides minority claims for exemptions and assistance, multiculturalism also draws attention to symbolic claims that are sometimes presented by the marginalised communities. Generally, symbolic claims challenge the way a community is represented in the public arena and in the symbols of national life. Minorities asserting such claims maintain that the cultural symbols of the nation-state—e.g., the national anthem, declared public holidays, recognised national languages and even the name of the state—tend to reflect the orientation of the majority. Through symbolic claims minorities seek to challenge their exclusion from the cultural expressions of the nation-state. In positive terms, they attempt to alter the way in which they are represented in the public arena through the chosen symbols of national life.

For the minorities, symbolic claims signify their struggle for equal status within the nation-state. To find a space in the name of the polity, its insignia, flag or public holidays suggests that they belong to the political community and are its full members. Consequently, even when symbolic representation yields sparse gains for the minorities in substantive terms, they influence their perceptions of the nation-state. Since these claims are closely associated with the prestige of the community in the public arena, they have a special place within the framework of multiculturalism, and are strongly supported by it. Besides, unlike other claims for cultural rights, these only challenge the majoritarian biases of the nation-state and place no costs upon internal members.

Claims for Recognition

Along with claiming symbolic space within the democratic state, minorities may, at times, seek recognition for specific community practices. Recognition rights do not simply grant communities the opportunity to continue with their customary practices, they acknowledge and protect traditional community structures and systems of authority. As such, recognition claims are generally a means of preserving cultural practices and maintaining a certain degree of continuity with the past. Almost everywhere, religious communities seek legal recognition of marriages performed by authorised religious persons. In some states, for example, India, they have sought, and received, recognition for their family laws. Indigenous people in North America have repeatedly demanded recognition for tribal laws, particularly in dealing with criminal offenses. They have also sought recognition for their special land rights, hunting and fishing rights and rights to govern themselves in accordance with traditional rules. Thus, recognition has been claimed for diverse cultural and religious practices, but in each instance it is desired to protect traditional community norms and institutional practices.

Although preservation is often favoured to protect these communities from external forces of disintegration, nevertheless, it

is important to note that recognition is aimed at sustaining existing community structures. It provides official state recognition to
community structures and systems of authority. Hence, it does
not simply enhance religious liberty or equality. It achieves something more by granting a legal status to traditional institutional
structures. One might even say that recognition rights set up an
alternative system of authority, and in this specific way, limit the
nation-state. They challenge the use of universal principles by
the nation-state and suggest that there are areas of collective
social life which could be governed by multiple codes that are
determined by particular communities.

As recognition rights honour multiple codes of social and cultural interaction, they tend to uphold traditional and customary
laws. In some cases, these traditional norms receive exclusive
jurisdiction over their members, but on other occasions, traditional laws are placed alongside the laws of the nation-state.
This can be done in a variety of different ways: by dividing the
area of jurisdiction, establishing a parallel system of governance,
or by giving members the option to choose and subject themselves to a specific set of laws. For instance, in some states of
America, jurisdiction is shared between the tribal governments
and the state. While certain kinds of criminal actions are tried
and punished in accordance with traditional tribal law, cases
involving death penalty are placed under the jurisdiction of the
federal authority. In some other states, recognition of tribal customs has meant the existence of a parallel system of jurisdiction
wherein indigenous people are tried under tribal laws while the
white population, living in the same area, is governed by the
laws of the state. In many other countries, for example, India,
recognition is accorded to family law of the community so that
individual members can choose to be married and governed by
the law of the state or the law of the community.

Recognition rights thus provide for competing jurisdictions in
a variety of different ways. At times, they place certain spheres
of individual life under the exclusive jurisdiction of the community, on other occasions, jurisdiction is shared or divided between the state and the community. Whatever be the chosen
arrangement, these rights accept the presence of community-based

authority. In fact, it legitimises such forms of authority and is among the most strongly contested collective rights. In most liberal polities, recognition for community practices, e.g., female circumcision, continues to be area of major debate. The crucial issue being whether the community should have the right to define its practices and implement them for its members. Should, for instance, communities have the right to excommunicate members? Should community members be governed by the Personal Laws of their community? These are issues that lie at the heart of the debate on multiculturalism. There are several votaries of multiculturalism who maintain that we cannot have a general theory by which all such hard cases can be decided, however, the general inclination of multiculturalism is to say that the perceptions of the agents and the community should be privileged over those of outsiders. While all forms of community practices are rarely justified, state intervention is usually considered undesirable. It is this assessment of the state that tends, implicitly at least, to legitimise autonomy for the community to determine its own practices unhindered. Thus, recognition rights do not merely introduce parallel systems of jurisdiction, they provide a rationale for giving greater power and control to the community in matters of cultural life.

SELF-GOVERNMENT RIGHTS

Self-government claims supplement recognition rights. Like the latter, these claims affirm the need for dual jurisdiction. However, there is one significant difference between these two kinds of minority claims. Self-government rights are generally linked to territorial claims. Usually communities that are concentrated in a specific region, or those that have occupied a given territory over a long period of time, seek the right to govern themselves. On most occasions, communities that ask for self-government rights see themselves as distinct nations; and it is in this capacity that they ask for special status within the polity. By comparison, recognition rights are not accompanied by analogous claims to territory. While the groups claiming recognition see themselves as culturally distinct entities, they do not bolster their identity claims with rights over territory. Moreover, the right to self-government can be claimed only when communities are concentrated in a given region. Recognition rights, on the other hand, can be claimed by, and given to, communities whose members are scattered in different regions of the nation-state. Thus, for example, religious minorities may seek special recognition for the family law of the community even though their members live in different parts of the country. However, self-government rights can be demanded only when a given minority constitutes a majority in a specific area.

Within the framework of multiculturalism, self-government rights are also justified as measures necessary for protecting a culturally distinct way of life while simultaneously affirming the territorial integrity of the polity. It is argued that in conditions where a way of life is collectively valued by its members, communities that are a minority at the national level but a majority in a given region may be given special rights to govern themselves. Usually these rights entail greater devolution of power to the identified region so that the group can take decisions on key matters such as education, immigration, language, land and resource use, family law, cultural rites, and administrative structure. A degree of political and territorial autonomy is favoured within the framework of a federal system in the belief that it will help to protect marginalised cultures and allow them to shape policies in consonance with their distinct way of life.

Since self-government rights give certain degree of political authority over a defined territory to communities who perceive themselves as separate nations within the polity, these have met with the considerable resistance. Mapping a region where the community is in majority and has the right to govern itself is viewed with suspicion by other communities. In most nation-states where claims of self-government have been made—for example, India, Sri Lanka, Canada—it is widely believed that granting these rights would weaken the nation-state. It would create dual loyalties and divisions that may challenge the territorial integrity of the state.

Theorists of multiculturalism challenge this reading of self-government rights. Instead of perceiving claims for limited political autonomy as threats to the nation-state they maintain that

accommodating the demands of existing nations within a federal
system may prevent the fragmentation of the polity. Indeed, devolution of political power may be the only viable way of maintaining cohesion in a polity split by internal cleavages (Bauböck,
2001). Pragmatic considerations of this kind apart, multiculturalists feel that fears about self-government arise from the unitary
model of citizenship. Within that framework it is assumed that
sovereignty must be pinpointed and narrowly located in an autonomous central state and that the individual must have a single
political membership. Approaching this issue through the framework of differentiated citizenship, multiculturalism argues that
both these assumptions are deeply flawed. First, 'multiple, overlapping, and even conflicting identifications and loyalties are a
widespread phenomenon in the modern world' (Carens, 1995:
18). Second, dual citizenship does not exacerbate the problems
posed by multiple identities and loyalties. For most people 'these
psychological attachments are only marginally affected by legal
status' (*Ibid.*). Taking the case of Native Americans in Canada:
'Whatever problems aboriginal identities and loyalties create in
the unity of the Canadian political community, these identities
and loyalties have existed for a long time in the absence of aboriginal government and in spite of systematic efforts at assimilation. Aboriginal self-government is, in part, a recognition of
and a response to this reality, not the cause of it' (*Ibid.*: 19).
Third, 'sovereignty and statehood should no longer be viewed
as coterminus.... Sovereignty should be accepted as something
to be spread around and as something that simultaneously bears
a multitude of meanings' (Scott in Carens, 1995: 19). It must be
seen as being 'permeable, fluid and partial' (*Ibid.*). And, likewise citizenship should be viewed as 'open, multifaceted and
contested' (*Ibid.*). Once these dimensions of sovereignty and citizenship are accepted, we realise that a unified integrated state
would not vanish with the institution of self-government for a
community. Indeed, when the unitary conception of citizenship is
abandoned, the presence of self-governing nations, dual allegiances and overlapping obligations would not appear as divided or incomplete loyalty to the nation-state.

Differentiated citizenship assumes that people can belong to a particular cultural community as well as the political community or the nation-state. One could, for instance, retain one's identity as a Native American and yet be a Canadian citizen; or, advocate a separate province of Jharkhand or Mizoram and yet be loyal to the Indian State. Multiple identities and loyalties of this kind could exist simultaneously without threatening each other; and people, or even regions, could be incorporated into the polity in different ways with different sets of rights.

The framers of the Indian Constitution put into practice this idea of differentiated citizenship, even though they did not conceptualise it in this form. Thus, for instance, special rights and special status were given to the state of Jammu and Kashmir when it was included into the Indian federation. Under Article 370 of the Indian Constitution it was agreed that this state would be governed by its own Constitution so that the jurisdiction of the central Parliament would be restricted only to such matters as foreign affairs, defence and communication. In another instance, the state of Nagaland and the state of Mizoram were also bestowed special privileges by the Indian Constitution. Under Article 371A and G, special provisions were made to limit immigration so as to protect the identity of the region of Nagaland. In addition, the Naga and Mizo customary laws were recognised and the respective legislatures were accorded supreme power over ownership and transfer of land. All these provisions for special treatment or inclusion of communities with special status gave effect to a system of differentiated citizenship wherein individuals were seen not merely as citizens but also as members of specific cultural communities. Accordingly, in some areas consociational arrangements were devised to incorporate individuals as members of both these communities (Lijphardt, 1996 and 1977).

To underline the idea that people may see themselves as having multiple identities, Charles Taylor suggests that we think in terms of 'deep diversity'. That is, we should consider diversity of identities and diverse modes of belonging to the polity instead of simply diversity of opinions or lifestyles as permitted by constitutionally given rights (Taylor, 1993: 180–85). We should further accept that a person may see herself or himself as a Canadian citizen as well as a Cree; there may be French–Canadians and Canadians of Italian origin and each of them may be included into the polity with distinct rights. Quebecois may receive special rights within Canada, rights that are not given to other provinces and communities. Thus, plural identities and allegiances may exist, and so may multiple patterns of inclusion and belonging to the polity. As and when genuine inclusion and the realisation of equal citizenship require special rights for specific communities they may be extended, specially when they assist in protecting collectively valued ways of life.

Self-government rights are clearly located within the framework of differentiated citizenship. In a manner of speaking, they manifest the most complete expression of differentiated citizenship. Contemporary theories of multiculturalism in the West have defended these rights primarily for the indigenous populations and national minorities such as the Quebecois. In fact, it is in terms of the experiences and demands of these communities that they have defined and justified these rights. It must be noted here that self-government rights are significantly different from other claims for cultural or polyethnic rights. Unlike the latter, they give political autonomy to a particular community in a defined geographical area. In other words, they convert a minority at the national level into a majority in a given area and allow it the right to deliberate upon its own affairs in the hope that this would allow a community to protect its own interests. The need to govern oneself invokes, among other things, the idea that a community is the best judge of its own interests and it alone can give due recognition to the collective concerns of the community. A somewhat similar argument is also used to support the third category of special rights: namely, special representation rights.

SPECIAL REPRESENTATION RIGHTS

Justifications for special representation rights are predicated upon the basic multicultural understanding that to ensure equal citizenship and genuine inclusion, group differences should not be eliminated. Rather diverse communities should have an opportunity to set public agendas and enrich policies by contributing their distinctive cultural perspectives and experiences. Although separate representation rights also enable minorities to protect their special needs and interests, what is emphasised here is that they allow differences to be counted and weighed in decision making. From the multicultural perspective, '[P]eople in different groups often know about somewhat different institutions, events, practices, and social relations, and often have differing perceptions of the same institutions, relations, or events. For this reason, members of some groups are sometimes in a better position than members of others to understand and anticipate the probable consequences of implementing particular social policies. A public that makes use of all such social knowledge in its differentiated plurality is most likely to make just and wise decisions' (Young, 1990: 186).

Separate representation rights are thus conceived as a mode of enriching the public domain. By bringing to bear upon all deliberations the diverse experiences and perspectives of various groups, they augment a better understanding of social and political issues. In addition to it, the deliberate inclusion of various groups, particularly oppressed minorities, can be a powerful tool in redefining the public norms and creating a deliberative consensus. While acknowledging the role of separate representation rights in enhancing diversity in the public domain, most multiculturalists justify these rights only for oppressed or marginalised minorities. However, the multicultural defence of these rights has, at times, been appropriated by numerically small but politically or economically powerful communities to bolster their demands for separate representation. For instance, in Zimbabwe the white population asked for, and were given, 20 per cent of the seats in the Parliament for the first few years of black rule. In India too various communities have presented claims for separate representation. At the time of independence all religious minorities, including those that were economically quite powerful, asked for, but were not given, separate representation. In recent times, the Jat community in North India has demanded special representation to protect their community interests. Indeed, in a situation of considerable scarcity, similar demands from culturally distinct communities have escalated and the multicultural framework has been appropriated to voice and protect specific economic and political interests. Multiculturalism does not, in principle, defend all such claims for special rights. It supports the claims of *oppressed* or *marginalised* minorities who are disadvantaged in the nation-state and whose cultures are susceptible to disintegration due to the pressures that come from the state and society. However, since these rights are justified on grounds of including culturally distinct groups, they have been used by many numerically small communities. Indeed, communities that feel they are insufficiently represented in state institutions, or economically vulnerable, or culturally distinct but small in numbers, often present themselves as vulnerable minorities that need special representation rights.

Minority claims for separate representation have been entertained in many liberal democracies. In fact, such claims have been accommodated in a variety of ways. At times, formal procedures have been instituted for accommodating communities; at other times, societies have relied upon informal practices. In France, for instance, political parties have informally agreed that 30 per cent of the candidates nominated would be women. This arrangement has been devised to accommodate women's demand for separate representation. Belgium, on the other hand, has instituted formal procedures to ensure that all the three linguistic communities in the country are equally represented in the Parliament. Further, it has stipulated that any legislation dealing with the issue of language must receive the approval of the majority of Parliamentarians from each linguistic community. In Canada, special representation is given to Quebec in the Supreme Court as well as the Department of Immigration. In India, similarly, seats are reserved in legislative bodies, government services and educational institutions for members of the Scheduled Castes and Scheduled Tribes.

Quotas and reservation of seats is by far the most common way of providing special representation to specific communities. While some countries such as Belgium, choose to give equal representation to each cultural community, many others (including India) opt for reservation of seats in proportion to the size of the community within the state. A few (e.g., New Zealand) have

created a more flexible system. Here, the number of seats reserved for the Maori community depends upon the number of
people voting from the reserved electoral roll. A lot of variation
also exists in the way reserved seats are filled. In some cases,
only members of the community vote to elect their representative, while in other contexts members of a particular community
are chosen in identified constituencies by the entire electorate
in the area. The latter ensures that members of a particular
community are represented in the Parliament. It focuses on the
identity of the chosen representatives. The former, on the other
hand, gives a community the right to decide who would be its
spokesperson in the Parliament. Hence, it stresses the identity
and special interests of the electors rather than the identity of
the chosen representatives (see Levy, 1997: 44–45).

Although liberalism only recognises the individual and strongly
favours geographically defined single-member constituencies, liberal democracies have not always been hostile to claims of separate and special representation. In colonial India, for instance,
the British introduced separate group-based representation for
the Hindus and the Muslims. Similarly, in Fiji they devised a
scheme of separate representation for the Native Fijians, Indians
and the British. In New Zealand, special representation is provided for the indigenous people; and in Belgium and Netherlands,
group representation is given to different cultural communities.
In America, an attempt was made to accommodate claims of special representation for the black community by redistricting (i.e.,
redrawing the boundaries of the electoral constituencies to create black majority areas).

Thus, the idea of special representation is not alien to liberal
representative democracies. Time and again such claims have
come from minorities and the liberal state has attempted to in-
vent institutions so that the different constituent groups in the
polity could be adequately represented. Liberal democracies
have, outside of the colonial context, been sympathetic to the
demands of minorities that have suffered injustice on account of
social prejudices and those that seek an equal voice within the
political system. Multiculturalism adds a new dimension to these
views by arguing that the presence of diverse communities in

the parliaments and the public arena would enrich society. It would bring in new perspectives and insights. Since separate representation is likely to enrich political life by enhancing diversity of perspectives, multiculturalism suggests that constituent groups, particularly groups that have been marginalised by the policies of the state, need to be represented in the democratic polity. In fact, special arrangements must be made to include their point of view so that public norms and spaces reflect the cultural diversity that constitutes the polity.

Sorting Minority Claims

Within the framework of differentiated citizenship, multiculturalism envisages the possibility of extending cultural rights, self-government rights and special representation rights to minorities within the nation-state. However, not all claims of minority communities are endorsed by theorists of multiculturalism. On the question of 'which special rights and for whom?' there are, in fact, vast differences within the multicultural camp. Some theorists, most notably, Iris Marion Young, advocate special rights for all oppressed and subordinated minorities, which include, for her, all non-dominant groups and communities that are discriminated against. All of them may demand and expect to be given special consideration in the form of cultural as well as representation rights. Other advocates of multiculturalism begin with a narrower definition of minorities. Will Kymlicka, for instance, stipulates that only communities which have a distinct societal culture are to be considered for special rights. By this definition, groups which express differences of lifestyle, such as homosexuals, are not seen as candidates for special rights. Jeff Spinner makes a distinction between oppressed and non-oppressed minorities. He maintains that only those groups which face discrimination by public and economic institutions on account of their identity deserve special consideration. Even here the claims of identified oppressed groups are only 'privileged provisionally' (Spinner: Forthcoming). In other words, even oppressed groups cannot claim that they deserve special rights in perpetuity or that the special rights that they have at the present should be continued permanently. Minority claims, including those of oppressed minorities must, in his view, be considered in the context of their history. However, identified oppressed communities that are victimised on account of their cultural identity, can expect to receive a wide spectrum of special rights. When such minorities are territorially concentrated they may even claim right to self-government. Others who are dispersed may justifiably ask for all those rights that are necessary to protect their cultural identity.

Joseph Carens introduces another caveat. He argues against any attempt to devise a general theory of minority rights. Although he endorses special rights for culturally distinct minorities, especially rights that allow them to protect their identity, he favours a context-specific approach. That is, while discussing the claims of minorities, he maintains it is necessary to consider at least the history of the group asserting the claim, the precise nature of its demands and the character of the state in which these demands are being made. It is only in the context of these and other related considerations that diverse minority claims for special rights must be assessed. Carens' context-specific approach thus disaggregates minority claims and suggests that the endorsement of differentiated citizenship does not entail the acceptance of all minority claims. In fact, as we will notice later, he places moral limits on the rights that can be claimed by minorities (see Carens, 1999 and 2000).

Votaries of multiculturalism who attempt, nevertheless, to provide a theory of minority rights, sort claims for special rights on the basis of the community making the demand. Perhaps the most systematic schema in this regard is developed by Will Kymlicka. He differentiates between 'national' and 'ethnic' minorities (Kymlicka, 1995: 6). That is, he separates people who are 'a historical community, more or less institutionally complete, occupying a given territory or homeland, sharing a distinct language and culture' (Ibid.: 11), and communities which retain their ethnic particularity but do not constitute a nation with their own distinct homeland. By this reckoning, indigenous populations of North America or the French in Quebec constitute national minorities, while Hispanic immigrants to the US or the African–

Americans who were brought in as slaves and prevented from integrating into the institutions of the majority culture, are conceived as ethnic minorities. The former, it is said, represent 'intact and rooted communities' that have lived on 'land that they had occupied for many centuries' (Walzer in Kymlicka, 1995: 20). By comparison, ethnic minorities are not nations that have been dispossessed of their original homeland and territory. As such, they are not keen to maintain themselves as separate societies alongside the majority culture. Typically these communities wish to 'integrate into the larger society, and to be accepted as full members of it' (*Ibid.*: 11).

For Kymlicka, these two categories of minorities have a moral right to quite distinct sets of special rights. National minorities are distinct and potentially self-governing societies, living on lands that they had occupied for many centuries. Many of them have, in the recent past, been dispossessed of their land and established rights over resources. In addition, they have been denied the use of their language and culture, and forced to assimilate into the larger society. These communities as independent nations within the multinational state can, in his view, legitimately seek special consideration and rights. In particular, they can claim the right to self-government, or at least greater political and administrative autonomy. In other words, liberal democracies need to incorporate them as nations; they must therefore allow these communities the right to maintain their own distinct societal culture.[2]

Immigrant groups, on the other hand, 'are not "nations", and do not occupy homelands' (Kymlicka, 1995: 14). Most 'immigrants... choose to leave their own culture. They have uprooted themselves, and they know when they come that their success...depends on integrating into the institutions of English-speaking society....

---

[2] Kymlicka uses the term societal culture to denote a 'culture which provides its members with meaningful ways of life across the full range of human activities, including social, educational, religious, recreational and economic life, encompassing both public and private spheres. These cultures tend to be territorially concentrated, and based on a shared language' (1995: 76). For Kymlicka, a societal culture can flourish in the modern world only when it is embodied in the institutions of society, such as school, government, media and economy.

The expectation to integrate is not unjust, I believe, so long as immigrants had the option to stay in their original culture.... In deciding to uproot themselves, immigrants voluntarily relinquish some of their rights that go along with their original membership' (*Ibid.*: 95–96).

Here, the fact that immigrant groups make a *choice* in leaving their national and societal culture and going to another place, differentiates them from national minorities. It also determines their moral claim to specific group rights. Immigrant groups are aware while making their choice that they will leave behind their known cultural space and will be expected to adopt a different cultural orientation. Consequently, it is said that they cannot claim special rights to protect their distinct societal culture. 'For example, if a group of Americans decide to emigrate to Sweden, they have no right that the Swedish government provide them with institutions of self-government or public services in their mother tongue. One could argue that a governmental policy that enables American immigrants to re-create their societal culture would benefit everyone, by enriching the whole society. However, the immigrants have no *right* to such policies, for in choosing to leave the US they relinquish the national rights that go with membership in their original culture' (*Ibid.*: 96; emphasis added).

Kymlicka does acknowledge that there are times when groups are compelled to leave their home country. Political repression and ideological differences may force them to seek refuge elsewhere. Similarly, the prospect of better jobs and life-conditions may induce people to immigrate to a new country. Hence, the choice may not always be a voluntary one. However, for Kymlicka immigrants can only make limited cultural demands on the state. They can justifiably expect minimum healthcare provisions and social benefits; they can also expect equal civil rights. But they cannot expect rights to sustain a separate societal culture. In effect, this means that these communities cannot ask for separate representation for their cultures and distinct ways of life in public institutions. Immigrant populations can keep their culture alive at the private level by teaching their children at home the values they cherish and the language that they speak.

Kymlicka argues that equal treatment for immigrants implies equal opportunity to integrate into the mainstream culture. Some cultural rights may be needed, and given, to assist the realisation of this goal of integration. For instance, bilingual education, representation of the heritage of these communities and their contributions in the educational curricula, exemptions or holidays for their religious or cultural festivals, may be necessary to ensure that immigrant communities can integrate and participate successfully in the mainstream culture. However, in this framework, the rights of immigrant groups to continue with their distinct ways of life or gain recognition for them is, to a considerable extent, dependent on the largesse of the state.

In principle, Kymlicka considers culture to be a valued collective good and maintains that all communities should have access to their culture. They should be able to live with the assurance that their cultural identity is secure. Yet, he places few obligations upon the host state to protect or preserve cultures of the immigrant people. These communities remain largely marginalised. Kymlicka defends this on the ground that these communities make a choice in leaving their own country. They are aware that their culture, however important it might be to their self-understanding, is likely to be eroded. For this reason, he does not justify substantial safeguards to protect their culture. Indeed, Kymlicka claims that these communities cannot expect the host country to allow cultural practices that contradict the law of the land. Nor can they expect their culture and identity to be accommodated in the public institutions of the state. In effect, they cannot expect to re-create their culture in the public domain. Kymlicka however accepts that the presence of immigrant cultures is valuable for they can contribute new options and perspectives to the national-majoritarian culture. Yet, while sorting the claims of different minorities he states that these minority communities cannot possibly expect to establish 'distinct and institutionally complete societal cultures' (Kymlicka, 1995: 78).

Thus, in this framework it is primarily the rights of national minorities for recognition and protection of their cultural community that are entertained. Since self-government rights are considered essential for protecting and sustaining a specific societal culture and identity, they are extended only to national minorities. It is assumed that these rights will allow a community to govern itself in conformity with its own social, political and economic institutions.

The immigrants have limited moral claims for special rights because granting the latter is not a part of the contract. The host state does not assure them that it will protect their cultural institutions and practices, and while entering the new country the immigrants understand this dimension. Consequently, in general terms, the immigrant groups remain more or less unrepresented in the public arena. Only the rights of those immigrant communities (e.g., the Hutterites in Canada) which came voluntarily but with the explicit promise that they would be allowed to protect their distinct cultural identity and remain a self-governing community, are acknowledged. It is argued that only communities of this kind can justifiably ask to be treated differently from the broad-spectrum immigrants. Here, the state would need to honour its historical agreement and respect all those practices that define the group's identity.

The implication of this line of argument is that groups such as the Amish, the Hasidic Jews and Mennonites, could reasonably expect to receive exemption from the common requirement of integrating in the host society. They may pursue and protect their specific way of life even though, as is well known, this entails placing restrictions upon internal members. But communities which immigrated to the new world to fulfil the labour needs of the capitalist economy, and whose presence was essential for the growth of the productive systems, cannot claim public recognition for their cultures. As many of these immigrants are from Asia and other erstwhile colonies, it is these groups whose cultures receive no state recognition and support.

Kymlicka, however, accepts that concessions may be given to ethnic groups and religious sects that have lived in the country for long and been allowed to continue with their distinct cultural practices. Although length or duration of one's stay is a fairly ambiguous criterion for sifting between minority claims, it suggests, implicitly at least, that concessions that have previously been given to communities, even some immigrant communities, need not be withdrawn. Historical agreements must be honoured but new demands in this regard need not be entertained. Kymlicka devises this framework keeping in mind the specificity of the experience of North America. A distinction between national minorities, such as the indigenous populations and the Quebecois, and immigrant communities gains significance in that context. It is, indeed, comprehensible only in that milieu.

In India, by comparison, it makes little sense to speak of original inhabitants or immigrant populations. But setting that aside, even in societies where these distinctions can be made, they remain fairly problematic. As was mentioned earlier, the assumption that immigrants can expect no rights to re-create their societal culture in the public domain perpetuates discrimination of the kind that multiculturalism is most concerned about. If non-representation in the public sphere and cultural assimilation is a form of discrimination then immigrants are as vulnerable as national minorities. If special rights are given to shield people from discrimination, the distinction between old privileges and new demands appears facile.

The distinction that Kymlicka makes between self-governance rights and cultural rights recurs in one form or another in much of the literature on multiculturalism. Theorists allude to this difference to allay the fears that granting any kind of special rights to minorities would lead to a spiral of unending demands from them. However, by placing the rights to self-governance in a separate category, these theorists differentiate the rights of immigrant communities and national minorities. This has, as we noticed, important implications in the North American and European context. Even though multiculturalism provides a philosophical defence of minority rights, separate institutional representation and political–territorial autonomy is supported primarily for the national minorities. In the case of immigrants, only different degrees of cultural rights are justified.

Even those who differ sharply from Kymlicka's assessment of the legitimate claims of ethnic minorities only make a case for relatively greater acceptance of minority cultural practices. These theorists argue that by coming to another country immigrants do not relinquish their right to use their own language or customs (see Carens, 1997: 43–46; Parekh, 1992; Carens and Williams, 1996). All communities, including immigrants, would like to pass on their cultural identity to their children. Non-realisation of this aspiration, in their view, is likely to alienate a community from the rest of society. It also creates serious difficulties for the younger members of these minority communities. Children who are distanced from their cultural context, face psychological and emotional trauma that affects their wellbeing and performance in society. It also creates inter-generation conflicts. Consequently, they maintain that immigrants should have some rights to continue with their cultural way of life. In particular, they claim that second-generation immigrants cannot be denied equal cultural rights. Since the children of the immigrant groups did not consent to being born in these countries they cannot be expected to give up the right to their culture. They can demand that the state protect their culture and give it some public recognition. Thus, differences exist about the nature of cultural rights that may be supported in the case of different immigrant communities. However, what remains more or less unquestioned in these debates is the belief that separate representation or self-government rights are not for the immigrant communities.

These differences about who gets which rights have arisen in a framework where the dominant trend is to relate special rights claims with the people asserting the claim. Kymlicka provides a typology of the different kinds of minorities and the rights that they may justifiably seek. Carens rejects the idea that the claims of different categories of minorities can be determined in advance. He suggests that the rights of a specific group must be discussed keeping in mind the history and identity of the minority community, the character of the nation-state of which these communities are members and the nature of the claims asserted. Thus, in his view, we need a case-by-case analysis rather than a general theory of minority rights.

These differences notwithstanding, most multiculturalists accept the distinction between cultural rights, rights of group representation and self-government rights. And what is perhaps even more important is that all forms of minority claims are represented in expressivist terms. They are perceived to be a means of protecting the cultural identity of the concerned minority community. Even rights of self-government are seen and justified as a means of making minority communities secure. It is this stipulated link between cultural identity and minority claims that sets multiculturalism apart from other modes of differentiating or assessing group claims. Ted Gurr, for instance, sorts minority group claims on the basis of their political and material ends. Thus, he separates claims for 'autonomy' or 'exit' from the nation-state, from those that merely seek to enhance a community's 'access' and 'control' over resources within the polity (Gurr, 1994: 15). In this framework, the desire for a secure cultural context is at best a secondary consideration. What matters is whether the minority wishes to remain a part of the nation-state, or not. Moreover, minority rights are seen as a political and economic resource. They are, to reiterate, not intended to protect a cultural identity but to ensure a better share of the limited national resources for a given community.

Multiculturalism, as is quite evident, approaches the issue of minority rights very differently. It focuses on the value of a cultural community membership for the individual, and the ways in which individuals are disadvantaged when this fundamental condition of human life is not met. Moreover, when special rights are advocated, be they cultural rights or self-government rights, for national minorities or for immigrants, they are seen as a way of incorporating differences of perceptions, beliefs, and even practices, in the public domain. Furthermore, as expression of a parallel rationality, special rights are not seen as being segregationist in intent. Instead, the framework of differentiated citizenship is invoked to discuss minority claims that are to be accommodated within the nation-state. Within it, it is assumed that people have dual membership: they are members of a political community as well as members of a cultural community, and that they value both these memberships. Hence, their cultural identities have to be taken into account along with their political identity. In fact, cultural identities need to be protected and preserved so as to ensure equal treatment to diverse communities.

5

Feminism and Multiculturalism

Theorists of multiculturalism sharply disagree about which special rights should be given to whom. Nevertheless, they do agree on certain fundamentals. All of them accept that marginalised and discriminated communities within the nation-state deserve special rights. At the very least, identified minorities must have access to their culture and the freedom to live by the norms of their distinct way of life. The majority culture and the nation-state must not prejudge these cultural communities or impose its own way of life upon them. In its place, the state should be sensitive to the self-perceptions of the community and its members. It should permit, and even encourage, the expression of differences in the public domain. This could be done by granting recognition to the cultural practices and codes, exemptions from the prevailing laws, provisions for separate self-government, or even separate representation. Whatever be the means devised within the framework of differentiated citizenship, the state and the citizens should be willing to explore options that will enable marginalised minorities to be included as equals.

The idea that the unitary model of citizenship may not be adequate for accommodating subordinated groups as equal citizens is today endorsed by many feminist scholars. Yet, there are also strong reservations about the multicultural agenda. Feminist writings thus stand in a paradoxical relationship with multiculturalism. While most of them support the concept of differentiated citizenship, there is anxiety in most quarters that women may remain unequal and subordinated even after minority communities are empowered. Apprehensions of this kind have been articulated by women from different cultures and communities. This chapter takes up some of these issues to draw attention to the questions that need to be addressed when the goals of group equality and protecting minority cultures are deliberated upon within multiculturalism.

Feminism and the Politics of Difference

Multiculturalism accords positive value to group difference. It suggests that a democratic society should realise, what in a different context Lyotard calls, 'justice of multiplicities'. Instead of transcending group differences, it should respect these differences and ensure equality for culturally and socially diverse groups. The notion of difference and group-specific rights that is advocated here finds a powerful and systematic defence in contemporary feminist writing.

The first wave of liberal feminists fought against existing social prejudices and division of functions by demanding equal political rights for women. They claimed that women should have the same rights and the same opportunities as men. Public offices and institutions should be open to women and they must have an equal opportunity to participate in the public domain. Nineteenth century feminists appealed to the ideal of formal equality to challenge the exclusion of women from political and professional life. They argued that 'all distinctions between persons grounded on the accidental circumstance of sex' (Harriet T. Mill and John S. Mill, 1998: 96) should be abolished so that the existing 'legal and moral subjection of women' (*Ibid.*: 97) could be eliminated.

The second wave of women's movement built upon the relative success of its predecessors. Having received legal and political rights, these feminists focused on the special needs of women. They referred to the biological differences between men and women to argue that women require special treatment and, with it, special rights. From their perspective, equal political rights were necessary but not enough in the case of women. Women had special requirements. They needed, on the one hand, special assistance to overcome the disadvantage they had suffered on account of their subordinate position in society. On the other, as mothers or child-bearers, they had special claims that the state must now address. For instance, they required maternity leave, child support, healthcare for their family, crèches at workplace, and even flexible hours of work. Thus, they used the concept of difference to justify special treatment and special welfare facilities for women (see Phillips, 1992: 206–11).

Subsequent writings added a new dimension to the notion of gender difference. They affirmed the 'politics of difference' and maintained that having the same rights as men could never be the basis of women's emancipation in society. Women would always remain disadvantaged in a framework that expects them to be the *same as* men in the public domain. So long as they were expected to fit into slots that were devised for men, they would always remain subordinate. Consequently, if women are to be equal partners in public life, the world 'should change its tune'; it should not ask women to 'shape themselves to a world made for men' (Phillips, 1992: 219). Women should be included as women. However, to realise this goal, theorists of difference felt that it was necessary to deconstruct the social symbolic system and to understand, first and foremost, that the public world is not neutral. It is structured by the dominant group, i.e., men, and through qualities that express their difference.

Men are systematically advantaged because the public realm is almost entirely defined by them. 'Men's physiology defines most sports, their needs define auto and health insurance coverage, their socially designed biographies define workplace expectations and successful career partners, their perspectives and concerns define quality in scholarship, their experiences and obsessions define merit, their objectification of life defines art, their military service defines citizenship, their presence defines family, their inability to get along with each other—their wars and rulerships—defines history...' (MacKinnon, 1987: 36). In other words, the socialised qualities and experiences of men shape the different spheres of social life. As a consequence, men are continuously advantaged; to use MacKinnon's words, something akin to an 'affirmative action plan is in effect' in society which privileges one-half of the population while disadvantaging the other half (*Ibid.*).

The fact that the socio-symbolic world is not neutral, however, constitutes only one part of the story. For theorists of difference, what is equally important is to realise that men and women are different. They 'perceive and experience the world, experience their bodies and express their experiences in fundamentally different ways' (Duchen, 1986: 20; see Irigaray, 1985 and Cixous, 1976). This difference needs to be acknowledged and reflected in the public domain. Being aware of the difference between men and women allows one to recognise that the standards that prevail in the public domain are culturally and experientially specific, and that they disadvantage women (Young, 1990: 156–91). At the same time, they argued, incorporating women's difference 'would inevitably alter the way we think, open new possibilities and make oppression in social discursive practices no longer inevitable' (Duchen, 1986: 71). It would, at the very least, restructure the public domain by bringing in feminine qualities and new principles of public ethics.

Feminist writers who emphasise the principle of difference point to the distinctiveness of women's experiences, capabilities and perspective. While they articulate the specificity of women's experience differently, many of them draw a contrast between the aggressiveness of men and the receptivity of women. They maintain that '[I]t is the woman who "embodies" in a literal sense the promise of peace, of joy, of the end of violence. Tenderness, receptivity, sensuousness have become features (or mutilated features) of her body—features of her (repressed) humanity' (Marcuse quoted in Shiva, 1988: 52). Others speak of the politics of care. In their view, women have a natural inclination to nurture, care and sustain life. These qualities are a valuable resource, both for deconstructing western rationality, and for restructuring our moral sensibilities and societal norms. Thus far, the suppression of the feminine ethic has resulted in the oppression of women and the repudiation of nature. It has dichotomised the world and reinforced hierarchies. Dualisms, such as those posited between male/female, reason/emotion, West/non-West, civilised/primitive, man/nature, have justified domination and control. Eco-feminists allude to the nurturing and life-giving qualities of women. They compare them to mother earth and nature, and argue that women are protectors of life. As such, they are naturally inclined to a model of development that is not anchored in the masculine vision of aggression, indiscriminate appropriation and exploitation of nature (see Harding, 1986; Keller, 1985; Mies, 1986; Shiva, 1988).

Jane Mansbridge and Carol Gilligan have applied the feminine ethic in the field of politics (see Mansbridge, 1996; Gilligan, 1982). Based on women's capacity to recreate and nurture, they outline the ethic of care as opposed to the ethic of power and rights-based justice (also see Noddings, 1984; Hartsock, 1984; Ruddick, 1989). Mansbridge argues that women are particularly sensitive to inequalities of power. At the same time, their experience of child rearing makes them 'especially concerned to transform "I" into "we" and to seek solutions to conflict that accommodate diverse and often suppressed desires' (Mansbridge, 1993: 11). Hence, their experiences can enrich our understanding and realisation of deliberative democracy. Women's perspective could assist in creating a framework of democracy that requires representatives to think not only of self-interest, but of collective concerns; not only of 'I' but also of 'we'. It could, in their words, provide a conception of politics without domination.

In these, and many other feminist writings, women's difference is used both to critique and to alter the norms that shape the public realm. Although within this framework, modes of accessing women's experiences and transcending the logocentric masculine rationality vary considerably. Yet, all of them underline the need to focus on the socially constructed differences between men and women. More importantly, they point to the limits of the principle of formal equality. In their view, the language of formal equality is insensitive to the gender-specific nature of the dominant value. It fails to see the ways in which the male-dominated intellectual and political heritage has suppressed and subordinated women. It has also failed to attend to the specificity of gender difference. It must, therefore, be abandoned in favour of a structure that acknowledges the presence of group differences. Further, since some groups, especially women, are 'actually or potentially oppressed and disadvantaged' (Young, 1989: 261), their experiences and way of thinking are excluded or suppressed, we need to include them as equal members of the polity. Minimally, we need a framework where these diverse groups can voice their interests and enrich the deliberations on public policies by bringing to bear their unique and distinctive perspectives (Young, 1990: 183–91).

This idea that women embody a distinctive perspective—one that can add something new and different to our world-view—has transformed the thinking on group rights. It has provided a new justification for group representation and differentiated rights. While affirmative-action policies had been defended on grounds of compensating and reversing the effects of social discrimination, radical feminists seek group representation for women on account of their difference. They maintain that men differ from women; their experiences vary. Hence, men cannot be expected to understand or defend the needs and interests of women (Phillips, 1992: 76). Even if they were to understand the other, they could not effectively represent women because there is a fundamental conflict of interests involved. On issues, such as family, income, child-care, discrimination, men and women have divergent interests, so men cannot adequately represent women (Minow, 1990: 286). Issues of representation aside, women's experiences and their perspectives need to be included for their distinctive quality. Women, as a group, need to be included in all deliberative bodies because they are likely to offer a new and different perspective which in itself is a valuable input in all discussion on social and political issues.

The feminist critique of formal equality, its positive valuation of difference and its plea to incorporate individuals as members of groups in various public institutions, initiated the politics of difference—a politics that is affirmed even by multiculturalism. Indeed, their arguments for special representation provide a new rationale for group-specific rights. It constructs difference as a source of desirable diversity. This association of difference with diversity and the accompanying belief that negating differences merely reinforces the privilege of the dominant groups, are themes that multiculturalism and, along with it, the discourse of minorities, incorporates within its framework. In fact, multiculturalism endorses the politics of difference and the claims for special group rights that are strongly voiced within feminism.

The idea of difference that is central to much of contemporary feminism is also privileged within multiculturalism. Both multiculturalism and feminism speak of the continued exclusion and marginalisation of some groups from the public domain. They point to the biases inherent in theories that claim to be neutral or universalistic, and reveal the limitations of the liberal understanding of equality as sameness. As both approach the world from the vantage-point of difference, they seek—in their own ways—respect for difference. Difference or 'foreignness', they maintain, should not be perceived as a threat. Liberal theory as well as political practices of the nation-state should be open and receptive to diversity of norms. Instead of imposing a set of universal rules, they should listen to the agents' self-perception and allow them to make their own choices. Finally, both multiculturalism and feminist theories of difference argue that a system of individual rights is insufficient to overcome the marginalisation of minority groups. We require special rights to attend to the specific needs of these vulnerable groups, and to ensure that difference is not a source of discrimination in society.

Yet, despite the shared commitment to the value of difference, women's groups and analysts are among the most vocal critics of multiculturalism. Despite their anxieties about liberal theory and their recommendations for special group rights, at least some feminists maintain that multiculturalism is bad for feminism. They feel that the limited gains that have been achieved by women's movements may be lost if the multicultural agenda is accepted. In the words of Susan Moller Okin, 'when minority cultures win group rights, women lose out' (Okin, 1997: 25). Okin's perception derives from her analysis that women occupy a subordinate position in most minority cultures. Under these circumstances, special rights to minority cultures may easily justify prevailing community practices that discriminate against women.

In critiquing multiculturalism, Okin and several other feminists single out gender discrimination that exists in minority communities. They sometimes write in a voice that suggests that similar inequalities do not exist in modern liberal societies. Against such unidimensional representations of minority cultures and the accompanying stigmatisation of these communities, it is important to assert that majority cultures are not devoid of patriarchal domination. Gender discrimination exists even in the cultures of the majority, and women in liberal societies are also victims of unfair treatment. While minority communities alone cannot be accused of perpetuating gender injustices, the issues that these critics have raised, and those that have emerged from the experiences and struggles of women everywhere, cannot be dismissed. They need to be considered seriously in a democratic polity committed to ensuring that no one is discriminated against on account of their ascribed social identities.

Feminist Critiques of Multiculturalism

The issues raised in feminist scholarship are particularly significant because they come primarily from the perspective of difference. They are cognisant of the homogenising and oppressive nature of the policies of the state and are equally committed to the ideal of group equality. However, despite sharing these concerns with multiculturalism, they question the possibility of realising the goal of non-discrimination and equality by granting special rights to cultural communities. The multicultural reading of culture, community and differences, in their view, leaves many structures of discrimination untouched, and it is to draw attention to this dimension that they interrogate the agenda of multiculturalism (see Shachar, 2000).

For feminist theorists perhaps the most striking inadequacy of multiculturalism is that it addresses the issues of inter-group equality but remains more or less indifferent to concerns of intra-group equality. In part, this neglect of intra-group equality surfaces because multiculturalism endorses the private–public distinction and operates within that framework. Like liberalism, it discusses the issue of justice with reference to the inequalities that exist in the public domain. Discrimination that occurs in the private domain, or the sphere of the family, remains a non-issue within this framework. It is not the subject of justice (Okin, 1997 and 1998). One concrete manifestation of this is that multiculturalism deals with discrimination of minority communities that we witness in the public domain but the subordination of some groups within the community remains relatively unattended. In fact, through a system of special cultural rights for communities, it leaves the private sphere almost entirely in the hands of the community. This impacts upon the lives of women much more, and often allows communities to continue defining social roles and division of labour within the family in a way that works to the disadvantage of women.

Disadvantages of this kind get compounded as multiculturalism takes note of one specific kind of difference: namely, cultural differences. Through this category of difference it points to cultural discrimination within the nation-state, and to remedy that it seeks to resurrect cultural differences. In the process, it inevitably essentialises cultures. It presents each as a homogeneous and univocal entity with clearly defined practices and norms. This picture obliterates differences that exist within each tradition and culture. It effaces the fact that cultural norms and community practices are not simply given; they are the subject of continuous contestation and appropriation. Even though multiculturalists are not unaware of the presence of internal plurality, yet this dimension remains unrepresented within their framework of cultural differences.

The presumed univocality of a culture becomes a matter of concern as it tends to privilege prevailing community practices. When current observances of a community become markers of group identity, then resistance to them becomes exceedingly difficult. In fact, all such attempts get transformed into acts of complicity with the state's homogenising agenda. Contemporary discourses on multiculturalism offer many examples of this. In the case of immigrant Muslim communities, for instance, the prevalent practices of female and male circumcision have come to be seen as a sign of their difference. Votaries of multiculturalism invariably defend these practices as being an integral part of the creation of a community identity (see Gilman, 1997), or as voluntary actions of individuals belonging to a community (Parekh, 1997). What is lost in this image of the community and its traditional way of life is that 'clitoridectomy…was falling into desuetude in Kenya when nationalists revived it as [a] part of their rejection of British colonialism' (Pollitt, 1997: 29).

The point that is worth recalling is that when existing cultural practices get represented as a sign of a community's way of life, or as traditional practices, the space for contesting the meaning of cultural practices within the community is steadily eroded. A de-historicised reading of cultures and their practices necessarily diminishes the existing room for the expression of differences. When multiculturalism presents operating practices as being collectively valued, endorsed by community members and sanctioned by tradition, it overlooks the disputes that exist around community practices. It ignores the fact that tradition is open to interpretation; it is multivocal and subject to a variety of different constructions (see Chakrabarty, 1998).

The reification of tradition that occurs on account of the presumed homogeneity serves the interests of patriarchy and disadvantages women. To take an example: when *Sati* (the practice of self-immolation by a wife on the funeral pyre of her husband) is viewed as a traditional cultural practice defining the Hindu way of life, then preserving the practice becomes the rallying point for the community. This allows the community leadership to suppress and marginalise internal voices of dissent and reinforce existing structures of patriarchal domination. It is to resist such appropriation of tradition that several feminists challenge the multicultural conception of culture. Instead of viewing culture as the realm of shared practices, they present it as the domain of contested meanings and practices (see Sangari, 1999).

Culture can, however, be viewed as an arena of contested meanings and practices only by treating tradition as a socially and historically constructed object. It is only when tradition is historicised that attention focuses on differences within the tradition. A historical reading, for instance, reveals that the practice of *Sati* is neither endorsed in all Hindu texts nor uniformly observed by all Hindu communities (see Sangari and Vaid, 1991). It also shows that there has been a revival of this practice in the last four decades, and in some cases, at least it has coincided with the changes in the inheritance laws. In other words, a historical reading allows cultural practices to be treated as sites of contestation. What is represented within multicultural framework as a sacred practice—defining cultural community identity—now gets transformed into a practice that can be questioned and discussed. The representation of cultural practices as points of conflict creates room for the expression of internal dissent. The multicultural perspective, by comparison, supports preservation of practices and closes the space for the expression of difference.

What needs to be recognised then is that acknowledging the presence of difference is important for challenging the hegemony of the dominant majority, but it is by no means enough. The discussion of differences that exist across communities must be supplemented with differences that exist within a community. What is perhaps even more important is that differences must also be viewed as being socially and politically constructed. They need to be located in time and history. If this dimension is forgotten, then multiculturalism is likely to sanction all prevailing practices, including those that express gender discrimination and perpetuate the subordination of women. Likewise, if the constructed nature of differences and diversity is ignored, then again multiculturalism may lose sight of the complex processes by which homogenisation occurs within the nation-state.

The latter needs to be emphasised because in multiculturalism diversity is most often equated with the mere presence of heterogeneity. Against the homogenising agenda of the nation-state, multiculturalism argues for accommodation of community codes, institutions and practices within the public sphere. Here, the presence of many diverse community codes is itself taken as a signal of desirable diversity. This perception of diversity has led many Indian feminists to conclude that the formulation of a uniform civil code may be a means of assimilating communities into the culture of the majority. The association of uniformity with homogenisation has thus provided strong support for the continuation of community Personal Laws. Indeed, the presence of multiple community codes is seen as an expression of diversity and defended on that ground. What is, as a consequence, lost in this simple equation is the awareness that the prevailing diversity is itself a political construct, and that it too acts as an instrument of homogenisation.

Against the imposition of a uniform code, the presence of multiple codes may appear as a sign of heterogeneity but if we see the community codes as historical objects, it becomes evident that each code has emerged by obliterating differences that existed within the community (see Sangari, 1995: 3287–310). Different practices that governed issues of family, marriage, separation and inheritance across regions, castes and class have been obliterated to construct a Personal Law that applies uniformly to people belonging to a specific community. Thus, the apparent diversity of forms and codes camouflages the erosion of internal diversity and variation.

In 1772, when the British colonisers decided to codify the practices of different communities so that the subject population may be governed by its own community norms, they began by inviting religious scholars and theologians to assemble a Personal Law. In the case of the Hindu community it was the Brahmin priests from Bengal who interpreted tradition and deliberated upon collective codes by which the law was defined (Chhachhi, 1994). The non-inclusion of other castes itself meant that their practices remained excluded and the Brahmanical tradition prevailed over all others. Even within this group, there were differences in interpretation of texts. However, as a homogeneous code for the entire community emerged, these differences of reading were also set aside. The Hindu Personal Law came into existence through a series of erasures, and at each stage, heterogeneity had to make way for the enunciation of a coherent and homogeneous Personal Law (see Mani, 1985).

The process of codification of the Hindu Personal Law serves to illustrate the ways in which homogeneity prevailed as diverse community codes came into existence. It reminds us that the emergence of community Personal Laws has 'helped to homogenize five fixed identities' (Sangari, 1999: 27) in the form of Hindu, Muslim, Christian, Parsees and Jews. Furthermore, some of these identities have been culled by assimilating a variety of different sects and religious groups. For example, for purposes of family affairs, Sikhs, Jains and Buddhists have been included within the category of Hindu, and accordingly, they are governed by the Hindu Personal Law. Even though each of these communities assert their separate identity and represent themselves as distinct religious groups, the Hindu Personal Law obliterates these distinctions and imposes another overarching identity within which the individuality of each of these communities is submerged (see Sangari, 1999: 3287–310 and 3381–389). Similar forms of assimilation and absorption also occurred in the codification of other community codes. When the Shariat Act of 1937 came into effect, the customary legal practices of Mer, Mopilla, Meo, Bohra and Khoja communities were set aside to construct a homogeneous Muslim identity. Indeed, the practices of these 'little communities' were deemed as being 'corrupt and deviant' (Mayaram, 1999: 395).

These aspects involved in the construction of cultural diversity have, however, received little attention within multiculturalism. Contemporary theorists work most often with homogenised categories and seek to preserve and protect the existing diversity of cultures and practices. They are concerned primarily with the fate of diverse cultures as they have come to be defined in their present form. As a result, they have remained inattentive to the concerns of heterogeneity and equality within the community. If heterogeneity is to be protected at all levels, across communities and within communities, and if practices are to be instituted in a way that they do not become a source of further discrimination, cultures and communities need to be viewed as historical objects. Only when we see them in this non-essentialising manner is there a possibility of carrying forward the agenda of democratic citizenship.

Multiculturalism begins by locating individuals within a specific community. It sees individuals as members of a given cultural community and assumes that their lives are shaped by the cultures in which they live. Several feminist writers argue that this conception of the self ignores 'hybridity' as an experience. It does not take cognisance of the fact that in the modern world, people, particularly women, find themselves inhabiting many different cultures. They see themselves caught between cultures, and, in the case of many Asian and Islamic societies, they often find membership of the traditional culture as being restrictive and oppressive (see Ziai, 1997; Lateef, 1998; Bano, 1999). The specificity of this transactional experience needs to be acknowledged; and accordingly we have to be cautious about preserving cultures or their practices because they might well be appropriated to legitimise the perspective of the traditional elite (see Alund, 1999).

In presenting this alternative picture of diversity and cultural memberships, most feminists accept that community locations matter, and cannot be ignored. The struggle for women's rights and equality cannot be delinked from their membership to other communities. However, from their perspective, recognising the significance of community membership does not imply preserving that identity. It is quite probable that even though people derive their history and obligations from membership to a community, they may still like to reconsider these inheritances. They may, therefore, seek the option of choosing communities and group memberships. Instead of preserving and protecting their received identities, they may wish to abandon them or even take on new identities. Consequently, acknowledging the role of cultural communities does not, or must not, sanction the need to preserve cultures.

There is also the additional question of whether we should try to preserve cultures which people do not wish to preserve or those that they themselves find oppressive (see Tamir, 1993: 8; also see Gutmann, 1994: 6–7). Given the unequal position of women in society and in almost all cultures, several critics ask whether rights should be given to uphold what people cherish or what they have inherited on account of their history and tradition. Questions of this nature have been repeatedly raised in different quarters. In fact, the attempt to justify cultural practices for the sake of protecting an identity or promoting diversity has met with a lot of resistance. For the liberal feminists, this has been a matter of grave concern for cultural differences and diversity have 'often been an excuse for cruelty' (Minow, 2000: 130). They have been a means of legitimising oppressive practices; most often practices that allow communities to control women. In the hands of defence lawyers, they have been a tool for explaining away violence towards women and seeking a reduced and lenient sentence for the male offenders belonging to cultural minorities (Okin, 1997: 27; Coleman, 1996). Community spokespersons have used these to maintain the status quo and to continue with existing practices, even when they disadvantage women.

The apprehensions about multicultural agenda here, are on account of the ways in which multiculturalism has been, and can be, appropriated to the disadvantage of women. Although theories of multiculturalism are not hostile to the concerns of gender equality, nevertheless, the feminist critique points that these concerns cannot be accommodated within a framework that aims to preserve cultures. Particularly, since cultures are not gender-neutral. Almost all cultures, those of the majority as well as those of the minority, are embedded in patriarchy. They endorse in various ways, and in different degrees, the subordination of women. Most culturally sanctioned customs make women subservient to men. They deny them agency and control over their own person. Under these circumstances, the multicultural agenda of preserving cultures is, it is said, likely to perpetuate the oppression of women. In fact a few feminist scholars maintain that to promote the ideal of equal citizenship, it is necessary to respect only those practices within cultures that are supportive of this goal (Pollitt, 1997: 29).

Multiculturalism is, however, reluctant to make distinctions of this kind. While it applies the concept of difference to question the hegemony of the dominant perspective, it does not interrogate the power relations that are at work in the diversity that exists. Examining the practice of clitoridectomy, for instance, it makes us aware of the liberal bias involved in representing this practice as 'Female Genital Mutilation' (Shweder, 2000). It suggests that this act may not necessarily be one of injury or mutilation; that for some community members it might be about 'cleanliness, beauty and adulthood' (*Ibid.*). However, it does not probe the structure of power relations in which this practice has arisen and by which it is sustained.

In these and many other cases, multiculturalism does not merely use the category of difference to critique the prevailing laws and state policies, it makes a deliberate effort to preserve cultural community practices. It considers the presence of difference positively and assumes that the presence of diversity is itself liberating. On the issue of polygamy, for instance, it does not just suggest that non-recognition of the practice may disadvantage women and children who are necessarily left behind when the husband immigrates to a country that does not recognise all his wives. It often goes further to say that polygamy may well provide a sense of sisterhood; it places women 'in a situation of solidarity' (Honig, 1997: 31), one that is not available to 'monogamous wives against their husbands' (*Ibid.*). The celebration of difference here again glosses over the inequalities within which the practice of polygamy is located. By representing all differences as positive, it neither acknowledges those structures of discrimination nor does it allow space for their discussion.

It is this uncritical attitude towards difference that—along with an ahistorical reading of culture—limits the democratic agenda of ensuring equal citizenship. Even as it exposes the majoritarian cultural biases of the liberal state, it leaves the structures of discrimination within cultures and communities undisturbed. It is limitations of this kind that compel rethinking on the multicultural agenda of protecting minority cultures and promoting diversity. If equality for all is to become the operative norm, then it is imperative to create room for disclosing and correcting discriminations of diverse kinds, and not merely those generated by the majoritarian cultural biases. But this is possible only when the goal of non-discrimination rather than enhancing diversity becomes the central principle. And this, needless to say, requires a fundamental shift in the theory of multiculturalism.

Issues of discrimination within the community have so far received insufficient consideration within multiculturalism. As and when these questions have been raised, they have been readily dismissed on the assumption that gender inequalities and other forms of discrimination within the community will vanish when communities have the right to determine their own affairs. In Canada, for instance, the issue of gender equality has been raised by Aboriginal women organisations. Recording the widespread oppression of women within the community and the violence that is directed against them in the family, the Native Women's Association in Quebec has argued that the First Nations must accept the equality of women. The Canadian Charter should 'continue to apply to Aboriginal governments until such time as one or more aboriginal charters provide with equal or greater protection' (Public Hearing of the Royal Commission of Aboriginal People, 1993: 10). Since no band council had so far adopted any 'anti-violence regulation or code of ethics' in this regard, self-government to these populations must be linked with the acceptance of the Canadian Charter that protects the equal status of women. Many other women's groups, including the National Action Committee on the Status of Women, have reiterated this. In their view: '[U]nless Aboriginal women are guaranteed the right to share equally with men the powers to develop the forms of self-government and the instruments required for dealing with poverty, conjugal violence, incest, the consequences of unemployment, the exclusion of Bill C-31 women and children from their communities,[1] there will be no significant improvement in living and social conditions' (*Ibid.*).

Objections of this kind have met with two responses from the multicultural camp: (*i*) It is said that such forms of discrimination are a legacy of colonisation. They are not intrinsic to these indigenous communities. Consequently, there is no reason to assume that these will persist after communities regain control over their own practices (see Turpel, 1994). (*ii*) A few theorists argue that these practices, which are perceived as being discriminatory towards women, are not an integral part of indigenous people's way of life. It is, as it were, incidental to their way of

---

[1] Bill C-31 was legislated to amend several sections of The Indian Act. It has, among other things, removed Section 12(1)(b) of the Indian Act by which Indian women who married 'any other than an Indian' were deprived of their status and rights as Indians. The amendment makes it possible for women who had lost their status upon marrying non-Indians or non-status Indians, and for their children, to apply for status and band membership. This has, to some extent, rectified the discrimination of women that ensued from the Indian Act. However, several indigenous communities have objected to Bill C-31 on the ground that it (*i*) violates their right to determine band membership and (*ii*) it will place new economic burden upon the limited resources of the reservation. The Bill, in their view, allows large numbers to women and children to be reinstated as band members but it does not provide any corresponding assurance that land or funds would be provided to these communities to take care of the new members. The women's groups have, however, been arguing on behalf of the disenfranchised women and their children. Since the provisions of the Indian Act disadvantaged many Indian women, depriving them and the children of property and access to reservation land on marrying outside the community or even divorce, Bill C-31 has been seen by many as a step in the right direction (Green, 1985).

life and something that is likely to be changed. This conclusion is backed by the claim that communities whose way of life is being protected within multiculturalism have societal cultures. They have institutions by which the community conducts its affairs and takes decisions. Consequently, there is no reason to assume that women will be excluded and their perspective marginalised within the community (see Kymlicka, 1995).

Responses of this kind to gender inequality within the community are not peculiar to the North American experience. These sentiments have been expressed frequently in India, both by the spokespersons of minority communities as well as the critics of the nation-state. Time and time again, it is argued that the state must refrain from interfering in the affairs of the community. Instead of reforming and modernising the community by imposing its will, the state should allow communities to govern their affairs and determine their Personal Laws (Chatterjee, 1994). In the recent past, these claims were strongly asserted in the events that followed the Shah Bano case. When the Supreme Court of India ruled in favour of Shah Bano, a 65-year-old Muslim divorcee, who had appealed for child support and maintenance from her ex-husband, it came under severe criticism from the community leadership and political representatives.

Although strong condemnation was, to some extent, provoked by the Court's comments on the discriminatory practices within Islamic Law, the community spokespersons criticised the judgement for legislating upon matters of Muslim Personal Law. Shah Bano had petitioned under the Indian Criminal Procedure Code (ICPC), Section 125, which deals with *destitute* women, yet the community asserted its right to deal with all issues pertaining to family matters. They not only defended the right of the community to preserve its own way of life, they also iterated that gender equality is a part of Islamic Law. There were laws within the framework of *Sharia* to protect the interests of women and no external interference was needed in this regard. Even though personal laws of all communities disadvantage women, and Shah Bano, like many other women of her community, was vulnerable within the existing structure of community laws and institutions, this dimension received little attention (Jayal, 1999: 112–43).

In the debate on the right to culture of the minorities, a dichotomy was posited between the state and the community and this invariably marginalised the goal of women's equality. Forced to choose between the state and the community, Shah Bano opted for the latter. She was persuaded to voluntarily relinquish the maintenance on the ground that her actions were detrimental to the interests of the community. Living in a context where communal conflict along religious lines was a part of her experience, Shah Bano could not be expected to put her faith in the actions of the state. Indeed, when the state is perceived as an oppressor, it is exceedingly difficult for women of minority communities to take a position which aligns them with the state rather than the community (see Ziai, 1997; Mukhopadhyay, 1998; Menon, 1999). Shah Bano's struggle for her rights, therefore, took a backseat as the rights of the community to protect and preserve their culture was accepted.

In fact, the elected representatives from the community, both in the state legislative assemblies as well as in parliament at the Centre, worked along with the religious leadership to assert the autonomy of the community in the personal sphere of individual life (Hasan, 1994). In the months that followed, the state, in order to distance itself from the actions of the Court, negotiated with the community leadership. The Congress government that was in power at the Centre, passed the Muslim Women (Protection of Rights on Divorce) Bill. The new Bill placed Muslim women outside the purview of ICPC, Section 125, under which the Supreme Court had entertained the appeal by Shah Bano. It also stipulated that maintenance after *idaat* (a short period of separation preceding divorce) was the responsibility of the natal family rather than the ex-husband. Thus, as the community received priority, cultural practices were certainly protected but only at the expense of subordinating women.

The Shah Bano episode did not merely reveal the subordinate position of women in the community. It showed that women's rights for equality may not be protected even though there is, in principle, some place for them within the culture of the community. The votaries of multiculturalism, like the community leadership in this episode, almost always speak of tradition, as opposed to operating practices, and assume that the latter will be negated or set aside when the community is in a position to determine its own affairs autonomously. The fact that women are rarely ever represented in community institutions, and that community structures on which multiculturalists pin their hopes currently function in a way that undermines women's rights, are elements that are often neglected. It is believed that institutions within the community need to be activated, and when this happens, there will indeed be opportunity for all to influence and shape the decisions collectively.

From this point of view, when minority communities seek a right to culture they are saying that 'we will not give you reasons for not being like you' (Chatterjee, 1994: 1775). However, in asserting their difference they are also accepting, at least implicitly, that 'we have our own reasons for doing things the way we do' (*Ibid.*). In other words, communities accept that there are reasons for doing things the way they do, except that these are 'their' reasons which can only be appreciated by members of the group. Consequently, they cannot deny the necessity of validating their reasons even if that is only done in the institutions of the community. So, institutions in which debate takes place may differ but the fact that community practices must receive the consent of the members is not in question. Also, if the community has to have regulative power over its members, then the forums and institutions in which the discussion takes place 'must have the same degree of publicity and representativeness that is demanded of all public institutions having regulatory functions' (*Ibid.*).

In this and other related arguments, minority communities have a moral responsibility, as it were, to initiate a process of internal democratisation because that follows from their rationale on which their own claims for special rights are based. If they expect rights to protect their difference then they must also allow space for expression of internal differences (Bhargava, 1991: 165–71). Or, if they justify their demand for special representation on grounds of their marginalisation and exclusion from the public sphere, then they must also acknowledge the rights of subordinated groups within the community for the same representation. The idea that reforms for democratisation should be initiated by the community and that its cultural claims have the support and consent of all members of the community offers an attractive way of negotiating the current impasses between multiculturalism and liberalism. It allows communities to justifiably claim a right to their own culture. At the same time, it assures the liberal critics that rights that enable communities to protect their way of life will not reinforce the hegemony of the dominant groups within the community; nor will they institutionalise practices that are seen as being oppressive by some of the community members.

There is no doubt that democratisation of communities is desirable, and that communities should also recognise the implicit commitment to this when they seek special rights for themselves. Nevertheless, it is necessary to recognise that responses of this kind act by imposing liberal–democratic procedures, though not liberal values. They suggest that communities may express and endorse their values so long as they deliberate upon these differences in a way that conforms to the accepted patterns of decision making in a democracy. In a democracy, it is not entirely unreasonable to have this expectation but what we need to note is that we cannot simply say that this follows from the site from which cultural rights are claimed by communities. Indeed, communities seeking rights to protect their way of life most often express a different rationality. They maintain that the right to one's own way of life also implies the right to continue with traditional decision-making procedures that have existed in the community, even if they appear unreasonable to others. It is on these grounds that many indigenous communities in Canada and America have resisted pressures to endorse the principle of gender equality as a pre-condition for self-determination. It is by the same interpretation of the right to one's culture that traditional institutions of tribal councils have been protected for territories that have been scheduled as autonomous and semi-autonomous regions in India. While the Panchayati Raj Bill, which became effective in 1994, has provided reservation to women in these local bodies (Panchayati Raj institutions) in all other areas, these scheduled regions have been exempted. Even though in most of these areas women do not have a presence in the political domain, these regions have been left free to determine their own policy, and so far communities have made little effort to include women in these decision-making institutions (see *Panchayati Raj Update*, 2000: 8).

This is not to say that minority communities work in ways that are non-democratic; or that indigenous populations are opposed to women's equality. What is important is to recognise that the right to culture or one's way of life is most often seen as a right to determine the procedures of decision making. These may change and become more representative of the different groups within in a society where the liberal–democratic ethos is deeply rooted; or in situations where pressures to change that come from within the community are backed strongly by external institutions. In any case, democratisation of community institutions is not the crucial issue here. While it is desirable, the difficulty with the multicultural agenda is that it privileges the right of a community, or more accurately, a minority community, to protect its own way of life. It is the right to preserve a way of life that enables traditional authority structures to prevail in a community.

Multiculturalism approaches the issue of minority discrimination by affirming the value of cultural diversity. It is the centrality accorded to promoting diversity of cultures that sustains the right of a community to its way of life. Moreover, even when multiculturalism acknowledges the value of cultural community membership for the self, it underlines the need to protect a cultural context of experience. Through each of these arguments it thus asserts the right of communities to have access to their culture, and this again entails the right to protect a distinctive way of life. In a framework where a cultural way of life is thus privileged, instituting new procedures and sustaining options for members of the community is rarely a weighted preference. More importantly, multiculturalism focuses only upon one aspect of community life. It examines the threat that is posed to it by a state that is actively seeking to assimilate or annihilate that identity. It does not explore the equally important threat that is posed by a community that does not allow members to exercise their option to deviate from the received way of life.

Communities oppress, not by denying individuals the right to exit, but by imposing a very heavy cost for differing from the accepted way of life. For people who value their community identity and see themselves as a part of that collectivity, ex-communication or forced exit from the community is often the hardest punishment. It is this that they challenge even when they deviate from a community's accepted codes. It is, therefore, of the utmost importance that valuing a community identity must not become a way of closing options and choices for the members. Indeed, since community memberships are crucial to the identity of the self, individual members should have the possibility of differing while belonging to a community. This may not, however, be possible in a framework where identity and community membership is associated with a definite way of life; or where protecting a way of life is of highest priority and rights are given to a community to realise that goal.

6

The Limits of Multiculturalism

Multiculturalism is not just a statement on the discrimination of cultural minorities in the nation-state, it represents an agenda in which promoting cultural diversity is considered an essential condition for ensuring equal treatment for all communities within the polity. What is specific to this agenda is that it links group-differentiated rights to equal citizenship, and more importantly, it sanctions special rights for minorities to protect their culture. Based on the perception that marginalisation or exclusion of minority communities is responsible for the disintegration of their culture, it underlines the need to protect minority cultures and create conditions in which they grow and flourish. This agenda of sustaining minority cultures is reinforced, on the one hand, by the value accorded to diversity of cultures in a society, and on the other, by the belief that individuals value their community memberships. It is this twin reading of the value of community identity and cultural diversity that sustains the need for protecting and preserving minority cultures.

Multiculturalism thus links the programme of protecting marginalised cultures with promoting diversity and enhancing equal treatment. It assumes further that valuing a community identity necessitates, if not implies, the desire to protect and preserve that identity. This understanding of community membership and the importance of protecting minority cultures and their distinct way of life invariably privileges the community. As was noted in the previous chapter it tends to legitimise existing practices and encourages ahistorical readings of culture. This minimises the space for the expression of dissent within the community, and can be an equally important source of discrimination within the community. Within a democratic polity, it is vital that both kinds of discrimination be reduced, if not altogether eliminated. At present, the discourses on multiculturalism are mostly silent about the community as a site of discrimination. Indeed, in much of this literature, the community is perceived as a place of adversarial politics by which the hegemony of the nation-state can be challenged. Consequently, it is the rights of the community against the state and the accompanying agenda of protecting cultural identities that has received centrality within this framework.

Beyond Liberalism and Multiculturalism

To address the issues of discrimination that arise from the policies of the nation-state as well as the practices of cultural communities, it is necessary to move away from both the liberal and the multicultural conception of individual, culture and community. For liberals, communities and collective identities have no intrinsic value. While they do exist, they derive their value from the contribution they make to the individual wellbeing. Hence, the only thing that has an independent or irreducible worth is the individual. Groups and communities are desirable only when they contribute to the wellbeing of the individual; and their claims matter only if they enable individuals to exercise their rights more fully. It is the life of the individual that alone has any moral worth; communities have only secondary and derivative value. Further, and more importantly, individuals become moral agents when they exercise choice. The freedom to choose is central to a meaningful life. What is of the utmost value then is that individuals have the opportunity to make their own choices. As autonomous persons, they must be able to 'lead a life which, on reflection, they have come to value, rather than a life imposed upon them by history and fate' (Tamir, 1993: 8). The problem with traditional communities built around ascribed identities is that they do not allow individuals to lead a meaningful life of this kind. Communities fix roles and identities; encourage conformity and function in a way that suppresses the growth of the individual self. Consequently, they stifle those aspects of the individual self that have the most value. To quote Amy Gutmann, human beings are 'unique, self-creating and creative individuals.... Part of the uniqueness of individuals results from the ways in which they integrate, reflect upon, and modify their own cultural heritage and that of other people with whom they come into contact' (Gutmann, 1994: 6–7). Communities, by putting a high premium on adherence to collective norms and goals, stifle just this dimension of the self. To protect the individual from the oppression of the community and to create space for the exercise of choice, liberals therefore ask for a 'right to exit'.

If cultures are valuable only to the extent that they give meaning to the life of the agents, individuals alone must determine for themselves whether they feel attracted to a given way of life, and whether they wish to abide by it. If, for some reason, they wish to make different choices or opt for another way of life, they must have the option of making that choice. They must, in other words, have a right to exit from that culture and community. What also follows from this line of reasoning is that individuals should have the opportunity 'to live within the culture of their choice, to decide on their social affiliations, to re-create the culture of the community they belong to, and to redefine its borders' (Tamir, 1993: 8). It is, therefore, meaningless to assume that cultures or communities have a right to preservation. Indeed, what needs to be preserved is not the unique and distinct form of each culture but the right of individuals to create and construct a unique world of their own, a world which they inhabit by choice and treasure for the same reason. Individuals should have the freedom to choose their way of life, freedom 'to form communities and to live by the terms of those associations' (Kukathas, 1992: 116). The right to free association could well provide this. Therefore, from the liberal perspective, there is no need for group rights, for the right to association can allow individuals to live by cultures that they find suitable and desirable for themselves.

Multiculturalism, in sharp contrast, begins by asserting the value of collective community identities for the individual. It speaks not only of the influence of community membership in structuring experiences, but suggests that recognition and respect for the community is crucial for a life of dignity. It is only when one's cultural community is secure and treated as an equal that one can meaningfully explore choices and options. Hence, it advocates rights to protect communities and to allow them the opportunity to determine their own way of life. To this end, it favours a range of special community rights, as distinct from individual rights that are given equally to all persons as citizens. These include rights to promote a collectively valued way of life, to live and be governed by the norms of that culture, and to observe the cultural practices of one's community.

While liberalism acknowledges the value of only those ties that are freely chosen, multiculturalism recognises the fact that individuals do cherish bonds and memberships that are not entirely chosen by the self. It also realises that communities are not voluntary associations which individuals enter for the sake of realising some shared purpose. Often, they 'find' themselves in them, but this does not make these collectivities any less significant. However, in accepting the significance of community memberships, multiculturalism assumes that we must strive to protect these identities and memberships. If liberalism makes the mistake of assuming that individuals move freely between cultures, picking and choosing what they like, multiculturalism makes the analogous error of assuming that because individual identity is shaped in part by community memberships, we must try to make community cultures secure. Thus, if one accords centrality to the right to exit, the other speaks of rights to sustain and protect cultures. Neither considers the reality that because people cherish and value identities, they seek the right to differ and the space to explore options while remaining within the community. In other words, most often individuals do not seek the right to opt out of the community. Because the community identity matters, they wish to be members but at the same time they do not want conformity to be the basis of that membership. Both liberalism and multiculturalism ignore this dimension of individual and collective life. While liberalism associates the expression of difference with the right to exit, multiculturalism gives primacy to differences that exist across cultures and communities. Hence, the former approaches from the vantage-point of an unencumbered self while the latter examines from the point of view of preserving and protecting cultures. We need to move away from both these perspectives so as to consider the possibility of creating discursive space for a right to non-conformist membership.

Right to Non-conformist Membership

The difficulty with liberalism is that it is often inattentive to the cultural orientation of the nation-state; consequently it is reluctant to give communities and its members the right to differ from the culture of the state. Multiculturalism recognises that the state expresses a culture and this culture frequently places minority communities at a disadvantage, but to correct this bias it seeks rights to sustain a community's way of life. Rights that are granted for the sake of protecting a minority community invariably help to secure a way of life. Consequently, these rights must be separated from those that are demanded and given for ensuring that individuals have the *option* of continuing with a way of life. The latter emanate from a respect for community membership but provide room for individuals to differ and not conform to a prescribed way of life. The former, by comparison, empower communities. Even though they enhance diversity, they give communities, and not individuals, the right to determine the values and practices that are essential to their way of life. For instance, when rights are directed towards protecting and sustaining minority cultures, then the Amish community can withdraw its children from schools at an early age if it perceives this to be an essential condition for the survival of its faith community. Likewise, when protecting the French culture and way of life is the desired goal, the Quebecois can enunciate all those policies that allow it to realise that end even if it entails limiting the options of members. It can stipulate that French will be the official language and medium of instruction in educational institutions. It can also legislate, as it has, that the French-speaking population must send its children only to schools where teaching is in French language. It can further state that Quebec must have a voice in determining who immigrates to this province; and it can also prescribe that immigrants must send their children to French-speaking schools and be committed to living in Quebec for certain number of years. All these, and may be many more, restrictions may legitimately be placed upon the members of the community for the sake of protecting the French way of life.

Quebec does not represent a unique case. In fact, rights aimed at making cultures secure and ensuring that they survive, most often place limitations on the choices of community members. They privilege what is supposedly a collective goal, stipulate conditions that are necessary for sustaining that valued way of life, and expect members to conform. The agenda of preserving diversity and protecting minority cultures invariably leads to closure of options for internal members. While the Anglophones in Quebec have the option of sending their children to English schools, it is the options of Francophones, along with those of the immigrants, that are limited and curtailed when the French culture is sought to be protected. Some measures may, at times, be initiated to offset the restrictions that are inevitably placed while acting to sustain cultures. The re-organisation of states along linguistic lines in India, for example, created a world in which diverse languages could flourish. This enhanced diversity within the country, but by insisting that the language of the region be the official medium of communication for all public offices in the area and instruction in educational institutions. This policy allowed a linguistic community to grow and increase in numbers, but primarily by encouraging that the regional language be the medium of instruction in all schools. The schools that were funded and run exclusively by the state only taught in the official language; and even though the Constitution provided for minorities to be taught in their language, this has not been provided in most states.

The goal of promoting recognised languages meant creating pockets in which each would be the official language and enjoy a privileged position. In most cases, this special position has been sustained by formally or informally putting pressure on others to conform. Even privately-run schools are expected to teach in the language of the state. The effects of this closure have, however, been mitigated a little by the fact that the goal of protecting and promoting these linguistic cultures and communities is qualified by an equally strong commitment to allow minority communities to establish their own educational institutions to promote their own language. And the State has specified conditions that have encouraged these institutions to be open to members of other communities.

Minority institutions can receive financial assistance from the State only if 30 per cent of the seats are filled by students from the general public (i.e., not belonging to the minority which established the institutions). Even members of the majority community can send their children to these schools. There are thus no restrictions, for instance, that Bengalis living in Bengal must send their children only to schools where Bengali is the medium of instruction; they can place them in Christian missionary schools where English is the medium of instruction. Options, to some extent, also exist because the State permits schools to teach in the two officially recognised national languages, namely, Hindi and English. Hence, in principle, a few options do exist, and are at times exercised, but only because complete conformity is not being enforced in the interest of promoting collective good. The Indian case is by no means an exemplary one. As is well known, options exist only for a very small proportion of the population; and unlike the situation in Quebec, the officially recognised minorities within the state do not usually receive education in their own language. However, the point is that the perspective of protecting and promoting diversity of cultures often operates by restricting options for members. We need to explore and create space for the exercise of options so as to create space for non-conformist membership of a community. Indeed, rights of communities and cultures need to be considered from this latter perspective.

Limitations of the Multicultural Response to the Issue of Minority Discrimination

There are, of course, a number of other difficulties that inhere in the multicultural agenda of preserving and protecting cultures. The one that needs closer attention is the claim that multiculturalism cannot adequately address the issue of minority discrimination within the polity. Multiculturalism works with a picture of discrete communities with clearly identified boundaries and membership. It places people in specific communities, identifies some as minorities and another as the majority. The entire enterprise of identifying vulnerable and marginalised minorities assumes that there are fixed groups to whom special rights may be given to protect their culture. Furthermore, and this is perhaps even more important, it tries to minimise discrimination by pinpointing oppressed minorities and granting rights to these identified few.

In recommending special community rights for marginalised minorities multiculturalism assumes that (*a*) a sharp and fairly unambiguous distinction can be made between the majority and the minority communities and (*b*) the minority communities can be identified categorically. That is, we can know in advance just who is a minority. The idea that minority communities can be clearly identified once and for all, and that there are some identifiable and permanent minorities within a nation-state, ignores the complex process by which communities get 'minoritised' (Gupta, 1999). This notion of fixed minorities ignores that 'bigotry...refuses to be shackled along predetermined lines' (*Ibid.*: 50). Consequently, minorities can, and do, emerge without prior warning or foreknowledge. In India, for instance, up until 1984, the Sikhs did not see themselves as a minority. However, the communal riots that followed the assassination of Mrs Indira Gandhi, in which Sikhs were systematically targeted and killed, created a new minority. Likewise, the policies and rhetoric of Shiv Sena in the mid-1960s transformed a hitherto dominant community of South Indians, living in Mumbai and Maharashtra, into a victimised minority (*Ibid.*).

Thus, new minorities emerge from time to time and even the most exhaustive listing of minorities can never be complete. Given this historical reality, Dipankar Gupta maintains that it will be preferable to dispense with the idea of specific rights for identified and fixed minorities. Instead, we should focus on the process of 'minoritisation'. This is necessary because the issue of minority discrimination cannot be adequately dealt with by simply extending special rights to some recognised minorities. To counter group-based discrimination, what is required is that we protect those rights that shelter all communities, irrespective of their history and status, from being victimised and transformed into vulnerable minorities.

This shift in perspective is recommended for another reason. The practice of giving special rights to officially recognised minorities creates a scenario of patrons and enemies. It allows some individuals and parties 'to play "back-room politics" and to grandstand as heroes of minority communities' (Gupta, 1999: 52). The politics of patronage, engendered by the majority–minority framework, creates the impression that the rights and wellbeing of the minorities is dependent on the largesse of these leaders. Political parties in power tend to co-opt the leaders of the minority communities or win their support by offering small concessions, such as public holidays, benefits for minority educational institutions, special schemes for loans, reservation of seats in public offices and legislative bodies, etc. Instead of strengthening structures that could ensure equal treatment to all minorities, the political leadership identifies some communities as possible beneficiaries of their sponsorship. This leaves minorities permanently vulnerable and susceptible to political manipulation.

In countries like India that are marked by acute scarcity and non-availability of basic amenities, the scenario of patronage invariably strengthens identity-centred politics. To win votes, parties offer a few sops to the favoured few, and communities competing for limited public resources try to get ahead by consolidating their identity. As more and more communities employ the same strategy, it is the organised, economically or politically powerful groups that manage to corner benefits. As a result, the politics of identities leaves the most marginalised communities unattended. They continue to remain disadvantaged within this framework. Consequently, extending special rights to a few communities can never be an adequate response to the issue of minority discrimination and marginalisation.

It is equally necessary to approach the issue of difference and discrimination with the understanding that communities are not stable formations with clearly identified boundaries and commonly held traditions. The belief that groups have fixed or naturally given boundaries obscures the fact that identities, like group boundaries, are often context-specific. They are malleable and open to multiple constructions depending upon the social and political context. Far from being 'permanently inscribed on our psyches...they undergo context-related changes' (Gupta, 1996: 2). Likewise, group boundaries shift. They alter with changes in the political context, government policies, emergence of new interests and other groups in society. New identities, for instance, emerged in India with the linguistic reorganisation of the states. People living in the same region and practicing the same religion began to identify themselves as Tamil or Telugu speakers. The latter, living in the state of Madras, were now transformed into a minority and the former into a majority. The creation of the state of Punjab consolidated the Punjabi identity as Hindus and Sikhs living within the state fore-grounded their linguistic identity. However, these identities were redefined significantly in the 1980s. The demand for Khalistan and the actions of Bhindranwale split the Punjabi community as cleavages appeared between the Hindus and the Sikhs. Further, in 1984, the riots against the Sikhs in Delhi created conditions in which members of the Sikh community began to perceive themselves as a minority community that was distinct and separate from the Hindu community.

Thus, identities change and so do group formations. The enumeration by the Government of India (SC) Order, 1936, of certain castes that were placed at the lowest rung of the hierarchy and treated as untouchables, created the category of Scheduled Castes. Initially, these castes were listed in a schedule for purposes of electoral arrangements. Subsequently, after India gained independence, the schedule formed the basis of identifying communities for whom positions and jobs were to be reserved in public institutions and legislative bodies. Likewise, using a different criterion for granting reservations to socially and economically deprived classes, the Mandal Commission constructed a new group in the form of Other Backward Classes (see Sheth, 1998). The latter brought together fairly disparate castes and communities and welded together a new identity. The point to note here is that public policy and government actions created a shared interest that cut across earlier group boundaries and forged new bonds of solidarity and distinctions.

The history of every society provides examples of the dissolution of existing, and apparently stable groups, and of the emergence of new ones. On some occasions, the new formations arise from the sublimation of existing identities and, at other times, divisions internal to the group ossify and create new groups and identities. Since identities are subject to reconfiguration it makes no sense to preserve a given identity; or, for that matter, to use existing groups and communities as the basis of political settlements. In fact, it may be quite inappropriate to determine political institutions and practices by appealing to the interests of existing groups (see Kukathas, 1992: 111).

Neither group interests nor community identities are naturally given; they are shaped by historical circumstances and political institutions. Indeed, they are, at times, constructed and used in the struggle for power and control over scarce resources (Nagata, 1987). Even though individuals value community membership, their self-identification and identity-construction are not entirely independent of instrumental ends. In post-independence India, for instance, linguistic identities have been continuously fashioned to seek public recognition as well as to protect specific group interests. In Assam, to take an example, a collectively valued cultural identity was a potent instrument in the hands of the 'Sons of Soil' movement. The movement invoked linguistic identity to categorise Bengalis settled in Assam as 'foreigners' who should be excluded from public offices and positions. Here, a collectively valued cultural identity was designed to consolidate the material interests of one group while simultaneously questioning the dominance of the Bengali population in most walks of social life. A couple of decades before this, in the 1960s, the Bengali people living in this region had also constructed their identities to suit instrumental ends. By declaring Assamese as their native language they identified themselves as 'natives' so that they could be eligible for land that was reserved for the indigenous people (see Horowitz, 1985: 195).

Multiculturalism tends to neglect the instrumentalist dimension of group identities. It works almost exclusively with a romantic picture of communities. It sees them as collectivities whose members are tied together by affection and non-contractual bonds of sharing. In the present world, these communities surface as 'havens of security, places where they can escape from the alienating workaday world of post-technological society. Ethnicity provides a sense of group belongingness and rootedness, i.e., a focus for ethnic identity and cultural continuity' (Kallen, 1982: 54). This representation of communities in purely expressivist terms takes attention away from the 'instrumental' side of ethnic collectivities

(*Ibid.*). It ignores the reality that communities have political and economic interests; they are often designed to meet survival needs and gain access to limited public resources (see Bullivant, 1981).

This instrumental dimension of collective community identity is almost entirely eclipsed in theories of multiculturalism. The latter represent cultural communities only as collective entities that give value and meaning to the life of the participants. They are cherished and sought to be preserved for this reason. *Vice-versa*, community claims for preserving a collective identity are also stripped off all instrumental aspects. They are seen as claims for public recognition that aim to protect a collectively valued good in society. Thus, for instance, the demand for special status for Quebec is translated as the realisation of a shared public definition of good life (Taylor, 1994: 58–60): namely, the 'survival and flourishing of French culture in Quebec' (Taylor, 1993: 175). What is almost entirely effaced in this reading is that these cultural demands emerged against the backdrop of sharp polarities in power exercised by the Anglophones and Francophones in the Quebec region. Also, that the call to promote French culture and language challenged the near-complete domination of the Anglophones in urban life, bureaucracy and industry. Likewise, within multiculturalism the demands of the Native Americans are also translated as claims aimed to protect and preserve their distinct cultural identity. Once again, what is forgotten is that the assertion of this collectively shared value is, for these people, a way of challenging the hegemony of the white settlers. The indigenous peoples' movements inevitably defy the power equation that exists currently in North America. In both instances, the expressivist assertions of community identity are intertwined with claims of political and economic rights (see Slattery, 1996; Benson, 1992; Allen, 1994; Asch, 1984; Cardinal, 1977). They cannot be understood independently of the latter. In fact, to represent them merely, or even primarily, as movements of cultural identity necessarily denies issues that are central to these cultural assertions.

Struggles of different groups for equal treatment as well as the issue of minority discrimination have therefore to be placed in a wider context. These cannot be adequately understood when they are represented as assertions of a cultural identity. Although it is important to take cognisance of culture-related discrimination, it is equally necessary to remember that discrimination is not merely a cultural phenomenon. In its discussion of minorities, multiculturalism often 'separates the issue of cultural deprivation from issues of socio-economic inequalities in society' (Joseph, 1999: 34). The dissociation of cultural marginalisation from other processes has resulted in an impoverished view of social conflict and discrimination in society. It neglects the links between disputes over resources, distribution of goods and citizenship rights, and remains inattentive to the ways in which cultural identities are manipulated and constructed in the competition for scarce resources. Indeed, it fosters the impression that social conflicts are primarily contests of identity, or *vice-versa*, that identity assertions are simply statements of deeply felt cultural needs. Furthermore, the construction of a 'purely cultural identity' (*Ibid.*: 32) delinked from the social context in which the individual and the community exist, provides very limited solutions to problems of discrimination in society. In everyday life, a 'person's social location and self-identity would normally be overdetermined by complex, structured patterns of identities which tend to reinforce each other. Therefore, measures to grant cultural protection may be only partially successful in ensuring equal dignity and non-discrimination for members of such (minority) communities' (*Ibid.*).

There are two other issues associated with the multicultural agenda that need also to be taken into account. First, even though multiculturalists speak of protecting minority cultures and making them secure to minimise the discrimination faced by minorities, this agenda is open to appropriation by the traditional elite. One needs, therefore, to be cautious on this count. Second, when preserving a culture is the vantage-point for deliberating upon policies, existing priorities and perspectives get privileged. Although theorists such as Will Kymlicka argue that making cultures secure will enable individuals to rethink their inheritances, this is not usually the case. Indeed, when policies are devised to protect what are supposedly collective goods, they invariably create conditions in which these goods and values are likely to be affirmed rather than challenged.

Protecting a minority culture in situations of tremendous group inequality poses serious difficulties. In situations where there are vast disparities in the power and prestige of majority and minority cultures, community members themselves feel attracted to the majority culture and wish to be a part of it. At the very least, they desire goods, particularly material goods that the dominant culture has to offer. The fact that the outside culture can provide for more opportunities and general wellbeing often draws members to them. Studies of the Arctic region of Canada, for instance, show that Eskimo communities, exposed to the outside world, eagerly adopted their way of life. New economic projects or activities, such as employment at construction sites, increased demand for white foxes and trapping, gave community members access to goods, standard housing and other amenities that were not previously available to them. Attracted by these benefits many, particularly 'younger men … said that this was the life for them. The older men tended to look at DEW Line employment as a way to buy store goods at a time when trapping was relatively unprofitable. It was also a way to buy boats, outboard motors, and all other types of useful goods' (Ferguson, 1971: 23).

In all such encounters between cultures and communities with unequal power, protecting and preserving the culture is not an attractive option for members. Indeed, the call for cultural preservation comes frequently from the dispossessed leadership. People who have been deprived of their traditional status by the changes that are introduced, actively support the need to preserve culture. And, *vice-versa*, accepting the demand to preserve community culture necessarily reinforces the position and control of the traditional leadership over its members (see Nagata, 1987). Moreover, as social, cultural and economic structures are very closely linked together in many of these communities, protecting a culture often implies building an artificial fence around it. It is only when the culture is shielded from new economic interactions and aspirations that necessarily arise from contacts with the outside world, can it continue with its traditional way of life. However, this course of action does not resolve the problem of marginalisation in society. While it protects these communities temporarily by building artificial fences around them, it does so by keeping them in a subordinate position. In other words, it does not always minimise their disadvantage. It is, therefore, hardly surprising to find that these communities too do not use the language of protecting their culture. They speak, instead, of the rights of the community to determine its own affairs and control its resources.

The multicultural agenda of preserving minority cultures is anchored in the belief that members of a community share a commitment to a substantive good. Also, that these shared notions of substantive good that are valued by the community as a whole, need to be pursued by the political society as a whole. The presumption of a collective goal obviously obliterates the differences that exist within the community but, more importantly, it operates with the belief that the given goal will remain unaltered. Policies of preservation assume that goals that are, at present, shared will persist and remain more or less unaltered. Indeed, they create conditions in which the present goals are continuously affirmed. For instance, in the case of Quebec, French culture and identity are sought to be protected by making French the official language of the province, and by controlling immigration policies so that the French character of the society can be maintained. While both these policies create conditions in which French culture can survive and flourish, they also help in the constitution of a society that is likely to affirm the present commitment to preserving the French identity. Promoting continued commitment to the prevailing collective norms thus forms an integral part of policies that seek to preserve a culture, and it is this element that protects the interest of the dominant groups in society. Multicultural agenda needs to take note of the ways in which it creates space for these appropriations and readings.

Multiculturalism needs to be cognisant of these difficulties. In particular, it needs to abandon the notion of fixed and clearly identified minorities and the accompanying assumption of homogeneous communities with a shared conception of good. This is necessary because 'minoritisation' is an on-going process and existing community identities are often themselves constructed by assimilating several communities. Multiculturalism, therefore, needs to have a more complex picture of discrimination, marginalisation and minority formation. If individuals are to have the option of continuing with a way of life in any meaningful way, then resisting assimilation by the state or the national culture must not imply affirming the culture of the community. The state must also not assume that non-assimilation entails accommodating communities as homogeneous entities. Multiculturalism needs to question these binary oppositions through which the self and the community are conceptualised.

Diverse and Unequal: Representations of the 'Other' in Multiculturalism

So far we have focused primarily on problems that arise from the agenda of protecting minority cultures and making them secure. Before concluding this discussion on the limits of multiculturalism it is, however, also necessary to look at the notion of the 'other', the culturally different that needs to be preserved and protected which surfaces in the discourses on multiculturalism.

Multiculturalism as a theory values cultural differences. It also cherishes cultural diversity. In part, at least, the discourses of multiculturalism challenge the ways in which minority communities and cultures are presented and accommodated in the public sphere. Yet, paradoxically enough, the images of the 'other' that emerge within multiculturalism bear a striking resemblance to the nineteenth century representations of non-western cultures. Indeed, the multicultural agenda affirms and reinforces these representations. The similarity of constructs manifests itself at various levels: in the identification of cultures that require protection as well as in the deliberation of policies that are required to sustain these cultures. By and large, the communities that multiculturalism seeks to protect are presented as being tradition-bound societies that are supposedly carrying on with practices that have been in existence for a long time. They appear to be unmarked by any significant conflict of values, and are therefore seen as sharing some substantive notion of good and a way of life. The 'other' remains, in a fundamental sense, the antithesis of everything that the West stands for: lacking the attributes of the latter it remains constant, univocal and tradition-bound (see Tamir, 1997).

This de-historicisation of non-western cultures is a necessary, even if unintended, consequence of the multicultural logic. Indeed, the issue of preserving cultures and traditional practices is predicated upon such a perspective. If non-western cultures are treated as entities that are evolving and redefining their value systems in the process of responding to new challenges, then the question of preserving cultural practices does not even arise. Moreover, the de-historicised picture makes minority cultures exotic. They surface as upholders of quaint customs and primordial identities. The idea that minority cultures are historical entities that undergo change, that their customs are often of recent provenance and contested history, are aspects that are never adequately accommodated within multiculturalism.

As a result, what multiculturalism debates is the nature of a specific cultural practice. It discusses whether a given practice, for instance, clitoridectomy, conforms to liberal sensibilities. The fact that this and many other traditional practices are of recent vintage, or that they are, or have been, contested, are elements that are almost entirely lost in this framework. The reality that clitoridectomy was revived in Kenya during the struggles against British colonialism; or that 'Israeli family law, which is extremely unfair to women…is the result of a political deal between the religious and secular Zionists who founded the state' are easily ignored here (Pollitt, 1997: 29). Multiculturalism tends to gloss over these specific histories of practices in their cultural contexts. Eventually it is this de-historicisation that allows existing practices to be valued as symbols of tradition and identity that cannot be easily open to reconsideration and negotiation by internal members.

The fact that prevalent cultural practices are products of historical negotiations needs to be emphasised because the language of collective community rights often 'motivates group leaders to foster social and cultural homogeneity'. It allows them to claim that 'every deviation from "the tradition"…risks the continuous existence of the community' (Tamir, 1997: 32). This rationalises internal oppression and disadvantages groups and individuals that dissent from the perceived traditional practices. At another level, in defending special rights for communities that are threatened by the policies of the state and market, multiculturalism, at least implicitly, assumes that these tradition-bound cultures cannot withstand the changes that are introduced by modernity. Although 'we' can 'reinvent ourselves and our culture time and again...."they" must adhere to known social and cultural patterns in order to survive' (*Ibid.*). That is, 'they' must preserve their culture but 'we' can endure the transformations that come with modernity. Further, multiculturalism presupposes that 'our' identity is strong and stable but 'their' identity is fragile; it needs to be protected by preserving their traditional way of life. While Americans 'from Virginia can retain their identity despite the fact that they live very different lives than their agrarian predecessors' the Native Americans cannot (*Ibid.*). Consequently, they must continue with their traditional lifestyle and patterns of economic and political life.

In this way, the dichotomies between 'us' and 'them' that informed the colonial discourse, persist even within multiculturalism. Although it does not represent the 'other' as barbaric or uncivilised, multiculturalism continues to treat the 'other' as unequal in many respects. The 'other' remains in a subordinate position because the qualities that define the self and make it a vibrant historical entity are almost always excluded from the 'other'. If the self is secular, technologically advanced, economically strong and constantly changing, the 'other' is unchanging, religious entity, steeped in tradition, rich in cultural form, myths and folklore but with a fragile economy and traditional modes of authority and power. Even though multiculturalists often weigh these differences positively, by denying the 'other' qualities that define the self, they subordinate them. In fact, multiculturalism transforms them into objects of admiration and even perhaps aesthetic value, but never as entities that can compete with the West in terms that the latter prizes for itself.

The point that also needs to be underlined is that the absolute privileging of difference creates an unbridgeable distance between the self and the other, and it is this that stands in the way of equal respect. Arguments about difference have, therefore, to be used with the utmost caution. They can cut either way. They may sanction special treatment or exclusion and discrimination. In the Sears case, for instance, feminists realised that their arguments about gender differences had been used to defend the apparently discriminatory hiring practices of Sears. The legal defence of the American retail giant, argued that 'fundamental differences—the result of culture or long-standing patterns of socialisation—led to women's presumed lack of interest in a commission sales job' (Scott, 1992: 258). The gender imbalance in certain spheres of the labour force was thus explained away in terms of existing differences between the experiences and attitudes of men and women. While feminists had invoked the difference argument to critique dominant values in the public domain and to draw attention to the specific needs of women, in this instance, the difference principle was appropriated to keep women out of certain positions.

The difference argument in every sphere is open to such interpretations. In recent times, the idea of cultural differences has been used effectively in some criminal cases involving minorities in America. A 'Chinese immigrant man in New York who battered his wife to death for committing adultery and a Japanese immigrant woman in California who drowned her children and tried to drown herself because her husband's adultery had shamed the family, relied on cultural defences to win reduced charges (from murder to second degree or involuntary manslaughter)' (Okin, 1997: 27). The 'four types of cases in which cultural defences have been used most successfully are: kidnap and rape by Hmong men who claim that their actions are part of their cultural practice of *zij poj niam* or 'marriage by capture'; wife-murder by immigrants from Asian and Middle-Eastern countries whose wives have either committed adultery or treated their husbands in a servile way; mothers who have killed their children but failed to kill themselves...; and ... [in] clitoridectomy' (*Ibid.*). In all these cases of violence (violence among men, violence against women, harsh treatment to children), and in situations involving ritualistic practices, such as those of animal sacrifice, cultural difference has been used as a legal strategy to get reduced sentences for individual members of minority groups. Actions that would otherwise have merited severe punishment or treated as murder, have been effectively transformed into acceptable practices that conform to traditional cultural norms.

   The unconditional privileging of cultural differences often creates difficulties of this kind. Accompanied by statements about absolute differences between cultures and communities, the difference principle is open to a variety of appropriations, including some that justify discriminatory practices. The possibility of multicultural agenda being used to defend strong communitarian structures and unacceptable practices is an important concern in all democracies. Most theorists of multiculturalism accept this; in fact, they maintain that multiculturalism does not empower communities or justify unfair treatment of groups in society. Whether recent theories of multiculturalism have taken cognisance of the limitations pointed out here, and whether they adequately address the issues raised, are questions that the next chapter will explore.

7

Responses to the Critics

Critiques of multiculturalism have not gone completely unheeded. Votaries of multiculturalism have, in the recent past, tried to respond to the concerns of the critics. In particular, they have tried to assure the sceptics that group-differentiated rights will not empower communities or legitimise practices that sanction discrimination of vulnerable sections of the population. This chapter looks closely at some of these formulations of multiculturalism to see if these adequately address the difficulties that we previously noted in the multicultural notion of culture, community, minority discrimination and diversity.

There are, in the main, four fairly distinct arguments that have been offered in defence of the agenda for preserving cultures, protecting diversity and sanctioning special rights for minorities. The first invokes the principle of difference. By privileging differences absolutely, it argues that respect for difference requires unconditional protection of diverse cultures and practices. Limiting the latter in the name of democratic or human rights necessarily entails the imposition of a universal or liberal standpoint, and this must be avoided at all costs. The second argument addresses liberal apprehensions by limiting special rights to only a few minorities and stipulating that these rights are not intended for use against internal dissent or difference. These rights are to be given only to protect and empower communities against pressures of assimilation that come from the outside. The third accepts that protecting minority cultures does not entail preserving all types of minority practices. We need to discuss the limits of 'permissible' diversity in society. It further suggests that the parameters of permissible diversity may be defined with reference to the values enshrined in the Constitution of the land. The fourth response introduces two caveats. It states that special group rights are to be given only if they enhance genuine inclusion of the minority communities within the polity; and when minorities exercise these rights in a way that is compatible with the principle of fair treatment to all members. Here, special rights of minorities are intended only for protecting collectively valued conceptions of good life. The aim of these rights is to ensure equal treatment to minorities in ways that do not place additional costs to other groups, including the majority.

These four arguments represent four fairly distinct positions on multiculturalism. While each responds to the charge that multiculturalism promotes conservative and communitarian sentiments, they do so in quite different ways.

The Difference Argument

The strongest and most strident defence of the multicultural agenda of protecting and preserving minority cultures has come from theorists who privilege the principle of difference unconditionally. Multiculturalism, it is argued, is defined by its commitment to the idea of difference, diversity and heterogeneity. Rejecting the ideal of assimilation and the corresponding ideology of the 'melting pot', multiculturalism values cultural diversity. It allows the free and unrestrained expression of differences. The agenda of preserving cultural diversity follows from the positive evaluation of differences and is doubly affirmed by a dismissal of the goal of assimilation. It is, therefore, a primary and non-negotiable value within multiculturalism. Some community practices, specially those of marginalised cultures, appear to be threatening, or even dangerous, only when the vantage-point of difference is not adopted. For instance, when other cultures are approached and judged from the perspective and values of liberalism, they appear to be starkly different and, therefore, unacceptable. The element of 'foreignness' results in negative representation of these practices, and it is this that leads liberals to conclude that these are oppressive and even hostile to the interests of women.

However, advocates of this point of view argue that the unfamiliar ceases to threaten when the perspective of difference is used. The latter opens us to the possibility that practices take on different meanings in different contexts. What seems in one historical context to be a source of gender injustice, may be an enabling practice in another context. For example, to the liberal self '[V]eiling might be a sign of sexist, enforced female subservience...but many Moslem feminists...see veiling as an empowering practice. Veiling allows upwardly mobile professional women to move from the familiar settings of their rural homes and 'emerge socially into a sexually integrated' urban world that is still an alien, uncomfortable social reality for both women and men' (Honig, 1997: 31). Likewise from the liberal feminist perspective, polygamy, a practice 'permitted by premodern Judaism and contemporary Islam and once required by Mormonism', may appear to be 'a device whereby men control women' (*Ibid.*). However, the institution of monogamy that is regarded to be 'unambiguously preferable from a feminist perspective, famously isolates women from each other and privatises them. The struggles of monogamous wives against their husbands' power are small, individual rebellions, usually unsupported these days by any networks of belonging. Surely monogamy, every man's little dominion, is no less often turned into an instrument of male power than is polygamy' (*Ibid.*).

Theorists of difference use the example of veiling and polygamy to argue that different practices perform different functions, and they often signify different things in different contents. Consequently, to assume that they have one single, uniform meaning in all contexts, or that they have the same meaning for others as they have for us, is to privilege our historically and culturally specific vantage-point over all others.

The important thing then is to allow free play to difference and to relinquish the search for homogeneity. Instead of imposing our moral values and specifying what should or should not be permissible in other cultures, we should respect diversity in itself. The multicultural agenda of protecting diverse cultural practices, it is said, appears unacceptable only when we assert the superiority of our own social and cultural perspective and argue that others must conform to our world-view. By this view, liberal critiques stem from, and express, a basic hostility to cultural differences. They assume that other cultures can be accepted only if they conform to the liberal picture of a culture. More specifically, if they abandon their ritual practices and cultural distinctiveness (Gilman, 1997: 33). Respect for cultural diversity, on the other hand, necessitates that we relinquish our moral arrogance and allow diverse cultures to flourish and observe the customs and practices that are peculiar to them (*Ibid.*).

Advocates of the difference principle make two related arguments. On the one hand, they suggest that 'what constitutes inequality and discrimination needs to be kept open and interrogated continuously' (Post, 1997: 36). On the other, they maintain that respect for difference implies that we create space for diversity. Against the more specific charge that policies aiming to preserve minority cultures are likely to promote gender inequality and other such unacceptable practices, these theorists maintain that gender discrimination is a widespread phenomenon. It exists in all cultures and is not a peculiarity of minority cultures. Hence, to assume that protecting minority cultures is likely to promote or legitimise practices of gender inequality is to misrepresent the issue.

What is also argued here is that gender inequality is not intrinsic to minority cultures. In many minority cultures, gender inequality is a product of external intervention and imposition of new laws. Writing about the indigenous people, Mary Ellen Turpel states that in most aboriginal communities 'the belief is that women, children and elders come before men and the responsibility of man is to live life as a good helper towards women, children and elders' (Turpel, 1994: 33). As a consequence, 'traditional tribal control of property did not lead to the victimisation of aboriginal women' (*Ibid.*). The situation, however, changed with colonial intervention. While women enjoyed a high status in family and had real property rights in traditional society, the Indian Act by which the reservations are now governed, has resulted in the demotion of women. Now property is owned by men and certificates of possession are only issued to male members of the band. Hence, women have no legally recognisable rights over matrimonial property in the reservation. The current norms thus discriminate against women but this is so because of colonial intervention. Today, an aboriginal woman who lives on the reserve with her husband cannot, upon breakdown of her marriage, claim possession of her home. Gender discrimination of this kind was not intrinsic to tribal law. It is a consequence of assimilative policies and suppression of difference. Minority cultures cannot be blamed for, or held solely responsible for, the victimisation of women.

Against those who point to the link between culture, religion and patriarchy, these theorists of multicultural difference argue that 'culture is something rather more complicated than patriarchal permission for powerful men to subordinate vulnerable women' (*Ibid.*). To put it in another way, they maintain that in some cases culture may oppress but in other situations it may be enabling. It contains both these possibilities. Moreover, culture can be 'deeply oppressive in ways that neither involve minority rights nor formally violate political and civil liberties. Cultures can be oppressive because of the values or the social roles that they inculcate' (Post, 1997: 36). Hence, the 'oppressiveness of culture cannot be evaluated merely by contemporary notions of political and civil liberties' (*Ibid.*). Indeed, it is virtually impossible to define in advance which practices and liberties serve the interest of emancipation. Hence, from their perspective, special rights for minorities cannot be accused of promoting conservatism or inequality.

Theorists of difference rebut the critics by pointing to the oppressive character of liberalism and the majority cultures. They continuously refer to the possibility of seemingly restrictive cultural practices being used for empowering women and other marginalised groups. In other words, they question the dominant reading of minority cultural practices and remind us that majority culture, even in liberal democratic polities, is not immune to the charges that are commonly levied against minority cultures. Thus, against those who are anxious about minority cultures enforcing practices that are unjust to women, they show that all cultures are embedded in patriarchy. They do not deny the presence of cultural practices that discriminate against internal minorities but offer the consolation that this is not peculiar to minority cultures.

The difference argument performs an important task by questioning the majority culture's representation of minority practices, but in the process it endorses almost all community practices. It neither explores the issue of what is, or is not, acceptable within a democracy. Nor does it discuss the terms of enhancing non-conformist membership. Indeed, within the framework of difference, no suggestion can actually be made in this regard. Since no practice can be definitely categorised as being repressive or liberating, the question of striving to alter existing practices does not even arise within this framework. Eventually, agents are supposed to decide for themselves. The fact that decisions of agents, which in this case are communities, might echo the sentiments only of the dominant sections, is also not adequately addressed. None of these issues receive much consideration because most of these theorists counterpose the ideal of protecting diversity to liberal practices of assimilation. What needs also to be noted here is that they endorse diversity of all forms against the hegemony of the dominant norms and the principle of sameness endorsed by liberals. In other words, to avoid homogenisation or the endorsement of a single universal norm, they defend all kinds of diversity. Indeed, to challenge the dominant societal values, they represent practices as being not univocal but multivocal. That is, they can take on different meanings. Polygamy, for instance, can be oppressive but also a mode of creating solidarity between women. Thus, in this framework, almost anything can be said to be acceptable, or at least permissible, within democracy. It is equivocation of this kind along with a de-contextualised reading of agents' self-perception that leaves many of the original issues unresolved within this strand of multiculturalism.

Special Rights, Not Group Rights

In sharp contrast to this perspective, some theorists, most notably Will Kymlicka, take serious note of liberal anxieties about multiculturalism. To assure his critics that multiculturalism does not empower communities or restrict the freedom of internal members, Kymlicka adopts a two-fold strategy. On the one hand, he makes a distinction between two kinds of community rights:

those that protect a culture against external pressures and those that stifle internal dissent. On the other, he justifies special rights for only a few 'national' minorities. Kymlicka posits a distinction between two kinds of community rights—group rights and special rights. The former are given to communities independent of the rights of individuals who constitute them. The latter are 'owed to people as members of a particular community rather than as being universal and owed to all people as human beings' (Kymlicka, 1994: 18). Although both types of community rights protect cultural communities against forces of disintegration, they respond to two quite distinct sources of instability. Group rights protect the community from destabilisation that occurs on account of internal dissent, while special rights shelter the community from pressures of assimilation that come from external sources, such as the decisions of the larger society or the market (*Ibid.*: 18–20).

By this reasoning, special rights address the issue of intergroup relations and are granted to check the imbalances that exist in the cultural marketplace. Group rights refer to intra-group relations and can be a means of strengthening the community against decisions that come from within. Kymlicka distinguishes between special rights and group rights to underline that these rights need not go together and, what is perhaps equally important, that they serve quite different ends. Group rights have the danger of permitting individual oppression and sanctioning patriarchal domination. Since they give the community, or its leadership, the right to determine what is necessary for the sake of protecting group identity and solidarity, they can be used to quell internal dissent. Special rights, he claims, do not pose a similar threat. These rights can, and often do, exist alongside individual rights. Typically, special rights guarantee the community a voice in the polity and an opportunity to be counted as an equal (Kymlicka, 1991: 187–90). Communities may ask for, and receive, separate representation in specific institutions, veto power, language rights, greater degree of political autonomy or the right to self-governance within a territory (Kymlicka, 1995: 109). Each of these are intended to 'reduce the vulnerability of the minority communities to the decisions of the larger society'

(Kymlicka, 1994: 20). Using the case of Native American people, Kymlicka argues that different treatment for these communities is necessary and justified on account of the 'unequal circumstances' in which these communities are placed (Kymlicka, 1991: 187 and 247). 'Unlike the dominant French and English cultures, the very existence of aboriginal cultural communities is vulnerable to the decisions of the non-aboriginal majority around them. They could be outbid or outvoted on resources crucial to the survival of their communities...' (*Ibid.*). Giving special rights to such communities is therefore a pre-requisite for ensuring fair treatment to them. These rights are not *prima facie* concerned with controlling their members.

Special community rights entail different treatment for different groups but, for Kymlicka, this does not imply that multiculturalism sanctions discriminatory practices such as those of apartheid. In the case of the Black community in America, different treatment was a source of discrimination because in their case separation was a mark of inferiority. However, for communities that have been forcibly assimilated, separation is a condition of being treated as equals. Hence, in their case at least forcing conformity by overriding certain traditional practices is a source of discrimination. Special rights are supposed to prevent this latter predicament. Kymlicka defends special rights only for such communities who have been forced to assimilate, and whose distinct way of life is threatened by these pressures to assimilate (Kymlicka, 1991: 245–51).

Special rights are intended to protect the survival of a community in a hostile environment dominated by the majority. Consequently, Kymlicka maintains that they serve the interest of promoting equality and pose no danger to individual freedom. For instance, special land rights allow indigenous people to survive and protect their way of life. Absence of this right would not only destroy their culturally distinct pattern of life but will leave them open to exploitation by the wealthier and more powerful sections of the market. Kymlicka classifies special rights as a subset of community rights, for these are given to communities and not the individual. Land rights and the accompanying right to hunt and fish on reservation land are given to a specific community.

Eventually, it is the community that decides how best this land is to be used. Thus, for instance, what to hunt and when to hunt, is determined by the community and individual members cannot claim that regulation by the community is restricting their rights. Kymlicka also accepts that the exercise of these rights may place certain restrictions upon other people. For example, special land rights for Native Americans will mean that non-members cannot live or own property on reservations. Hence, the rights of outsiders are bound to be curtailed. But these restrictions, he argues, are essential for protecting their distinct way of life and for treating them as equals. Far from being a basis of discrimination, these rights are the basis of their equal status in the polity. Eventually, special rights are, in this framework, only extended to communities that have been disadvantaged by policies of assimilation.

Kymlicka's response to liberal and feminist critics rests, in large measure, upon the distinction between special rights (i.e., rights given to protect communities against external pressures of assimilation) and group rights (i.e., rights given to strengthen communities against pressures of disintegration that come from within). It is only special rights that he sanctions for marginalised minorities under the schema of differentiated citizenship. Further, these rights are to be granted to national, not ethnic, minorities. Ethnic minorities or voluntary immigrants, for Kymlicka, choose to leave their homeland and come to another country. While making this choice they know that they will have to live by the norms of the host country. Hence, they cannot expect to be granted special rights to protect and preserve their culture in the public domain (Kymlicka, 1995: 96–97). Even when the people concerned are second-generation immigrants who have lived in the new country all their life, or those who had no choice but to leave their country for the sake of survival, Kymlicka maintains that they have very limited claims for special treatment. They must receive equal social welfare rights but cannot really ask for rights to preserve their culture. The latter can legitimately be claimed by national minorities 'whose homeland has been incorporated through conquest, colonisation or federation...' (*Ibid.*). Since these communities, at the time of being incorporated or assimilated, had a distinct societal culture, their position is said to be different. As victims of forced assimilation they have, and can claim, special rights to protect their distinct way of life. Special rights, intended to protect minority cultures against external threats, are defended only for these national minorities. Other minorities may expect some limited cultural rights. However, which of these rights are given to whom is open to negotiation.

This framework of multiculturalism addresses many liberal concerns. Through the distinction between special rights and group rights, it assures them that all community rights are not meant to empower communities against individuals. Further, by narrowing down the minorities that may expect to receive special rights, it states that multicultural schema of special rights does not justify all cultural practices, certainly not those that immigrants bring with them. Since it is the customs of the immigrants that the critics object to most of the time—be it polygamy, clitoridectomy or arranged marriages—Kymlicka's framework takes care of many liberal apprehensions. However, even as he softens the liberals by restricting special rights to only a few minorities, the distinctions that he makes between different claimants pose many difficulties. It is, indeed, questionable whether immigrants, who move to another place for the sake of improving their life-prospects or to avoid political repression, relinquish the right to their culture. Or, whether the children of these immigrants, who did not share in this choice, can be expected to give up the right to carry their culture in the public domain, particularly since culture is seen as being a crucial element of their personal identity and context of choice.

A number of other problems also present themselves. Kymlicka's defence of community rights rests upon the belief that rights given against external pressures and those extended to protect the community against internal pressures are quite distinct. The difficulty, however, is that in actual practice it is extremely hard to separate these two kinds of rights. Special rights may be granted initially to shelter the community from pressures that come from the outside, but once they are granted, the community may use them in a way that it deems best. The

Pueblo Indians could, with the right to self-governance, decide that protecting their religious identity is crucial to their identity. Hence, they may ban conversions, or penalise members who convert to another religion. Likewise, indigenous communities may receive special rights to land for the sake of protecting their culture against external pressures, but since land–population ratio is important for sustaining their way of life, these communities may well stipulate restrictions upon their members. The fact that many groups have denied women who marry outside of the community rights to reservation land only reaffirms the possibility of special rights being used for limiting the options of some members. Kymlicka realises that rights obtained for the sake of minimising external pressures to assimilate may be used to curb individual choices. But since the latter is not a 'logical' extension of multicultural policies, he mentions it but does not take it to be a significant problem (Kymlicka, 1995: 41).

In fact, while discussing cases where national minorities have endorsed policies that restrict liberty of their members, Kymlicka merely recommends caution. He argues that just as liberal states are extremely careful about intervening in the affairs of other independent states that do not endorse liberal cultures, likewise they should be extremely cautious about interfering in the lives of illiberal national minorities. This is significant because even though the imposition of internal restrictions is not supported in his framework, their absence is not regarded as a necessary condition for granting special minority rights. Thus, the possibility of special rights being used for perpetuating oppressive communitarian practices remains.

Indeed, in a framework where special rights are advocated for the sake of protecting a minority culture, there is a very real chance that the community would place restraints upon its members. Take the case of the Amish community, for instance. Kymlicka defends special rights for them on the ground that these communities came to America with the assurance that they could continue with their distinct way of life. Unlike other immigrants, the Amish, he maintains, made their choice on the assumption that they would have the freedom to rebuild their societal culture. It is, therefore, the obligation of the state to honour that promise. Kymlicka takes this position even though this community frequently seeks special rights to minimise choices for its members and to suppress internal dissent. In many countries, the Amish have asked for rights to withdraw their children from school at an early age so that the young members are sheltered from external influences. Exposure to other ways of life, in their view, is likely to result in the disintegration of their culture. Thus, special community rights that they seek to protect a distinct way of life involve internal restrictions on members. Yet, Kymlicka accepts their claims for protecting and preserving their culture. Since the state is expected to acknowledge historical agreements, it is assumed that it must respect the community rights of these minorities, even if that violates the general condition under which special rights are justified.

Kymlicka does not place any restrictions upon the exercise of special community rights. He finds the introduction of such constraints as being both inadequate and unnecessary. Using, once again, the example of the indigenous people, he argues that 'many Indian leaders seek exemptions from the Bill/Charter of Rights, but at the same time affirm their commitment to the basic human rights and freedoms which underlie these constitutional documents. They endorse the principles, but object to the particular institutions and procedures that the larger society has established to enforce these principles' (Kymlicka, 1995: 40). Hence, from his perspective, there is no real need to limit their exercise of special rights. Here, the entire weight of his argument rests upon the fact that minorities in western liberal democracies by and large endorse the societal ethos. They accept the basic human rights even if they do not, at times, endorse institutions of representative democracy and an individual-centred ethic. This may indeed be the case but it only underscores the consensus on basic rights and political values that exists in these societies. It shows that the dominant societal ethic defines the lives of almost all communities in western democracies. This may be on account of the success of the democratisation process or their history of assimilation. Whatever be the reason, the liberal perspective on fairness and equal treatment is widely acknowledged, and Kymlicka's argument relies on this historical condition. It also suggests that minorities within the nation-state cannot for long pursue policies that contravene the core principles endorsed in society. Sooner than later, these communities have to change and alter their practices. Here again, it is the dominance of the liberal ethos in society that generates confidence that national minorities are not likely to endorse policies that appear to be blatantly discriminatory. Consequently, this line of reasoning can at best apply to contexts where the democratisation process has been quite successful. It cannot be taken as a statement about the nature of all national minorities.

Kymlicka is reluctant to accept limitations on special rights for another reason. He assumes that the state whose assimilationist policies have been the source of minority discrimination does not have a moral right to stipulate conditions. Besides, he fears that any attempt by the state to specify conditions for self-government, or other special rights, is bound to be perceived by the community as an act of continuing hostility. As such, it is unlikely to be accepted by them. In his view, since special rights are intended to bridge the gap between the oppressor and the oppressed and reverse the conditions of discrimination, they must not be qualified by any conditions. For this reason, he does not limit the exercise of special rights. Instead, he restricts the communities that can expect to receive special rights. But the latter, as we noted earlier, also yields a whole host of difficulties. In particular, the distinction that he makes between immigrant and national minorities remains deeply problematic. Besides, Kymlicka deals with the problem of minority discrimination not by attempting to create space by which the majority cultural orientation of the state can be checked. Instead of compelling the state to include minorities as equal partners in determining public decisions, he redresses the imbalance by empowering communities and giving them the right to determine their own affairs in their carefully defined territories. While this builds islands where minority communities may feel free from the pressures of the majority, it does not ensure that they have an equal status and voice in the deliberative processes of the state.

While elaborating on his multicultural schema, Kymlicka believes that minority communities would, when their cultures are protected, be willing to change and rethink their community practices. He assumes, for instance, that Indian American communities would re-examine the property rights of women and rectify present-day anomalies when they receive the right to self-governance. Submission to the Canadian Charter cannot, or should not, therefore be imposed as a condition for granting communities the right to govern themselves. In making this argument, Kymlicka, at least implicitly, accepts that an encounter with others is bound to alter a given way of life. As such, it is reasonable to suppose that these minority communities cannot, and will not, remain sheltered from the wider society in which they live. They will make the necessary changes to correct gender injustice, albeit by their own initiative. Kymlicka and many other multiculturalists emphasise that changes should, and they will, come from within the community but it is important to note that pressures to change arise from an interaction with a society in which basic principles of equality and liberty are extended to all persons. Internal voices of dissent begin to be counted, or at least they cannot be discounted altogether, when there are external societal pressures to change and incorporate these points of view.

The wider context in which these communities are placed is, therefore, extremely important. Kymlicka tends to neglect this dimension as he works with the idea that there is a distinction between 'cultural structure' and the 'content of culture'. He assumes that 'members are free to modify the character of the culture' (Kymlicka, 1991: 167) if they do not find any part of it desirable. He further believes that changes in the content of culture do not have any bearing on the cultural structure, which is identified as the context of choice. The latter is associated merely with linguistic and historical processes. To quote Kymlicka: '[O]ur language and our history are the media through which we come to an awareness of the options available to us, and their significance....' (*Ibid.*:165). Religion and other social practices through which a community constitutes itself, and which are perceived by insiders and outsiders as markers of their membership, are not taken as the basic constituents of a cultural identity here. In this highly secularised reading of cultural structure, where language and history are seen as the primary sources of identity, internal structures of power and inequality receive little attention.

The neglect of internal inequalities and the non-specification of any conditions for the exercise of special rights, other than those of good intentions, and the pervasiveness of a liberal democratic ethos, leaves many problems intact. Above all, it leaves the possibility of special rights being used to compel conformity with community practices. Consequently, many of the anxieties associated with the multicultural agenda of preserving minority cultures remain despite the purported distinction between community rights that protect against external pressures and those that empower against internal dissent. In fact, many of these difficulties get compounded as this framework continues to operate with a notion of homogeneous community. Special rights are given to the community against the assimilationist policies of the nation-state and it is with the leaders of the community that the state negotiates. In all such deliberations, it is assumed that the community speaks in one voice. This assumption of homogeneity places voices of internal dissent at a disadvantage. In most communities, it tends to silence the differences that are expressed by women. While special rights enable minority communities to enter the public arena, most marginalised groups within the community remain unrepresented. The disadvantages faced by the marginalised groups are further accentuated as this paradigm aims to preserve minority cultures. In conditions where institutions of authority are monopolised by the dominant groups, giving the community rights to determine the core structure and the practices that are constitutive of it, is likely to reinforce the hegemony of the prevailing elite.

The Limits of Permissible Diversity

The third multicultural response does not address the concerns of critics by restricting special community rights to merely the national minorities. Instead, it accepts that all ethnic minorities—religious and immigrant communities included—have a right to culture. It also acknowledges that equal treatment requires that minority cultures be recognised and accommodated in the public arena. However, while accepting the distinctive character of diverse cultures, it maintains that public recognition to minority cultures does not imply protection for all ethnic cultural practices. While the majority cannot expect minority communities to restrict their culture to the private domain, the minorities too must accept that some of their cultural practices may not be accepted in a liberal democracy. This perspective on multiculturalism emerges most sharply in the writings of Bhikhu Parekh. He argues that no political community is tolerant of all practices. Every society permits certain practices and forbids others. Hence, all forms of diversity cannot be accommodated within a democratic state. One needs therefore to reflect upon the prescribed 'limits of permissible diversity' (Parekh, 1994c: 214–17). Multiculturalism needs to examine the criterion that is currently used by liberals for stipulating what is permitted in a society. It also needs to scrutinise the practices of liberal democracies to reveal the inconsistencies in their attitude towards diverse cultural practices (see Parekh, 1994a).

In other words, what is argued here is that multiculturalism need not, indeed it should not, simply endorse all forms of cultural diversity. It must, instead, stipulate a norm for sifting between practiced diversity. For Bhikhu Parekh, neither the idea of individual autonomy nor the 'no-harm' principle is appropriate for prescribing the limits of permissible cultural diversity. The former reproduces the errors of assimilationist liberalism. It is dismissive of cultural diversity and is unable to accommodate community cultural practices—tattooing or circumcision, wearing a *chador* or a turban. Also, it can provide no acceptable grounds for demarcating reservation land or for accepting common ownership of property. The no-harm principle is equally problematic. When harm is equated simply with physical injury, it provides no legitimate basis for disallowing incest or polygamy. And when it is defined more broadly in terms of 'damaging the capacity for autonomy' it expresses the difficulties that confront the application of the autonomy principle (Parekh, 1994c: 214–15). Hence, the most commonly applied liberal criteria remains inadequate for prescribing the limits of permissible diversity.

In lieu of the liberal criteria, Bhikhu Parekh suggests that the 'operative public values enshrined in the Constitution' (*Ibid.*: 215–17) provide a more adequate basis for determining what is acceptable diversity within a society. Values that are incorporated in the Constitution shape the social and political institutions of society, and they structure its collective life. What is perhaps equally important is that these values are cherished by the political community as a whole. Even those who do not believe in the existing public values have to abide by them in the conduct of their affairs; and people who wish to change these norms also have to work within the parameters specified by them. As such, the operative public values provide the most adequate basis for determining what might be allowed or disallowed within a polity.

Within this framework of multiculturalism, operative public values can be used to determine what may or may not be accepted within a liberal society. Effectively, this means that minority practices that do not violate the operative public values can be permitted within a given liberal democracy. Instead of being dismissed entirely, we need to see if these practices are opposed to the shared public values. Parekh accepts that in almost all liberal polities, operative public values include respect for 'human dignity, equal respect for persons, secure spaces for self-determination, freedom for dissent and expression' (*Ibid.*· 216). However, each society defines, limits and cherishes these values differently. The operative public values enshrined in the Constitution become important as they give concrete meaning to these collectively valued goods. Hence, in any given society, it is the latter that must be the basis of negotiating the permissible limits of cultural diversity.

Bhikhu Parekh also accepts that the core values endorsed by liberal societies 'do not represent the best, let alone the only rational or truly human, way of organising human societies, but they are central to the historically developed moral self-conception of the liberal society' (*Ibid.*). As such, they can prescribe the limits of what a society will find acceptable or unacceptable within its boundaries. Prescribing the limits of permissible diversity with reference to the operative public values would certainly not allow for full equality to all cultural groups; nor would it permit all cultural practices to be accommodated within each society. Yet, in his view, it can offer a viable way of sorting diverse claims and identifying minority practices that may be accommodated within existing liberal societies.

While discussing the issue of permissible diversity, Parekh assumes that each society has a distinct character—one that is shaped by its distinct historical experiences. This historically specific orientation, which defines the identity of the nation-state, cannot simply be erased. Minorities need to negotiate with the majority with this awareness. In other words, they have to accept that there are a set of core values and sentiments that need to be acknowledged and respected by them. And even as they aspire to alter some of these values, they must not simply expect endorsement of all forms of diversity. They have to realise that the society in which they live cannot negate its distinctive identity and embrace everything. At the same time, the majority also needs to interrogate its prejudices. In particular, it needs to examine whether minority practices that are currently disallowed violate the operative public values. For instance, it needs to be seen if polygamy or clitoridectomy by an adult are incompatible with liberal public values (see Parekh, 1994b). Both the majority and the minority thus need to take cognisance of the operative public values that are enshrined in the Constitution.

The basic assumption of this framework is that misunderstanding takes place when the majority and the minority fail to take cognisance of the cultural differences that separate them. To negotiate with the other and live as equals both need to appreciate the specifics of each other's way of life. The majority has to realise that non-recognition of minority cultures disadvantages the members of these communities; at the same time, the minorities also have to accept that certain practices violate the values that the majority cherishes deeply. Both groups need to act with the awareness that the self is culturally embedded and it is with this consciousness that they must interact with the other (see Parekh, 1992). For Parekh the values that are enshrined in the Constitution reflect what large number of people prize in society, and what they are most reluctant to relinquish. All communities need to acknowledge this and they are required to operate within the space defined by the operative public values. Effectively, this means that minority communities can justifiably claim protection for those cultural practices that do not challenge the operational public values, and the majority must accede these claims for recognition.

The idea that some cultural practices may be unacceptable in liberal democratic societies, departs quite radically from much of multicultural theory. While most theorists emphasise the need to accommodate diverse cultural practices, this perspective raises the question of what may or may not be permissible in a society. It also accepts that some practices, which are incompatible with the collectively valued public goods, may not be permitted in a given society. This acknowledgement takes care of some liberal worries, for it allows each society to sift through minority practices and permit only those that do not violate the operative public values. Instead of stipulating that cultural rights be given only to minority cultures that are liberal in spirit, it allows the society to consider each minority practice individually with reference to the particularity of its own national history, culture and political norms.

This framework of multiculturalism values cultural diversity but it does not privilege it unconditionally. It maintains that it may be necessary to sift between minority claims that seek protection for cultural practices. While all minority cultures, in its view, deserve public recognition, it does not necessarily follow that all cultural practices of minorities can be protected, or even preserved, in a given society. Moreover, public recognition can come in many forms, from optional holidays for minority religious or cultural festivals to participation of state officials and majority leaders in these festivals, and multilingual education programmes. By emphasising the need for recognition, Parekh suggests that representation in the public domain is essential for creating an environment in which minorities feel included and represented. Granting recognition to minority cultures would necessarily introduce diversity in the public arena but it does not require unqualified defence of all practices. This shift in emphasis is significant. While accepting the need to protect cultures, it creates some room to weigh this priority against others. For example, the right of gypsies to continue with their distinct way of life, with the rights and needs of their children who need to acquire skills that will help them survive in the modern world.

In placing the rights of minorities along other rights Parekh does privilege the concern for equal treatment. Even though this does not reject the pursuit of cultural diversity, it does not lend unqualified support to the agenda of protecting minority cultures. While protecting cultural diversity remains a valued goal, it is now qualified a little. It is accepted so long as the pursuit of this goal does not violate the core public values of a society, especially as they are enshrined in the Constitution. This qualification is important, not because it takes care of several liberal apprehensions, but because it does not unilaterally privilege the agenda of preserving cultures and diversity. Implicitly at least, it accepts that preserving minority cultures may not be either possible or desirable. However, its suggestion that we sift minority claims on the basis of operative public values is not entirely free of difficulties. In many societies, collectively shared values that are endorsed through interpretations of the Constitution reflect merely the preferences of the majority community. In France, for instance, the school authorities disallowed Muslim girls from wearing the headscarf (*hijab*) to school on the ground that the display or use of ostentatious religious symbols violates the operative public value of *Laicite* (secularism). In North America, the right to private property, which is an inviolable fundamental right and a cherished public value, was used to justify the parcelling of tribal land into separate allotments. Thus, operative public values have often been interpreted in a way that has disadvantaged minorities and promoted cultural uniformity.

Bhikhu Parekh does not address these problems because he assumes that in a liberal polity, the Constitution usually embodies principles that have shaped contemporary democratic sensibilities, namely, equal respect for all and freedom of belief and expression. Since there is a high degree of consensus around these values, they can easily be applied to draw the boundaries of what is or is not permitted in society. However, what needs to be inserted here is that constitutions often reflect the prevailing consensus in society. The goals that are stipulated within the Constitution and the priorities accorded to specific values express the aspirations of the citizens living in a determinate historical time. The Constitution is, therefore, to be viewed as a historical text.

What is perhaps equally important is that the Constitution does not always speak in a single voice. In India, for instance, the Constitution endorsed freedom of religious worship and practice and equality for all as basic public values. However, given the exigencies of that time, it accorded, in some places, priority to the first. Hence, community Personal Laws were permitted even though many realised that community codes tend to treat women unfairly. However, given the commitment to equality for all, the framers of the Indian Constitution stipulated the desirability of having a Uniform Civil Code which would be more just in its treatment to women. Here, reference to merely the operative public values is not enough because it can be used equally for continuing with practices that are unjust to women, or for legislating to change these practices. Consequently, the criterion of operative public values does not provide adequate safeguards against various forms of discrimination.

Parekh assumes that equal respect for all persons is an operative public value in almost all liberal democracies, and it could be used to interrogate existing state practices. However, as we just noted, this value co-exists with many other norms and it receives a specific meaning in association with them. Hence, it needs to be prioritised and defined in a way that allows respect for individuals as citizens and as members of diverse communities.

In Lieu of a General Theory of Community Rights

The fourth multicultural response addresses liberal concerns by prescribing moral limits to the exercise of special rights. While it endorses the concern for protecting the collective cultural identity of minorities, it maintains that all special rights for preserving cultures cannot be admitted unconditionally. Special rights may be given to minorities for protecting culture only when this goal is collectively valued and where it is viable and good for the community to pursue this goal. There is a further condition attached to the exercise of special rights by minorities: namely, that the pursuit of cultural preservation must not jettison the principle of human moral equality (see Carens, 1992). The justification of separate rights for minorities requires the fulfilment of all these provisions. Effectively, this means that all minorities, which claim to be oppressed or marginalised, cannot expect to get special rights, specially the rights to self-government or separate representation. A collective cultural identity and the fact of being oppressed are necessary but not sufficient conditions for getting special consideration in this framework.

Delineating this point of view, Joseph Carens argues that a collectively shared and valued cultural identity is only a minimum condition for seeking special consideration. Rights may be given to communities to preserve their identity, if preserving that identity is feasible and pursuing this goal is likely to include the community as an equal partner in the polity. He also stipulates, what might be called, moral limitations upon the exercise of minority rights. Rights given to minorities, he writes, cannot be used to deny equal political citizenship to other groups; nor can they be used for promoting practices that vitiate the equal moral worth of all persons. Thus, for instance, cultural difference cannot be applied to support the ritual killing of slaves or for genital mutilation of young girls (Carens, 1992: 623 and 653). Liberal democratic states can prohibit such practices, indeed, they may prescribe rules about the legal rights of individuals.

Thus, in this framework, separate rights for preserving the collective cultural identity of minorities are entertained but, in each instance, they require some justification. Moreover, Carens maintains that the conditions outlined only provide a minimum criterion under which differentiated rights might be considered. They do not offer an exhaustive schema for sorting all minority claims. Indeed, he argues against a general theory of minority rights. Instead of specifying the rights that should be given to a particular kind of minority, he recommends a 'contextual' approach (Carens, 2000: 21–28). The application of this approach means that specific claims of each minority have to be examined separately and with regard to such specifics as the history of the community, nature of the nation-state and the kind of rights that are claimed. In other words, one can no longer say what rights should be given to immigrants or religious minorities or national minorities. The claims of each community have to be judged individually. Hence, giving rights to one minority does not provide any justification for similar rights for another community. Each case is considered unique and has to be discussed in its specifics.

It is within the ambit of this context-specific approach that Carens considers all other questions; for example, whether special rights for cultural preservation are good for the community as a whole; whether the use of special rights is likely to violate the basic principles of democratic equality. Consequently, no one condition is considered to be absolutely crucial; nor can one say in absolute terms when a special right is warranted or when it should be withdrawn. All claims have to be judged individually and with relation to the specific context in which they are raised. Special rights may be considered if they help promote the integration of a minority community, or to minimise its sense of marginalisation, or even to protect a collectively valued good. These are all conditions in which we might approach the issue of differentiated rights positively. In general terms, all that can be said is that benefits of granting special treatment have to be weighed. Since a sense of exclusion and unfair treatment induce alienation among members of the community, what has to be considered is whether giving special rights would enhance 'genuine inclusion' of the community in the polity (Carens, 1996–97: 120). At the same time, the exercise of special rights by the minority is also a pertinent factor. When minorities protect their identity and exercise their rights in a manner that does not violate or undermine the basic rights of other communities, there is good reason to continue with these special rights.

Like all other theories of multiculturalism, Carens' contextual approach begins by acknowledging the value of cultural community identity. Hence, it accepts preservation of a collective identity as a viable and desirable goal. However, keeping in mind the liberal anxieties about community rights and preserving cultures, it suggests that we look at each case by itself. Instead of closing the option of special rights for minorities, we might see if a particular minority should be given these rights. In other words, its intention is not to question the goal of cultural preservation or to challenge the idea of group-differentiated rights. It endorses both these ends but accepts that we, as historical subjects, are also constituted by our contexts. Hence, the principle of equal treatment to all is an important concern for us. It cannot be simply ignored. It is a condition, one among many, which needs also to be taken into account while assessing minority claims.

Some of these aspects, particularly the consideration given to protecting collective cultural identity, become clear when we turn to his analysis and justification for special rights for specific minorities. In the case of Quebec, Carens argues that special rights are warranted as they allow the people to preserve their French cultural identity which they cherish deeply. That the people of Quebec protect the rights of their internal minorities and endorse the ideals of political community which are cherished in Canada further strengthens their claims for differentiated rights (see Carens, 2000: 107–39). Similarly, in the case of the aboriginal populations of North America, he supports special land rights as they are necessary for preserving their culture, and the latter are in the best interest of the community as a whole. Extending the same logic to the case of Fiji, Carens argues that restrictions upon the sale of native Fijian land were desirable because they were necessary for the economic and cultural stability of the community. Since alienation from their land resulted in the impoverishment and marginalisation of indigenous communities everywhere else, special laws for native Fijians in this regard were altogether justified. They enabled the native Fijians to 'maintain a relatively stable and coherent way of life over the last century or so' (Carens, 1992: 576). Even today, special land rights may be given if they are found essential for preserving that way of life. The only limitation being that preservation of culture should not be a means of denying the political rights of Indian Fijians who have lived there all their life.

In each of these cases, protecting a cultural identity is, to borrow a phrase from Jeff Spinner, contingently privileged (Spinner: Forthcoming). That is, a variety of other considerations weigh in assessing the claims of minorities for special rights. In the foregoing cases, the desire to protect a collective identity, the gains from preserving it, and the treatment towards internal minorities within the region, are conditions that justify special rights for each of these communities. Since special rights are given here, for instance, to Quebec as it fulfils these conditions, one cannot now say that similar rights should be extended to other provinces of Canada. However, when special consideration for Quebec is accepted, all measures that help realise the goal of preserving the French identity can be easily defended. Special representation for Quebec in the Department of Immigration and in the Supreme Court can be upheld. Likewise, the existence of laws that prescribe education for the children of immigrants in French schools and stipulate minimum years of residence for new immigrants to Quebec, are also endorsed for the sake of preserving French culture and identity (see Carens, 2000: 129–39). Here, the only internal minorities whose rights are upheld are the Anglophones, i.e., the dominant community in the rest of the country. The rights of the immigrants, as well as those of the members of the Francophone community, to differ from the collectively defined good merit no consideration. So long as the Anglophones have the option of sending their children to schools where English is the medium of instruction, it is said that Quebec can legislate to preserve its identity. Restricting the options of the immigrants who come to stay in Quebec as well as the French community is not a sufficiently important consideration for which the right of Quebec to preserve its identity should be reconsidered. It is assumed that all the people of Quebec collectively value their identity and are therefore willing to make these sacrifices. Having a community identity and valuing it is thus equated with the desire to preserve that identity.

Thus, despite all the qualifications, in this framework too special community rights are granted and supported for the sake of preserving a culture. In fact, the latter even justifies restrictions on internal members of the community. Even though special rights are not extended to all minorities, communities that receive special rights are given considerable space to pursue cultural preservation. Moreover, the assumption of human moral worth and accompanying liberal values only constitute normative commitments within this framework. Carens, for instance, does not stipulate adherence to these norms as a condition for granting special rights. Commitment to the Canadian Charter and the legitimacy of the demands for gender equality are thus acknowledged but they are not regarded as necessary conditions that must be fulfilled before special rights are granted to Native American communities. Similarly, he recommends the ideal of common franchise for Fiji but is willing to endorse the special claims of native Fijians with regard to land even though these necessarily deprive Indian Fijians (for whom Fiji is the only homeland) of the security and prestige that stems from ownership of land. In other words, liberal sensibilities notwithstanding, the concern for preserving cultures and cultural identities remains directly or indirectly the overriding concern, even in this framework.

This is, of course, not unique to this framework of multiculturalism. All theories of multiculturalism are equally steadfast in their commitment to the ideal of cultural preservation. While some accept the relevance of liberal objections in this regard, others see little merit in them. But all of them feel that marginalised minorities that have a distinct cultural identity, can seek special rights to preserve their cultures against external pressures. A few multiculturalists accept that liberal democracies may not permit all types of minority cultural practices, but they too agree that cultural identity is a collectively valued good that must receive due recognition from liberal democracies. Group-differentiated rights are expected to assist communities in preserving their cultural identity. Consequently, the commitment to preserve oppressed minority cultures remains the unquestioned value in all theories of multiculturalism; and it is this that needs to be interrogated seriously.

Focusing on the specifics of a context, nevertheless, adds a new dimension to the thinking of multiculturalism. It delinks diverse minority claims from one another and permits separate policies in each case. This leaves sufficient room for practical and pragmatic considerations to enter into the picture while discussing specific claims. It also enables a better appreciation of the implications of a specific policy. By focusing on the particularities

(such as the place of the Hindu majoritarian party in the government, its policy on cultural assimilation) we might, for instance,
understand why the minority community and the women's movements are reluctant to endorse legislation for a uniform civil code
at the present conjuncture. Likewise, one might also understand
why the Muslims and the Christians are unlikely to accept the
initiatives of the present Indian government in this regard. Thus,
dwelling on the specifics of a group history can sensitise us to
the point of view of the other. It can even assuage some liberal
apprehensions about special rights. But that is about all.

In a situation of considerable inequality, a contextual approach
that advises each case to be considered separately, allows a lot
of room for the politics of patronage. If special rights to one
community place no corresponding obligation to extend similar
rights to others, then groups which have the ability to effectively
mobilise political resources are likely to emerge as winners.
Communities that are the worst-off, small, marginalised and lacking in political skills of communication and mobilisation, may
well remain on the periphery. Hence, what is needed is a more
stringent criterion of inclusion and exclusion so that minorities
are not left searching for patrons in their quest for equality.

The contextual approach is not sufficiently attentive to this
dimension of group assertions. It does not also question the
ideal of protecting and promoting a cultural community identity.
It assumes that having a community identity and valuing it entails acting to preserve it, and the institutions that are constitutive of it. It is this understanding of the relationship between
community identity and cultural preservation that is deeply problematic and needs to be re-thought. This is not, however, a task
that this particular framework alone needs to undertake. All theories of multiculturalism endorse the goal of preserving a community culture. While challenging the assimilationist agenda of the
nation-state, they recommend special rights to protect minority
cultures and the practices that are collectively valued. It is this
commitment to preserving cultures and making them secure that
leaves many issues unresolved. In particular, it paints a picture
of fixed identities, clearly identified, near-permanent group formations, homogeneous communities and monolithic, timeless

cultures. These representations of cultural communities tend to privilege the voice of the dominant sections and foreclose choices for the members. Hence, it is this dimension of multiculturalism that needs to be reconsidered seriously.

Perhaps the most important element in this regard is to dissociate community identity and membership from the commitment to preserve it. It is not sufficient to say that cultures are being protected against external threats but not from those that come from within. As we noted earlier on, it is exceedingly difficult to maintain this distinction, and in most cases, rights given for safeguarding the community against pressures from the outside can, and are, used to place restrictions on the members. Shah Bano, for instance, was persuaded to give up the maintenance allotted to her by the Court on grounds of protecting the community against external interventions.

Examples of this kind can be found everywhere, and they point to the problems that invariably arise when protecting and promoting a culture is the primary consideration for sifting between minority claims for special rights. There is no doubt that cultural identities are important and they do define, in part, who we are. Individuals also cherish these identities; indeed, when these are challenged or vilified by the nation-state, members tend to coalesce together. At times, they even articulate a shared interest in asserting that identity publicly. However, all such assertions of identity in the public domain have to be contextualised and we need to be extremely cautious in assuming that they suggest the need to protect that identity. Besides, when we take a relational view of identity, it becomes evident that asserting an identity and acknowledging certain shared symbols as markers of that identity are instruments of challenging state policies. They seek to check attempts to marginalise or decry a community membership rather than suggest the commitment of members to protect that culture or the existing practices associated with it. To put it another way, in a democracy many assertions of community identity aim to limit or question interference by the state. What community members defy stridently are attempts by the state to redefine their identity and to alter or control community institutions. But once again, owning these institutions as symbols of one's identity is not the same as claiming that these institutions represent the community as a whole or that they are its sole spokesperson.

Take, for instance, the case of the Sikh community in India. The Shiromani Gurudwara Prabandhak Committee (SGPC) was set up in 1925 by Malcolm Hailey. The committee was an elected body and was open to all persons who averred their faith in the ten Gurus and the holy book, *Guru Granth Sahib*. Even though in 1934 the SGPC modified this a little to say that its members must observe the *'Rehat Maryada'* and endorse the five 'Ks', the membership is still quite unrestricted and dependent primarily upon the person's avowed commitment to the faith. The SGPC was constituted in this fashion keeping in mind the demands of the community for a separate body that could manage and control community institutions. It was then, and even today continues to be, a sign of Sikh identity. Its existence and autonomy from the state machinery is favoured and strongly desired. Yet, despite all this, less than 20 per cent of the Sikh population in the country have registered themselves as members of this body.

This is important, more so because this is an open and voluntary body which the community sees as being associated with it very closely. One needs to take cognisance of these seemingly paradoxical elements because these are constitutive of community membership in a democratic polity. They indicate both the fact that people value their collective membership and also that they see themselves as distinct from it. Respect for their group identity and equal space for it in the public arena may constitute the shared interests of the community, but beyond that there are differences and no one institution can be seen as representing the collective interest of the community. Indeed, there are no collective interests except in this minimal sense.

The problem with much of contemporary multicultural theory is that it often conflates membership with the demand for protecting and preserving a community culture. And, in line with this point of view the state too negotiates just with recognised community institutions that have existed over a long period of time. This inevitably empowers these institutions but the voices they express, whatever be the pattern of their membership, remain unrepresentative of the community because there is no one voice in the community that can claim to represent a collective interest, let alone a shared substantive good. Multiculturalism needs to acknowledge this dimension of community membership and abandon the priority it accords to protecting and preserving a collective community identity and culture.

8

Rethinking Multiculturalism

The significance of multicultural political theory is that it has raised the issue of culture-based discrimination in society. While previous theories of democracy emphasised the individual and were culture-blind, multiculturalism shows that indifference to cultural differences can shelter prejudices. In a liberal democracy, culture blindness often entails an unquestioned acceptance of the norms that express the culture of the majority. This does not mean that other groups and communities are excluded from the public domain; they may indeed be included but they are expected to conform to the practices of the majority. They can enter the public sphere, but in ways that their presence remains more or less invisible.

Multiculturalism reveals these biases of the dominant liberal model of democracy and demonstrates that cultural identities are also a source of discrimination in society. What is perhaps equally important is that multiculturalism shows that this form of discrimination exists even in western liberal democracies. Thus, even societies that pride themselves for affirming the ideal of fair and equal treatment to all are not immune to this form of discrimination. Indeed, culture-based discrimination may persist even after equal rights are granted to all persons in their capacity as citizens. The idea that cultural differences are also a source of disadvantage and discrimination in society is the unique contribution of multiculturalism to democratic theory.

In a democracy, the principle of non-discrimination is the central, if not the defining, value. The idea that no one should be discriminated against on account of his or her ascribed social identity is the distinguishing mark of a democracy—one that sets it apart from all other forms of political organisation. As and when an ascribed identity, such as race, religion or gender, becomes a source of exclusion, disadvantage or unfair treatment, it constitutes an injustice in a democracy and needs to be rectified. *Vice-versa*, when a social identity is used to differentiate between people in a democracy, it too needs to be justified. It must be shown that differentiation on the basis of an ascribed identity does not constitute an unacceptable disadvantage to others, and that it is necessary for enhancing equal treatment to all. Commitment to the notion of non-discrimination is, in this dual sense, an essential and inviolable norm of democracy.

Endorsing the principle of non-discrimination, however, entails constant vigilance. Democracies have to be continuously cautious about the possibility that ascribed and received identities can be a source of disadvantage and unfair treatment. Searching for these sites of discrimination and devising strategies to eliminate them is, therefore, the mainspring of the project of democratisation. Historically, democracies emerged by challenging the link between noble birth, landed status and political privileges. Subsequent struggles of the oppressed and marginalised pointed to other forms of identity-based discrimination. They perceived religion, race and gender as sources of discrimination in society. Their efforts to dismantle prevailing structures of unequal treatment assisted in the process of democratisation. Multicultural political theory has contributed to this project by pointing to the unequal treatment of marginalised minorities in the nation-state. By indicating culture-based discrimination that may exist even after political rights are granted to all persons as citizens, it has raised issues that no democracy can ignore.

The identification of cultural identity as a possible ground for discrimination has set a new agenda for liberal democracies everywhere. The awareness that assimilation and coercive inclusion, like forced exclusion, is a mode of discrimination, has added a new dimension to the idea of identity-based discrimination. It has, indeed, enriched the discourse of democracy. However, the issue of culture-based discrimination has received a specific articulation within contemporary theories of multiculturalism. Since most of the theorisation on the subject has come from liberal democracies of the West, it is structured and shaped by the uniqueness of that experience. It is anchored in the experiences of those democracies; and more importantly, it is structured by the specificity of that historical context.

The notion of culture-based discrimination, its precise nature and form, the language of multicultural discourse, the goal of cultural preservation, have all been shaped by the particularity of the western context. Theorisation on multiculturalism has, as a result, taken a distinct course: one where a nation-state is the main site of cultural discrimination, special community rights the most appropriate form of countering that discrimination, and preserving minority cultures a mode of minimising discrimination and enhancing diversity. Each of these dimensions of multicultural political theory need to be reconsidered carefully, because they conceptualise the issue of minority discrimination rather narrowly, and sanction rights for the sake of promoting cultural diversity rather than minimising discrimination.

Nation-state as the Site of Cultural Discrimination

All theories are context-specific and multiculturalism is no exception. The pronouncements of contemporary multiculturalists are structured by the historical experiences of western liberal democracies. While the questions of culture-based discrimination and minority marginalisation concern all democracies, and India was among the first few to reflect upon the position of minorities in the polity, nevertheless, these subjects have received a specific articulation in the western context. They have been imbued with meanings that express the particularity of that experience. Moreover, the delineation of the minority problem and the viability of special rights have also been assessed and interpreted in the light of American and European experience. It is, therefore, necessary to step outside this context to see the forms that cultural discrimination takes in different historical formations.

Diverse historical contexts reveal, as Hegel reminds us, the many ways in which the concept manifests itself in the concrete. So it is through the study of these concrete expressions that we can understand the distinct dimensions and meanings of the concept. If, however, we focus upon any one single expression, we are likely to end with an impoverished view of that concept.

What is perhaps even worse, we are likely to reduce the concept to a single form that it has in a given historical context. To avoid the pitfalls of this kind of essentialism, and to enrich the analysis of multiculturalism, it is therefore necessary to reflect upon the different expressions of cultural discrimination, and rethink the agenda of multiculturalism in the light of these concrete expressions.

The most distinctive feature of contemporary multiculturalism, as it has been theorised in the West, is that it locates the issue of cultural discrimination in the context of the nation-state. Most of these theories focus on discrimination that minority communities face on account of the cultural orientation of the nation-state. The policies of the nation-state, especially on language, education, public holidays, religious and cultural festivals, privilege the majority culture and simultaneously disadvantage the minorities. The discrimination that minorities suffer as their cultures are excluded from the public domain and the pressures that these communities face to assimilate into the majority culture, form the core of western multicultural discourse. Indeed, it defines their conception of cultural discrimination.

Within this frame of analysis, the nation-state is seen as the primary source of minority discrimination in society. Further, the twin notions of preserving minority cultures and granting group-differentiated rights are mooted to counter discrimination that occurs due to the ethnic and cultural character of state. The singular emphasis on the majoritarian cultural biases and the homogenising policies of the state thus structures the concept of culture-based discrimination in these theories of multiculturalism. This specific notion of cultural discrimination has emerged against the backdrop of a state that has, for almost four centuries, actively pursued policies of homogenisation and cultural assimilation. The nation-states in Europe and America played a critical role in constructing an ethnic majority. Through policies of an officially recognised national religion and language, these states welded an ethnic majority; at the same time, they excluded and systematically marginalised populations that failed to endorse the cultural identity of the nation-state. Thus, in these societies the public space was, for a long time, completely monopolised by the constructed majority. Indeed, the culture of the nation-state was inextricably linked to the culture of the majority. The implication of the state in the construction of an ethnic majority and its persecution of communities that did not affirm the cultural identity of the nation-state, are the distinguishing marks of the western experience. And it is this experience that informs the notion of cultural discrimination in theories of multiculturalism that has come from the West.

Endorsement by the nation-state of the culture of the majority and the accompanying policies of assimilation are almost always sources of minority discrimination. However, the singular emphasis on the nation-state as the site of discrimination is quite limiting. There are often other equally important sites of cultural discrimination and these too need to be considered within the framework of multiculturalism. For instance, in India, special rights have been granted to the minorities by the Constitution itself. At the time of framing the Constitution, the minorities were anxious that the independent state might take on the identity of the religious majority and impose an agenda of cultural homogenisation. Consequently, to allay these fears, the Constitution provided special rights for minorities to protect their distinctive cultural and linguistic identity. Among other things, the minorities were entitled to establish their own educational institutions and these were eligible for funding by the state. Although the state has no obligation to provide assistance to these institutions, nevertheless, if funds are given to other educational institutions, minority establishments cannot be excluded (Mahajan, 1998a: 97–101). In addition to it, the state gave recognition to community Personal Codes, which were to govern individuals on matters of family. It also accorded communities the right to continue with their religious practices. Although the state in Independent India has not been completely neutral or equidistant from all communities, minority cultures and practices have received some public recognition. Public holidays on religious and cultural festivals of the minorities, participation of state officials on these occasions, acceptance of multiple codes of dress and official recognition to several minority languages, are some of the ways in which public space has been created for minority communities. Although specific linguistic identities received recognition after considerable struggle by each group, and even today rights granted to cultural minorities are not always adequately protected; yet, in principle at least, cultural minorities are acknowledged and accommodated in the public domain.

Discrimination by Other Cultures Within the Nation-state

In India, the cultural rights of religious and other minorities are recognised by the Constitution. While there is lingering anxiety—especially at the present moment—that some political parties in government may try to introduce changes in the Constitution which may undermine the framework of group equality, so far the minorities have not been excluded from the public domain. At least non-recognition of cultural minorities and their practices is not the primary source of disadvantage and discrimination. Instead, it is the actions of other groups in society and the complicity of the government officials that is a major source of minority discrimination. To say this is not to deny the possibility that the state can—and at times even has—expressed the sentiments of the cultural majority, but only to highlight that the religious and cultural orientation of the state are not the only sources of discrimination of minorities in India. Time and again, communities have suffered on account of the actions of other communities and political groups in society. As collective identities are constructed in relation to the 'other', the way they are perceived and represented by others is crucial to their self-identification. Just as denying public recognition harms the other, similarly the representation of a community as an 'outsider' or 'anti-national' serves to exclude and discriminate it in the public arena. In India, the construction of specific groups as hostile 'others' has been a common form of discrimination of minorities, and it is not just the officially recognised minorities that have been victimised in this process. In the 1960s, the Shiv Sena targeted the South Indian community living in Mumbai and initiated a virulent attack on them. Labelling this community as 'outsiders' who had usurped the rightful place of the 'native' Maharashtrians, the Shiv Sena accused the South Indians of taking away jobs and positions from the 'natives'. To ensure that jobs in the city go to Marathi speakers, the Shiv Sena singled out and pressured individuals and groups into hiring Maharashtrians. The Shiv Sena subsequently targeted the Communists, and later, the Muslims, with a similar strategy (see Gupta, 1982). In both cases, they dubbed these groups as anti-national elements whose loyalty lay outside the territory of the nation-state. This gave them enough reason to castigate individual members of the group and demand proof of their loyalty to the nation-state. In all these instances, the representation of specific communities as 'outsiders' was a mode of discriminating against them and disadvantaging them in the public arena.

Discrimination that occurs through the representation of communities as hostile others is reinforced more stridently by acts of communal violence. In India, violence directed at members of a specific community is perhaps the severest but most frequent expression of minority discrimination in India. The trauma of sudden and sporadic violence that results in the death and destruction of innumerable community members, brings home the reality of being an alien and unaccepted minority. The irrationality of the act, and frequently, the complicity of state authorities, is a continuous reminder to the victims of their marginalised minority status. In a way, the perpetrators of communal violence seek to give this message repeatedly to the minorities. Just coping with this continuous reality of insecurity and fear reinforces minority consciousness among the victims. It makes them vulnerable and disadvantaged minorities, whose very existence and right to life is under threat.

Are Special Rights for Communities Enough?

The exclusion of minorities from the public domain on account of the ethnic orientation of the nation-state and their discrimination by sectarian groups in society constitute two distinct sources of minority discrimination, and they require different strategies. However, within the multicultural frame, the latter form of discrimination has received little attention. Since western discourses of multiculturalism focus primarily on the nation-state, its assimilationist policies and non-recognition of cultural differences in the public domain, cultural identity-based discrimination that stems from the actions of other communities and groups in society has not been seriously considered.

The neglect of other sites of cultural discrimination and the exclusive focus on the cultural identity of the nation-state as a source of discrimination, are relevant because they have shaped the multicultural response to the issue of minority discrimination. Most theories of multiculturalism advocate group-differentiated rights for identified minority communities in order to correct the majoritarian cultural biases of the nation-state and create space for minority cultures in the public domain. Rights claiming exemption, assistance, recognition, or even separate representation, are defended for the sake of minimising discrimination that arises from the cultural character of the nation-state. At times, they enable marginalised minorities to carry their culture into the public domain, but they are nevertheless ineffective in checking the discrimination that these communities suffer due to the actions of other groups in society. Indeed, they are not intended for that purpose and cannot provide any safeguard against the latter. When cultural identities are the basis on which majority groups target specific minorities, what is often required, as a minimum condition for fairness, is an unequivocal defence of the rights of individuals as citizens. Unless the state takes the responsibility of protecting the basic rights of all its citizens and punishing those who violate them, discrimination of this kind is bound to persist. Consequently, the state has to be pressured to uphold the universal rights of citizenship as a condition for equal treatment of all cultures and communities.

This needs to be asserted forcefully because in the debates around multiculturalism, community rights have been pitted against individual rights. Against the backdrop of a homogenising nation-state that almost always embodies the culture of the majority, cultural community rights and individual rights have been transformed into binary opposites. It is assumed that discrimination of minorities can only be overcome by granting special community rights. It appears that individual rights have little or no role to play in this. What is being argued here, particularly with

reference to Indian experiences, is that discrimination faced by
minorities requires that we do not think in terms of either cultural community rights or individual rights of citizenship. The
two are not mutually exclusive. While special rights given to
cultural communities can help to correct the majoritarian biases
of the nation-state and enable minorities to retain their identity,
individual rights are essential, and indispensable, for protecting
minorities from discrimination by the actions of other groups in
society. Oppression that emerges from the hostility and violence
of the dominant community and other groups in society require
unambiguous defence of individual rights of citizenship. Discrimination of marginalised and vulnerable minorities cannot
be eliminated in the absence of the latter.

Eliminating Cultural Discrimination
Or Preserving Minority Cultures

Another particularity of the western discourses on multiculturalism—and one that needs to be examined critically—is that it
privileges, contingently or otherwise, the task of promoting cultural diversity. On most occasions this goal is prioritised because it is
regarded to be the most appropriate way of challenging policies
of homogenisation and minority discrimination. Since multiculturalism sees the suppression or exclusion of minority cultural
practices as signs of their discrimination, it maintains that by
incorporating diversity in the public arena, minority communities would be able to protect their identities, make their cultures
secure and be included as equals in the polity. To a considerable
extent, this understanding of discrimination and the accompanying link between promoting cultural diversity and minimising
minority marginalisation has been shaped by the experiences of
the indigenous population in North America. Historically, the
indigenous people of North America were victims of the most
coercive forms of cultural assimilation. The Federal government,
through a series of laws, destroyed their way of life and systematically eliminated their aboriginal identity. Under 'Potlatch laws'
the government prohibited a number of aboriginal practices and
declared them punishable by law. In many cases, they took the

children away from their families and placed them in residential schools or in foster homes. Such oppressive measures of cultural assimilation were supplemented by changes in the economic and political life of the community. The tribal land was divided and portioned to individual families. At the same time, the communities were placed under the 'care' of the Federal government. They were deemed unfit for self-government and were expected to seek permission of the Federal government for selling land that was legally theirs. The communities were also not allowed to mortgage their land or form corporations without the consent of the Federal authorities. Thus, the cultural identity of these communities and, with it, their way of life was systematically destroyed.

It is against the background of these experiences, where the imposed homogeneity by the state was directly aimed at the destruction of the aboriginal identity that the ideal of protecting minority cultures and promoting cultural diversity was initially mooted and defended within multiculturalism. It has since been extended to include other national minorities, such as the people of Quebec. In all such cases, creating conditions in which a collectively valued way of life can be protected is represented as a way of minimising the discrimination faced by these minorities. This belief that safeguarding a culturally distinct way of life is necessary for promoting fairness and minimising minority discrimination is however quite problematic. As was observed in the preceding chapters, measures aimed at enhancing diversity and protecting minority cultures tend to sanction existing practices and traditional structures of authority. As they aim primarily to challenge the interventions of the state, they privilege the voice of the community and remain largely inattentive to the inequalities of power within the community. Since policies framed with a view to promoting cultural diversity almost always empower and strengthen communities, it is necessary to re-think this agenda. Besides, a close look at the indigenous people shows that even in their case the ideal of enhancing cultural diversity and preserving minority cultures remains inadequate, both for expressing their interests and for reducing their sense of discrimination. Indeed, many indigenous communities do not even present their claims in the language of protection and cultural preservation. Although within multiculturalism, the rights of Native Americans to their reservation land, control and management of their resources and tribal cultural practices are defended for the sake of making these cultural communities secure, these communities themselves assert their claims as rights due to them as First Nations. They challenge Federal authority and seek autonomy not to protect their culture but to assert that these are Treaty Rights that are justifiably due to them. That is, they wish to restore the status that they had as separate Nations within the polity and it is in this capacity that they seek these rights. While the endorsement of these rights may entail a framework of differentiated rights, but these are not simply measures aimed at preserving their cultures and identities. In fact, in several cases where indigenous communities have rights over land and other resources linked to it, they have used them not to continue with the traditional modes of economy, but to have the freedom to explore other options. Hence, it is perhaps inappropriate to represent their claims for independent status, most often within the framework of a federal polity, as rights to preserve their cultural context of experience. Indeed, as and when these rights to special status have been interpreted, or perceived as being rights to preserve the culture, they have met with resistance from many quarters, including some aboriginal women's groups.

Leaving the case of the indigenous people aside, there is a much deeper problem presented by the agenda of preserving cultures. The policy of protecting and preserving minority cultures assumes that the assertion of one's cultural identity manifests the desire to protect that culture. Since belonging to a community and valuing its membership is associated with collective commitment to a set of shared goods, affirming one's cultural identity is interpreted as a demand for protecting those shared goods and goals. It is this purported link between having/asserting an identity and seeking to protect and even preserve that culture that is deeply problematic. This understanding of cultural identity needs to be interrogated for it transforms the assertion of difference and distinctiveness into a policy of preserving a culture and its defining practices.

Theories of multiculturalism need to make a distinction between having an identity and protecting it. No doubt individuals belong to specific communities and, in part at least, their actions derive their meaning from these memberships. However, this does not mean that they affirm or seek to protect the different practices and symbols associated with that cultural identity. The expression and construction of an identity is context-specific. At times, people assert their distinctiveness to protest against assimilation, and at other times, they may express it to have the option of continuing with a particular practice. To take an example: when Sikhs protest against the law that requires all scooter/motorcycle riders to wear a helmet, they assert collectively that the turban is the prescribed headdress for members of their community. To challenge the action of the state and to assert their distinct identity, they rally together and underline the importance of the turban as a sign of their separate religious and cultural identity. However, wearing of the turban on this occasion and the collective assertion of the value of this symbol does not imply that all members of the community seek to protect and preserve that practice. In fact, many of the protesters may themselves not be observing this practice in everyday life. They may simply don the turban to oppose the actions of the state and support those who wish to continue with wearing the turban. The chosen expression of their identity here aims to secure for members of the community the *option of* wearing the turban. Even as the community members affirm the importance of this symbol, it does not imply that all members actually observe this practice and wear the turban, or that measures be taken to ensure that this practice survives. One needs to make this distinction between valuing an identity, or the practices and symbols associated with it, and seeking to preserve it.

In 1984, after the anti-Sikh riots in Delhi and elsewhere in the country, many individuals asserted their religious identity, valued it and communicated their solidarity with the victimised community by wearing the turban, even though they had not done that for several years. Wearing the turban was a sign that was privileged under the circumstances and there is nothing to say that this will not change if perceived threat and humiliation diminishes. Likewise, those who stopped wearing a turban for fear of being persecuted may also change their perception. Community practices, like the chosen symbols of identity, are thus subject to continuous redefinition and negotiation. The language of protection and preservation is for this reason quite inappropriate for discussing community membership. Indeed, it invariably helps restrict options for internal members. To say that community cultures be protected only against external pressures does not also solve the problem. It too restricts choices for internal members and promotes conformity with existing practices. Consequently, it is necessary to abandon the agenda of preserving cultures by making a distinction between accommodations made with a view to giving internal members the choice of continuing with a way of life, if they so choose, from rights granted to protect a culture.

Within a community, almost all practices, no matter how deeply valued they may be, are subject to multiple readings and assessments. Religious communities and sects do not always allow space for the expression of these differences. In order to define an identity around a set of core practices and encourage conformity, they set in motion a system of penalties. Some communities ex-communicate their members, others penalise in specific areas. They may, to take a hypothetical case, state that a Sikh who does not wear a turban cannot be married in the Gurudwara by the official priests. The point is that religious and cultural communities, at times, inculcate discipline by stressing conformity with a set of core practices, and the multicultural agenda of protecting and preserving minority cultures tends to legitimise such actions. At least, the policies that aim to give effect to this agenda justify these actions of communities. If to value the French culture implies that individuals must send their children to schools where education is imparted in French language and the state may legislate to ensure that people act accordingly, then a culture may survive, but only by compelling conformity. When multiculturalism supports the actions of the state which dictate that Francophones send their children only to specific schools, it not only privileges the goal of preserving that culture, it also echoes the communitarian belief that each community is defined by its commitment to shared goals. It assumes that as members of a community, individuals affirm those collective goods. Further, since they value these collective goods, the latter must be protected. Indeed, in this framework the only way to value that way of life is to act to preserve it. It is this stipulated link between cultural preservation and valuing a culture that creates problems and is open to a variety of conservative readings.

If multiculturalism is to be rescued from communitarian appropriations, then this notion of community membership needs to be abandoned. Along with it, we need also to jettison the claim that protecting a culture or enhancing cultural diversity is an appropriate way of addressing the issue of cultural discrimination in the polity. There is, indeed, no doubt that all cultures and communities need to be accommodated as equals within a democratic polity, and that policies compelling cultural homogeneity place minority cultures at a disadvantage. However, what must also be acknowledged is that protecting minority cultures and enabling them to preserve their identity and cultures does not redress that imbalance. In fact, it creates new forms of inequity and discrimination and it is this that multiculturalism must also guard against.

Policies aimed at protecting and preserving cultural diversity further privilege the politics of common good. In a democracy, cultural diversity has value mainly because its presence indicates the absence of cultural homogeneity which, as we noted earlier, is often a source of discrimination. However, when the pursuit of cultural diversity becomes an end in itself, it reinforces the problems presented by the agenda of preserving vulnerable cultures. Difficulties of this kind persist even when these policies are favoured for a few historically oppressed communities. This is so because enhancing cultural diversity is almost always accompanied by the belief that people sharing the same identity cherish and protect the same values. It, therefore, constructs the community as a homogeneous entity that is shaped by myths of common origin, a shared faith and past experiences— an image that bears close resemblance to the communitarian representation of community. One needs, therefore, to be extremely cautious about affirming the goal of preserving and protecting

cultural diversity. It is equally necessary to recognise that there
is a vast difference between policies that aim to enhance cultural
diversity and those that are aimed at checking homogenisation
and discrimination of particular cultures. The latter require the
presence of options: options that allow individuals to have access to their culture; but enhancing cultural diversity involves
that members of the group act in a way that enables the culture
to survive and flourish. Theories of multiculturalism must therefore aim to minimise cultural discrimination rather than enhancing diversity of cultures. Further, they should seek to realise this
goal of eliminating discrimination by creating options that may
be explored by internal members.

Reconceptualising the Issue of Special Rights

The significance of contemporary discourses on multiculturalism
is that they draw attention to the ways in which cultural discrimination may persist in democracies even after equal political
and civil rights are granted to all persons. However, as was noted
earlier, the current scholarship concentrates by and large on the
discrimination engendered by the ethnic character of the nation-
state. It further claims that indifference to the value of cultural
community membership to the self, and of cultural diversity to
society as a whole, is responsible for perpetuating culture based
discrimination. The multicultural insights about the sites of cultural discrimination in society and its discussion of the ways in
which minority communities continue to be disadvantaged by
the seemingly neutral policies of the state have surely enriched our
understanding of liberal democracies. Above all, they have made
us more attentive to issues of cultural discrimination within the
polity. However, its analysis of minority discrimination tends to
overwhelmingly collapse the state with the majority community.

Multiculturalism operates with the understanding that the state
embodies and expresses the culture of the majority community.
It is, in a manner of speaking, an arm of the latter, acting and
affirming the agenda of the majority community. This representation of the state and the majority community may well be warranted in countries where minority communities were systematically

emasculated, annihilated and excluded from the political and public domain. However, in India, where the Constitution began by taking note of the presence of several cultural and religious minorities and the dangers of cultural majoritarianism, it is preferable to begin with a triadic structure, comprising the majority community, the minority community and the state.

Since the actions of the state and those of the dominant groups in society constitute two distinct sources of discrimination, the relationship between the contextually specific majority and the minority community and the interaction of the minority community with the state need to be analysed and understood separately. If the state is continuously treated as an extension of the majority community, it is difficult both to take cognisance of the space accorded to the rights of minorities within the framework of the democratic Indian state as well as to appreciate the changing nature of the latter. If we are to make sense of the shifts in the relationship between communities living in a given region, it is essential to work with a more differentiated picture of the sites and modes of cultural discrimination within a polity. It is equally important to reconsider the multicultural response to the issue of cultural discrimination, particularly the primacy it accords to protecting marginalised minority cultures.

With regard to the strategies suggested for eliminating cultural discrimination, the responses of the multiculturalists present significant problems because they sanction special rights with a view to protecting and preserving minority cultures. While special rights take a variety of different forms, ranging from exemptions and state assistance to self-government, what is important is that they may be claimed and granted for the sake of safeguarding these cultures and their distinct way of life. A few caveats are occasionally introduced. For instance, it is said that cultures may be protected when they are collectively valued; when it helps take care of the interests of the members and enables them to make a positive contribution to social and public life (see Carens, 2000; Parekh, 2000). Or, that cultures may be protected against external pressures (Kymlicka, 1995) and perhaps only in the case of historically marginalised or oppressed communities, particularly those that respect the rights of their members (Bhargava, 1991; Chandhoke, 1999).

These qualifications, important as they may be, do not question the basic multicultural understanding of cultural discrimination and diversity. While they allow us to limit the minority cultures that may be granted special rights to protect their way of life, they nevertheless maintain that the identified few need to be protected and preserved, at least against assimilation by the nation-state, majority community and the market. This conclusion is reaffirmed by the accompanying belief that (a) cultural diversity is valuable and we need to protect it, and (b) cultural community identities are valued by individuals, and hence, we must make a special effort to protect them. In each of these cases, it is argued that cultural identities are being misrecognised, disintegrated and eroded due to policies of external bodies. Consequently, they need to be accommodated, affirmed and protected in the public arena.

To put it in another way, expressing differences in the public domain is only one aspect of the multicultural agenda. What is equally essential is that the cultural context be protected. Special rights are given to realise this end. They are granted both for including minority cultures into the public domain and for ensuring that their cultures survive and flourish. If the survival of the cultural community requires that permission be granted to protect certain practices from external intervention, or that the community has the opportunity to inculcate certain values in its members, then so be it. Special rights may be claimed and granted for this. Indeed, to protect a given way of life, it is argued that restrictions may even be placed upon 'some non-basic rights' of the members (Bhargava, Bagchi and Sudarshan, 1999: 10). Although statements of this kind do suggest that basic rights, such as freedom and equality need to be protected by all cultures and at all times, the underlying conception of special rights remains more or less the same. Here, too, these collective community rights are given with a view to protecting and nurturing a distinct way of life. There is also the additional difficulty of determining what are non-basic rights and which practices violate basic rights. Does polygamy, for example, violate the basic rights of individuals? Can communities curtail the choices of their members to marry outside the community so as to sustain their way of life? Can Quebec stipulate that children of new immigrants be taught in French language? Is the right to choose a spouse or to be taught in a specific language a basic right? Is receiving education in one's mother tongue a basic right? Or is the right to education alone basic? These are issues on which there can be no consensus because cultural practices take on different meanings and people in diverse cultures assess them differently. Some may say that polygamy is enabling for women for it allows them to build solidarities. Consequently, introducing this caveat and saying that basic rights be protected by all cultures acknowledges liberal apprehensions about the multicultural agenda, but does not address the assumptions from which these anxieties arise. In other words, it continues to conceive special rights as measures aimed at protecting vulnerable minority cultures. It also accepts that cultural identities need to be protected, that protecting them is necessary for eliminating discrimination, and that cultures have core structures and are defined by commitment to a shared set of values and practices.

What is being argued here is that apprehensions about multiculturalism can be addressed only by questioning (*a*) the stipulated relationship between eliminating discrimination and promoting diversity and (*b*) the notion of self and community membership that is invoked in this framework. Just limiting the claimants of special rights or prescribing moral limits of what liberal societies can be expected to accommodate does not change anything, for these responses accept the need to protect at least some minority cultures. More importantly, they continue to approach the issue of special rights from the standpoint of preserving minority cultures and making them secure.

Special Rights for Promoting Non-conformist Membership

Although multiculturalism points to an issue that is exceedingly important in a democracy, the question that needs to be asked is whether promoting cultural diversity can adequately check discrimination that occurs on account of cultural differences. Also, whether affirming the significance of a cultural community identity entails protecting that culture. These questions are essential because rights that are sanctioned from the perspective of promoting cultural diversity are significantly different from those that are justified to check policies of cultural homogenisation. As has been argued in the preceding sections, the latter requires primarily the presence of multiplicity and this can be fashioned in a way that does not close choices for internal members. The former, on the other hand, accords the highest priority to protecting the existing diversity of cultures and this permits communities to frame policies that preserve existing institutional structures and practices.

The difficulties that arise from this perspective of enhancing diversity cannot be simply redressed by making minor changes, such as including women and other marginal voices in the institutions of the community or by attending to other procedural dimensions of the community's functioning. They require a shift in focus: a move whereby special rights for minorities are not granted for protecting minority cultures or enhancing diversity. Rather, they are sorted with a view to sustaining options for internal members, including the option of continuing with their cultural way of life. In other words, the guiding norm must be the principle of non-discrimination rather than that of cultural diversity. Democracy requires commitment to the ideal of non-discrimination. In a democracy, the primary consideration is that no one should be excluded from the political domain on account of his or her social or ascribed identity. Further, individuals and groups should be included, not in a subordinate position, but as equals in the public domain. It is this concern for the ideal of non-discrimination, not the mere assertion of sameness or identity, that distinguishes democracy from all other social and political systems. And, it is this principle that needs to be privileged, even in a framework that challenges cultural majoritarianism and assimilation.

Both cultural majoritarianism and assimilation are undesirable, not because they impose uniformity, but because they privilege one cultural group and include all others in a subordinate position within the polity. In a similar vein, cultural diversity is to be valued to the extent that it assists in unravelling the structures of discrimination that are almost always present in a homogeneous national culture. Consequently, in a multicultural democratic polity, the pursuit of cultural diversity needs to be mediated through the concern for non-discrimination. Just as diversity is privileged *vis-à-vis* assimilation, likewise the principle of non-discrimination needs to be given priority *vis-à-vis* the unconditional pursuit of cultural diversity.

The centrality currently accorded by multiculturalism to the ideal of cultural diversity can, however, be displaced only if the multicultural conception of community life and minority discrimination is revised. At present, most statements on multiculturalism suggest that minority cultural communities need to be protected because individuals value these memberships and identities. Equality, by this reading, implies that minority communities have access to their culture and the latter, it is said, is possible when vulnerable cultures become secure and able to preserve themselves. This notion of community, which underpins the agenda of protecting and preserving minority cultures, has to abandoned. It is necessary to begin by recognising that valuing a cultural community identity is not a claim for protecting that culture, let alone the practices by which it is defined. All identities are subject to construction and re-configuration. Effectively, this means cultures and communities are, in a manner of speaking, under-determined, for the practices and institutions that constitute them are themselves changing. Consequently, special rights have to be structured in a way that takes cognisance of this under-determined nature of cultures. Instead of conceiving them as measures that enable communities to protect their culture, they must, instead, be designed to give individuals the choice of carrying on with a given way of life, if they so desire. What needs to be promoted and valued through them is, what I have called, a non-conformist membership.

Once we accept that belonging to a community involves valuing non-conformist membership, then the goal of protecting and preserving a culture will not follow from the premise that cultural community identities are deeply prized by individuals. Indeed, promoting cultural diversity will cease to be a necessary condition for minimising minority discrimination within the nation-state.

This is not to say that cultural diversity has no relevance for us. On the contrary, the presence of cultural diversity is both a condition for recognising the oppression of the majority as well as for challenging it. Since the majority asserts its hegemony by negating and suppressing differences, it is necessary to create space for the expression of cultural diversity in the public domain. However, creating space for the expression of differences is significantly different from pursuing the goal of enhancing cultural diversity and devising policies that promote this end. Multiculturalism has to be attentive to this distinction, particularly while sorting claims for cultural rights of communities.

Contemporary multiculturalism deconstructs the political community. It shows that the nation-state comprises diverse communities, but it does not subject the cultural community to the same scrutiny. As a result, the community remains a homogeneous entity; in fact, it is included in the public domain and represented in the deliberative process as a unified collectivity with a single voice. To promote the ideal of non-discrimination, multiculturalism has also to explore the differences and heterogeneity that exist within a community, both at the level of practices as well as substantive conceptions of good life. At present, when cultural community practices are discussed within the framework of multiculturalism, the general tendency is to counterpose the perceptions of the state with those of the community. The two are presented as binary opposites; since the state stands for the voice of the majority, the community is taken to symbolise the sentiments of the minority. As both entities are essentialised, it is assumed, at least for purposes of deliberation that the community speaks in a single voice and that there is a consensus within the community around certain core practices. If multiculturalism is to challenge culture-based discrimination then it is absolutely necessary to question this assumption about the homogeneity of the community. Minority discrimination cannot simply be addressed by accommodating marginalised communities in the public domain; space also has to be created for accommodating marginalised groups within the community in the same way. Accommodation of both kinds of minorities is necessary to ensure that some communities are not excluded from the public arena on account of their differences, and that the differences that they themselves incorporate are also articulated in that sphere.

Most theories of multiculturalism, particularly those that have come from the West, are silent about the inclusion of the community as a heterogeneous body. Perhaps, in societies where the secularisation process pushed the church and the community into the private domain, women were able to create some space for themselves in these bodies. However, in post-colonial societies such as India, men continued to control the private sphere constituted by their religion and community and women were represented only by their husbands in the family, and by their community, in society. As a result, there is a vast disparity in the positions of men and women in the community. Since these have been dominated almost exclusively by men, the community needs to be perceived and represented as a heterogeneous group. If multiculturalism is to contribute to the health and vigour of democracy, it cannot simply be about inter-group equality. It must also be sensitive to relations within the community.

In a democracy, cultural differences must not be a source of discrimination or marginalisation in the public arena. Policies that disallow public expression of differences or compel assimilation have to be challenged because the gains of citizenship should not come at the cost of erasing one's self-identity. Since identity of a person, to some extent at least, is shaped by community affiliations, citizenship must not imply negation of those memberships and identities. The public domain, therefore, must be open to differences; it must also create room for the expression of cultural differences. But along with this, it is also necessary to accept that cultural communities are not homogeneous entities; and they are continuously being defined and altered. Consequently, eliminating discrimination should not mean that cultural communities hold on to their differences, or that they be incorporated into the political system as a unified group with a congealed common interest or values. Multiculturalism needs, therefore, to explore ways by which the sense of alienation and disadvantage that come with being a minority are visibly diminished, but in a way that does not replace the power of the

homogenising state with that of the community. It must, therefore, aspire towards a form of citizenship that is marked neither by
a universalism generated by complete homogenisation, nor by the
particularism of self-identical and closed communities.

Bibliography

Allen, Mark (1994), 'Native American Control of Tribal Natural Resource Development in the Context of the Federal Trust and Tribal Self-Determination', in Robert N. Wells, Jr (ed.), *Native American Resurgence and Renewal: A Reader & Bibliography*, Native American Resources Series, no. 3, Metuchen, New Jersey: The Scarecrow Press Inc.

Alund, Alexandra (1999), 'Feminism, Multiculturalism and Essentialism', in Nira Yuval-Davis and P. Werbner (eds), *Women, Citizenship and Difference*, London: Zed Books.

Asch, Michael (1984), *Home and Native Land: Aboriginal Rights and the Canadian Constitution*, Toronto: Methuen.

Bano, Samia (1999), 'Muslim and South Asian Women: Customary Law and Citizenship in Britain', in Nira Yuval-Davis and P. Werbner (eds), *Women, Citizenship and Difference*, London: Zed Books.

Bauböck, Rainer (2001), 'Multicultural Federalism: Territorial or Cultural Autonomy', paper presented at the Conference on Philosophy of the Indian Constitution, Goa, India.

Benson, Bruce L. (1992), 'Customary Indian Law: Two Case Studies', in Terry L. Anderson (ed.), *Property Rights and Indian Economies*, Boston: Rowman and Littlefield Publications Inc.

Bhargava, Rajeev (1991), 'The Right to Culture', in K.N. Panikkar (ed.), *Communalism in Indian History, Politics and Culture*, New Delhi: Manohar Publishers.

Bhargava, Rajeev, Amiya K. Bagchi and R. Sudarshan (1999), (eds), *Multiculturalism, Liberalism and Democracy*, New Delhi: Oxford University Press.

Bullivant, B.M. (1981), 'Multiculturalism—Pluralist Orthodoxy or Ethnic Hegemony', *Canadian Ethnic Studies*, 13/2, pp 1–22.

Cardinal, Harold (1977), *The Rebirth of Canada's Indians*, Edmonton: Hurtig Publishers.

Carens, Joseph (2000), *Culture, Community and Citizenship: A Contextual Exploration of Justice as Evenhandedness*, Oxford: Oxford University Press.

Carens, Joseph (1999), 'Multiculturalism and the Idea of Justice as Evenhandedness', *Seminar,* vol. 484, pp 46–50.

——————— (1997), 'Liberalism and Culture', *Constellations,* vol. 4, no. 1, pp 35–47.

——————— (1996–97), 'Dimensions of Citizenship and National Identity in Canada', *The Philosophical Forum,* XXVIII, nos 1–2, pp 111–23.

——————— (1995), 'Citizenship and Aboriginal Self-Government', paper prepared for Royal Commission on Aboriginal People, Toronto.

——————— (1992), 'Democracy and Respect for Difference: The Case of Fiji', *University of Michigan, Journal of Law Reform,* vol. 25. nos 3 and 4, pp 549–631.

Carens, Joseph H. and Melissa S. Williams (1996), 'Muslim Minorities in Liberal Democracies: The Politics of Misrecognition', in Rainer Bauböck, Agnes Heller and Ari Zollberg (eds), *The Challenges of Diversity: Integration and Pluralism in Societies of Immigration,* Aldershot, England: Avebury Press.

Chahachhi, Amrita (1994), 'Identity Politics, Secularism and Women', in Zoya Hasan (ed.), *Forging Identities, Gender, Communities and the State,* New Delhi: Kali for Women.

Chakrabarty, Uma (1998), *Rewriting History: The Life and Times of Pandita RamaBai,* New Delhi: Kali for Women.

Chandhoke, Neera (1999), *Beyond Secularism. The Rights of Religious Minorities,* New Delhi: Oxford University Press.

Chaplin, Jonathan (1993), 'How Much Cultural and Religious Pluralism?', in John Horton (ed.), *Liberalism, Multiculturalism and Toleration,* London: Macmillan.

Chatterjee, Partha (1994), 'Secularism and Tolerance', *Economic and Political Weekly,* 9 July, pp 1768–77.

Cixous, Helena (1976), 'The Laugh of the Medusa', *Signs,* vol. 1, no. 4, pp 875–99.

Coleman, Doriane Lambelet (1996), 'Individualizing Justice Through Multiculturalism: The Liberals' Dilemma', *Columbia Law Review,* 96/5, pp 1093–167.

Collingwood, R.G. (1976), *The Idea of History,* New York: Oxford University Press.

Corrigan, Samuel W. (1992), 'Underground Policy: An Essay on Identity and the Aboriginal Victims of Non-Aboriginal Structures', in Joe Sawchuk (ed.), *Identities and State Structures,* Brandon: Bearpaw Publications.

Dilthey, Wilhelm (1988), *Introduction to the Human Sciences: An Attempt to Lay a Foundation for the Study of Society and History,* tr. and introduced by Ramon J. Betanzos, Hertfordshire: Harvester, Wheatsheaf.

_____ (1961), 'Pattern and Meaning in History', in H.P. Rickman (ed.), *Thoughts on History and Society: Wilhelm Dilthey,* New York: Harper and Brothers.

_____ (1949), 'The Understanding of Other Persons and their Expressions' (an Essay from *Gesammelte Schriften, Vol. VII),* reprinted in H.A. Hodges, *Wilhelm Dilthey: An Introduction,* London: Routledge and Kegan Paul.

Duchen, Claire (1986), *Feminism in France: From May '68 to Mitterand,* London: Routledge and Kegan Paul.

Eaton, Richard M. (2001), 'Temple desecration in Indo-Muslim states: Why, after the rise of pre-modern Indo-Muslim states, were some Hindu temples desecrated, some protected, and others constructed anew?', *Frontline,* 5 Jan., pp 70–77.

_____ (2000), 'Temple desecration in pre-modern India: When, where, and why were Hindu temples desecrated in pre-modern history, and how was this connected with the rise of Indo-Muslim states?', *Frontline,* 22 Dec., pp 62–70.

Ewing, Katherine Pratt (2000), 'Legislating Religious Freedom: Muslim Challenges to the Relationship between Church and State in Germany and France', *Daedulus,* Fall, pp 31–54.

Ferguson, Jack (1971), 'Eskimos in a Satellite Society', in Jean L. Elliott (ed.), *Native Peoples: Minority Canadians,* vol. I, Ontario: Prentice–Hall.

Ferrarra, Peter (1993), 'Social Security and Texas', in Donald Kraybill (ed.), *The Amish and the State,* Baltimore: John Hopkins University Press.

Galston, William A. (1996), 'Value Pluralism and Political Liberalism', report from the Institute for Philosophy and Public Policy, 16/2, Spring; also at http://www.puaf.umd.edu/ippp/galston.htm

Gandhara, Jagdish S. (1993), 'Multiculturalism and the British Nation-State', in John Horton (ed.), *Liberalism, Multiculturalism and Toleration,* London: Macmillan.

Gilligan, Carol (1982), *In a Different Voice: Psychological Theory and Women's Development,* Cambridge: Harvard University Press.

Gilman, Sandra (1997), 'Barbaric Rituals', *Boston Review,* Oct.–Nov., pp 33–34.

Gilroy, Paul (1987), *There Ain't No Black in the Union Jack,* London: Hutchinson.

Gray, John (1988), 'The Politics of Cultural Diversity', *The Salisbury Review,* Sept., pp 38–45.

Green, Joyce (1985), 'Sexual Equality and Indian Government: An Analysis of Bill C-31 Amendments to the Indian Act', *Native Studies Review,* vol. 1, no. 2, pp 81–95.

Gupta, Dipankar (1999), 'Secularization and Minoritization: The Limits of Heroic Thought', in D.L. Sheth and G. Mahajan (eds), *Minority Identities and the Nation-State,* New Delhi: Oxford University Press.

——————— (1998), 'Recasting Reservations in the Language of Rights', in Gurpreet Mahajan (ed.), *Democracy, Difference and Social Justice,* New Delhi: Oxford University Press.

——————— (1996), *The Context of Ethnicity,* New Delhi: Oxford University Press.

——————— (1982), *Nativism in a Metropolis: The Shiv Sena in Bombay,* Delhi: Manohar.

Gurr, Ted Robert (1994), *Minorities at Risk: A Global View of Ethnopolitical Conflict,* Washington D.C.: United States Institute of Peace Press.

Gutmann, Amy (1994), 'Introduction', in Amy Gutmann (ed.), *Multiculturalism and the Politics of Recognition,* Princeton, New Jersey: Princeton University Press.

Haksar, Vinit (1998), 'Collective Rights and the Value of Groups', *Inquiry,* 41, pp 1–23.

Harding, Susan (1986), *The Science Question in Feminism,* Ithaca: Cornell University Press.

Hartsock, Nancy (1984), *Money, Sex and Power: Towards a Feminist Historical Materialism,* Boston: Northeastern University Press.

Hasan, Zoya (1994), 'Minority Identity, State Policy and Political Process', in Zoya Hasan (ed.), *Forging Identities, Gender, Communities and the State,* New Delhi: Kali for Women.

Heckman, Susan, (ed.), (1999), *Feminism, Identity and Difference*, London: Frank Cass.

Herder, J.G. von. (1969), *On Social and Political Culture*, tr. and edited by F.M. Barnard, Cambridge: Cambridge University Press.

_____ (1966), 'Philosophy of History', in *Outline of a Philosophy of History,* tr. by T. Churchill, New York: Bergman Publishers.

Honig, Bonnie (1997), 'Complicating Culture', *Boston Review,* Oct.– Nov., pp 30–32.

Horowitz, Donald L. (1985), *Ethnic Groups in Conflict,* Berkeley: University of California.

Horton, John (1993), *Liberalism, Multiculturalism and Toleration,* London: Macmillan.

Irigaray, Luce (1985), *The Sex Which is Not One,* tr. by Catherine Porter, Ithaca: Cornell University Press.

Jayal, Niraja (1999), *Democracy and the State: Welfare, Secularism and Development in Contemporary India,* New Delhi: Oxford University Press.

Joseph, Sarah (1999), 'Of Majorities and Minorities', *Seminar,* 484, pp 30–34.

Kallen, Evelyn (1982), 'Multiculturalism: Ideology and Reality', *Journal of Canadian Studies,* 17/1, pp 51–63.

Keller, Evelyn F. (1985), *Reflections on Gender and Science,* New Haven: Yale University Press.

Kroeber, Alfred (1952), 'The Chibcha' (1946), in *The Nature of Culture,* Chicago: University of Chicago Press.

_____ (1952), 'Psychosis or Social Sanction' (1940), in *The Nature of Culture,* Chicago: University of Chicago Press.

_____ (1952), 'Areal Types of American Indian Culture and their Growth' (1939), in *The Nature of Culture,* Chicago: University of Chicago Press.

Kroeber, Theodora (1970), *Alfred Kroeber: A Personal Configuration,* Berkeley and Los Angeles: University of California Press.

_____ (1961), *Ishi in Two Worlds: A Biography of the Last Wild Indian in North America,* Berkeley: University of California Press.

Kukathas, Chandran (1992), 'Are There Any Cultural Rights', *Political Theory,* 20/1, pp 105–39.

Kymlicka, Will (1997), 'Liberal Complacencies', *Boston Review,* Oct./Nov., pp 29–30.

——————— (1995), *Multicultural Citizenship,* Oxford: Clarendon Press.

——————— (1994), 'Individual and Community Rights', in Judith Baker (ed.), *Group Rights,* Toronto: University of Toronto Press.

——————— (1992), 'The Rights of Minority Cultures', *Political Theory,* 20/1, pp 140–46.

——————— (1991), *Liberalism, Community and Culture,* Oxford: Oxford University Press.

Kymlicka, Will and Wayne Norman (1994), 'Return of the Citizen: A Survey of Recent Work on Citizenship Theory', *Ethics,* vol. 104, no. 2, pp 352–81.

Lateef, Shahida (1998), 'Muslim Women in India: A Minority Within a Minority', in Herbert L. Bodman and Nayareh Tohidi (eds), *Women in Muslim Societies: Diversities Within Unity,* Boulder, Colorado: Lynne Reinner Publishers.

Lerner, Daniel (1958), *The Passing of Traditional Society: Modernizing the Middle East,* Glencoe, Illinois: Free Press.

Levin, Michael (1999), 'Diasporas and the Nation: Finding Acceptance Abroad', paper presented at Nehru Museum and Memorial Library, New Delhi, 7 Dec.

Levy, Jacob T. (1997), 'Classifying Cultural Rights', in Ian Schapiro and Will Kymlicka (eds), *Ethnicity and Group Rights, NOMOS XXXIX,* New York: New York University Press, pp 22–66.

Lijphardt, Arendt (1996), 'The Puzzle of Indian Democracy: A Consociational Interpretation', *American Political Science Review,* 90/2, June, pp 258–68.

——————— (1977), *Democracy in Plural Societies,* New Haven: Yale University Press.

MacIntyre, Alasdair (1981), *After Virtue: A Study in Moral Theory,* London: Duckworth.

MacKinnon, Catherine A. (1987), *Feminism Unmodified: Discourses on Life and Law,* Cambridge, Massachusetts: Harvard University Press.

Macklem, Patrick (1996), 'First Nations Self-Government and the Borders of the Canadian Legal Imagination', in Thomas Issac (ed.), *Aboriginal People and Canadian Law: Readings in Aboriginal Studies,* vol. V, Manitoba: Bearpaw Publications.

Madood, Tariq (1993), 'Muslims, Incitement to Hatred and Law', in John Horton (ed.), *Liberalism, Multiculturalism and Toleration,* London: Macmillan.

Mahajan, Gurpreet (1998a), *Identities and Rights: Aspects of Liberal Democracy in India,* New Delhi: Oxford University Press.

——————— (ed.), (1998b), *Democracy, Difference and Social Justice,* New Delhi: Oxford University Press.

——————— (1992), *Explanation and Understanding in the Human Sciences,* New Delhi: Oxford University Press.

Mahajan, Gurpreet and D.L. Sheth (1999), 'Introduction', in D.L. Sheth and G. Mahajan (eds), *Minority Identities and the Nation-State,* New Delhi: Oxford University Press.

Mahajan, Sucheta (2001), 'Which Swaraj? Gandhi's RamRajya or Hindu Raj? Or the Making of Post-Independent Polity', paper presented at the *Dialogue on Democracy and Pluralism in South Asia,* New Delhi, 14–17 March.

Mani, Lata (1985), 'The Production of an Official Discourse on Sati in early 19th century Bengal', in F. Barker (ed.), *Europe and its Others,* Colchester: University of Essex.

Mansbridge, Jane (1996), 'Reconstructing Democracy', in N.J. Hirschmann and C. Di Stefeno (eds), *Revisioning the Political: Feminist Reconstructions of Traditional Concepts in Western Political Theory,* Boulder: Northwestern University Press.

——————— (1993), 'Women, Government and the Common Good', reprinted in *Span,* March, pp 10–15.

Margalit, Avishai and Joseph Raz (1990), 'National Self-Determination', *Journal of Philosophy,* 87/9, pp 439–61.

Mayaram, Shail (1999), 'Recognizing Whom? Multiculturalism, Muslim Minority Identity and the Mers', in R. Bhargava, Amiya K. Bagchi and R. Sudarshan (eds), *Multiculturalism, Liberalism and Democracy,* New Delhi: Oxford University Press.

Mendus, Susan (1989), *Toleration and the Limits of Liberalism,* London: Macmillan.

Menon, Nivedita (ed.), (1999), *Gender and Politics in India,* New Delhi: Oxford University Press.

Mies, Maria (1986), *Patriarchy and Accumulation on a World Scale,* London: Zed Books.

Mill, Harriet T. and John S. Mill (1998), 'Papers on Women's Rights', in Gurpreet Mahajan (ed.), *Democracy, Difference and Social Justice,* New Delhi: Oxford University Press.

Minow, Martha (2000), 'About Women, About Culture: About Them, About Us', *Daedulus,* Fall, pp 125–46.

_____ (1990), *Making All the Difference: Inclusion, Exclusion and American Law,* Ithaca: Cornell University Press.

Moore, G.E. (1977), *Ethics,* New York: Oxford University Press.

Mukhopadhyay, Maitrayee (1998), *Legally Dispossessed: Gender, Identity and the Process of Law,* Calcutta: Stree.

Mulhall, Stephen and Adam Swift (1992), *Liberals and Communitarians,* Oxford: Blackwell Publishers.

Nagata, Shuichi (1987), 'From Ethnic Bourgeoisie to Organic Intellectuals: Speculations on North American Native Leadership', in *Anthropologica,* vol. 29, pp 61–75.

Noddings, Nel (1984), *Caring: A Feminist Approach to Ethics and Moral Education,* Berkeley: California University Press.

Nozick, Robert (1974), *Anarchy, State and Utopia,* Oxford: Blackwell.

Okin, Susan Moller (1998), 'Feminism and Multiculturalism: Some Tensions', *Ethics,* 108, pp 661–84.

_____ (1997), 'Is Multiculturalism Bad for Women', *Boston Review,* Oct.–Nov., pp 25–28.

Panchayati Raj Update (2000), vol. 7, no. 12, 84, Dec., New Delhi: Institute of Social Sciences.

Pandey, Gyanendra (1990), *The Construction of Communalism in Colonial North India,* New Delhi: Oxford University Press.

Parekh, Bhikhu (2000), *Rethinking Multiculturalism: Cultural Diversity and Political Theory,* Massachusetts: Harvard University Press.

_____ (1997), 'Equality in a Multicultural Society', in Jane Franklin (ed.), *Equality,* London: Institute for Public Policy Research.

_____ (1994a), 'Superior People: The Narrowness of Liberalism from Mill to Rawls', *Times Literary Supplement,* 25 Feb., pp 11–13.

Parekh, Bhikhu (1994b), 'Equality, Fairness and the Limits of Diversity', *Innovation*, vol. 7, no. 3, pp 298–308.

_____ (1994c), 'Cultural Diversity and Liberal Democracy', in David Beetham (ed.), *Defining and Measuring Democracy*, London: Sage Publications.

_____ (1993), 'The Cultural Particularity of Liberal Democracy', in David Held (ed.), *Prospects for Democracy: North, South, East, West*, Cambridge: Polity Press.

_____ (1992), 'Britain and the Social Logic of Pluralism', in Sandra Coliver (ed.), *Striking a Balance*, London: Human Rights Centre, University of Essex.

Phillips, Anne (1993), *Democracy and Difference*, London: Polity Press.

_____ (1992), 'Feminism, Equality and Difference', in Linda McDowell and Rosemary Pringle (eds), *Defining Women, Social Institutions and Gender Divisions*, Cambridge: Polity Press and The Open University.

Pollitt, Katha (1997), 'Whose Culture', *Boston Review*, Oct.–Nov., p. 29.

Post, Robert (1997), 'Between Norms and Choices', *Boston Review*, Oct.–Nov., pp 34–35.

Public Hearing of the Royal Commission on Aboriginal People (1993), *Exploring the Options: Overview of the Third Round*, Ottawa: Canada Communication Group Publishing & Ministry of Supply and Services.

Radhakrishna, Meena (2001), 'In Search of a Gene for History' and 'Codifying Prejudice', *The Hindu*, Sunday, 11 March.

Ranke, Leopold von (1991), 'On the Epochs of Modern History' (1906), reprinted in Rolf Sältzer, *German Essays on History*, New York: Continuum.

Rao, Shiva B. (1968), *The Framing of India's Constitution: Select Documents, Vol. II*, Delhi: Indian Institute of Public Administration.

Rawls, John (1985), 'Justice as Fairness: Political Not Metaphysical', *Philosophy and Public Affairs*, vol. 14, no. 3, pp 223–51.

_____ (1980), 'Kantian Constructivism in Moral Theory', *Journal of Philosophy*, vol. 77, no. 9, pp 515–72.

Raz, Joseph (1994), 'Multiculturalism: A Liberal Perspective', *Dissent*, Winter, pp 67–79.

_____ (1986), *The Morality of Freedom*, Oxford: Clarendon Press.

Rickman, H.P. (1976), *Dilthey: Selected Writings,* Cambridge: Cambridge University Press.

Ricoeur, Paul (1981), *Hermeneutics and the Human Sciences,* edited and tr. by John B. Thompson, New York: Cambridge University Press.

Ruddick, Sarah (1989), *Maternal Thinking: Towards a Politics of Peace,* New York: Basic Books.

Said, Edward W. (1979), *Orientalism,* New York: Vintage Books.

Sältzer, Rolf (ed.), (1991), *German Essays on History,* New York: Continuum.

Sandel, Michael (1987), 'Discussion', *Dissent,* Spring, pp 202–11.

_____ (1984), 'The Procedural Republic and the Unencumbered Self', *Political Theory,* vol. 12, no. 1, pp 81–96.

Sangari, Kumkum (1999), 'Which Diversity?', *Seminar,* 448, Dec., pp 24–30.

_____ (1995), 'Politics of Diversity: Religious Communities and Multiple Patriarchies', *Economic and Political Weekly,* vol. 30, nos 51 and 52, pp 3287–310, 3381–89.

Sangari, Kumkum and Sudesh Vaid (1991), 'Institutions, Belief, Ideologies: Widow Immolation in Contemporary Rajasthan', *Economic and Political Weekly,* 26/17, pp 2–18.

Scott, Joan W. (1992), 'Deconstructing Equality-Versus-Difference:. Or, The Uses of Post-Structuralist Theory for Feminism', in Linda McDowell and Rosemary Pringle (eds), *Defining Women. Social Institutions and Gender Divisions,* Cambridge: Polity Press and The Open University.

Shachar, Ayelet (2000), 'On Citizenship and Multicultural Vulnerability', *Political Theory,* 28/1, Feb., pp 64–89.

Shahabuddin, Syed (2000), 'Future of Urdu in India in the Coming Decade', *Muslim India,* 205, Jan., pp 2–4.

Sheth, D.L. (1998), 'Reservation Policy Revisited', in Gurpreet Mahajan (ed.), *Democracy, Difference and Social Justice,* New Delhi: Oxford University Press.

Shiva, Vandana (1988), *Staying Alive: Women, Ecology and Survival in India,* New Delhi: Kali for Women.

Shweder, Richard A. (2000), 'What About Female Genital Mutilation? And Why Understanding Culture Matters in the First Place', *Daedalus,* Fall, pp 209–32.

Slattery, Brian (1996), 'Understanding Aboriginal Rights', in Thomas Issac (ed.), *Aboriginal People and Canadian Law: Readings in Aboriginal Studies, Vol. V*, Manitoba: Bearpaw Publications.

Suarez-Orozoco, Marcelo M. (2000), 'Everything You Ever Wanted to Know About Assimilation But Were Afraid to Ask', *Daedulus,* Fall, pp 1–30.

Svensson, Frances (1979), 'Liberal Democracy and Group Rights: The Legacy of Individualism and Its Impact on American Tribes', *Political Studies,* vol. 27, no. 3, pp 421–39.

Tamir, Yael (1997), 'Who Do You Trust', *Boston Review,* Oct.–Nov., pp 32–33.

—————— (1993), *Liberal Nationalism,* Princeton, New Jersey: Princeton University Press.

Taylor, Charles (1994), 'The Politics of Recognition', in Amy Gutmann (ed.), *Multiculturalism and the Politics of Recognition,* Princeton, New Jersey: Princeton University Press.

—————— (1993), *Reconciling the Solitudes: Essays on Canadian Federalism and Nationalism,* Guy Laforest (ed.), Montreal and Kingston: McGill University and Queen's University Press.

Thapar, Romila (1994), *Cultural Transaction in Early India,* New Delhi: Oxford University Press.

Turpel, Mary Ellen (1994), 'Family Conflict Over Matrimonial Property', *Canadian Journal of Family Law,* 10, pp 20–33.

Tylor, Edward B. (1959), (1871), 'Science of Culture', reprinted in Morton H. Fried (ed.), *Readings in Anthropology, Vol. II,* New York: Thomas Y. Crowell Company.

Van Dyke, Vernon (1977), 'The Individual, the State, and Ethnic Communities in Political Theory', *World Politics,* vol. 29, no. 3, pp 343–69.

Walzer, Michael (1997), *On Toleration,* New Haven: Yale University Press.

—————— (1994), *Thick and Thin: Moral Argument at Home and Abroad,* Notre Dame: University of Notre Dame.

—————— (1983), *Spheres of Justice: A Defence of Pluralism and Equality,* Oxford: Blackwell.

Wolf, Eric R. (1964), *Anthropology,* New Jersey: Prentice–Hall Inc.

Young, Iris Marion (1990), *Justice and the Politics of Difference,* Princeton, New Jersey: Princeton University Press.

Young, Iris Marion (1989), 'Polity and Group Difference: A Critique of the Ideal of Universal Citizenship', *Ethics,* vol. 99, no. 2, pp 250–74.

Ziai, Fati (1997), 'Personal Status Codes and Women's Rights in the Maghreb', in Mahnaz Afkhami and Erika Friedl (eds), *Muslim Women and the Politics of Participation: Implementing the Beijing Platform,* Syracuse: Syracuse University Press.

Index

About the Author

Gurpreet Mahajan is Professor, Centre for Political Studies, Jawaharlal Nehru University. She is the author of *Explanation and Understanding in the Human Sciences, Identities and Rights: Aspects of Liberal Democracy in India,* and the editor of *Democracy, Difference and Social Justice* and (along with D.L. Sheth) *Minority Identities and the Nation-State.*